P9-BVM-396

and

WITHDRAWN

LANGUAGE
AND THE POET

LANGUAGE AND THE POET

VERBAL ARTISTRY IN FROST, STEVENS, AND MOORE

MARIE BORROFF

THE UNIVERSITY OF CHICAGO PRESS
CHICAGO AND LONDON

THE UNIVERSITY OF CHICAGO PRESS, CHICAGO 60637
THE UNIVERSITY OF CHICAGO PRESS, LTD., LONDON

Library of Congress Cataloging in Publication Data

Borroff, Marie.
  Language and the poet.

  Bibliography: p.
  Includes index.
  1. American poetry—20th century—History and
criticism.   2. English language—Style.   3. Frost,
Robert, 1874–1963—Style.   4. Stevens, Wallace, 1879–
1955—Style.   5. Moore, Marianne, 1887–1972—Style.
I. Title.
PS3235.B64   811'.5'409   78-14567
ISBN 0-226-06651-7

MARIE BORROFF is the William Lampson Professor
of English at Yale University. She has been a
Guggenheim fellow and a Phi Beta Kappa
visiting scholar. She is the author of *Sir Gawain and
the Green Knight: A Stylistic and Metrical Study* and
has translated *Sir Gawain and the Green Knight*
and *Pearl* into modern English verse. She is also the
editor of *Wallace Stevens: A Collection of Critical
Essays.*

TO THE MEMORY OF MY FATHER

CONTENTS

ACKNOWLEDGMENTS

I wish to express my appreciation to the Guggenheim Foundation for a grant which furthered my studies at an early stage, and to Yale University for two triennial leaves of absence. Grants from the Griswold Fund, administered by the Council on the Humanities of Yale University, were of substantial help in defraying expenses for typing and assistance in research.

Parts of Chapter 1 were originally published in "Words, Language and Form," *Literary Theory and Structure: Essays in Honor of William K. Wimsatt,* edited by Frank Brady, John Palmer, and Martin Price (Yale University Press, 1973). I am grateful to Yale University Press for permission to reprint them, and to *Modern Philology* for permission to reprint the articles which appear here as chapters 2, 3, and 4.

Among those colleagues and friends from whom I have received valuable criticism, I should like to mention Professors Stephen A. Barney, Paula Johnson, Mark Lambert, and Fred C. Robinson.

Ashley Crandell, Jack Rawlins, and M. Teresa Tavormina were of great assistance in carrying out the tabulations in Appendix A, and M. Teresa Tavormina assisted me also with my work on scientific prose. The researches of Willis Buck, Mark Johnston, Anne Parten, and Diane Ross contributed substantially to the documentation of the study. In the final stages of preparation, Peter D'Epiro helped compile the Index of Proper Names and gave chapters 5 and 6 the benefit of an eye for accuracy of detail (not to mention a knowledge of baseball) that would have been pleasing to Marianne Moore.

Clive E. Driver, Marianne Moore's literary executor, and Patricia C. Willis, editor of the *Marianne Moore Newsletter* (both affiliated with the Philip H. and A. S. W. Rosenbach Foundation in Philadelphia) have been unfailingly prompt and courteous in responding to my queries.

I owe a special debt of thanks to Grace M. Michele for her meticulous and expert typing, and to J. Chris Kendrick for his cheerful assistance in assembling and checking the typescript.

INTRODUCTION

We should like to know how that was done.
—Marianne Moore, "The Icosasphere"

This book has grown out of two long-standing preoccupations: with poems, in all the particularity of their shapes and sounds, and with the English language and its history. The writing of it has confirmed my conviction that important things can be found out about poems by observing the verbal materials of which they are made, and trying to see how changes in these—in form at its most superficial levels—are attended by changes of a more deep-seated nature.

The poetry of Frost, Stevens, and Moore makes an ideal laboratory for studies so conceived. Each left us a rich legacy; each wrote a highly distinctive kind of poem; and—most important for my purposes—each wrote a highly distinctive kind of language. Since they were all American, born within thirteen years of one another, these differences cannot be explained away by nationality or historical period. An account of them can be expected to throw light on what matters most: the creative individuality of the poet.

Though I have something to say about each of these poets that has not been said before, I hope the book will prove of theoretical and methodological interest as well. In the first chapter, I work out in detail the conception of style that is implicit throughout, arguing that the style of any poem is an integral part of its form, and that the stylistic and non-stylistic aspects of form are distinct only in theory, the boundary line between them being drawn arbitrarily by the critic. Drawing examples from all three poets, I show that the characteristics of lexical meaning—what I call the characteristics of words as terms—are intimately linked with what we think of as the purely formal characteristics of language, and must, therefore, be taken into consideration in any adequate discussion of the relationship between language and style.

Some conspicuous feature of language furnished the starting point for my study of each poet. With Frost's pastoral lyrics, it was simplicity of diction. Trying to see in what sense simplicity was really there, in the language, and not merely an impression created by the language, I was inevitably led to a consideration of word origins. Students of English style have always known that native words sound plainer, as a general rule, than loan words from French and Latin, and that the presence of a large number of words of non-native origin in a passage will make it sound literary and ornate.[1] But no one had ever said what "a large number" was, nor had "Latin origin" in the relevant sense been clearly defined.

1

Introduction

The etymological breakdown, described in chapter 2, is a tool for the investigation of this aspect of language. It yields a statistical measurement for any passage which can then be seen in relation to a range between low and high, correlating with the extremes of perceptible simplicity and perceptible ornateness in English.

With Stevens, my starting point again was diction. Here, what seemed striking was not any single characteristic but variegation, unpredictableness. The etymological breakdown was of some value in examining this aspect of Stevens's language, but a more comprehensive account of the "kinds of words" available to him, as to other poets, was needed. The scheme I have entitled "the spectrum of diction in English," described in chapter 3, was designed to fill this need; it too provides a tool that can be used to talk about the language of any poet.

With Moore, it was syntax that stood out—not sentence structure so much as a seeming imbalance within the sentence or clause in the distribution of the parts of speech, with nouns and modifiers heavily outweighing verbs. Here again, as with diction, some quantitative ground-clearing was called for, with a view to determining how "low" the proportion of finite verbs in Moore's language really was, as compared not only to the language of Frost, Stevens, and other poets, but to language other than poetic, including the language of everyday. And given that the proportion of verbs in Moore really was extraordinarily low, what did this imply for her poems as representations of human thought? In dealing with this question, I found a valuable tool in the grammatical distinction, increasingly emphasized in recent years, between "stative" and "dynamic" words and meanings, and the corresponding conceptual distinction between the idea of stasis and the idea of process or flux.

As my work went forward, I became increasingly aware of the importance of the "generic affiliations" resulting from restrictive patterns of use in determining the perceived effect of this or that aspect of verbal form. Our experience when we read a poem presupposes a wide range of experience with language on occasions of many kinds, occasions differing from one another in atmosphere and emotional tone, from the solemnity of religious ritual and political oratory, through the seriousness of educational reading, to the playfulness of intimate conversation. Even the most superficial features of diction and syntax have "meanings" of this sort, inherited from the past and repossessed in the present.

Though I had not expected to draw any general conclusions about the three poets, I was interested in retrospect to see that the poetry of each defines itself in relation to two aspects of the cultural inheritance as it bears on our present-day use of language. One is Christianity: Frost, Stevens, and Moore, each in his own way and for his own purposes, use words in ways that allude to the writings and teachings of the Christian church and take on solemnity thereby. The other is the figure of the poet in the "high formal" tradition. Frost and Moore disassociate themselves in different ways and for different purposes from the language of the poet, Frost retreating into the reticence and understatement of New England country speech, Moore into prose, including certain journalistic genres whose affinities with her poetry have until now gone unremarked. Stevens, for his part, exploits to the full the power of the inherited forms of language to clothe the speaker in the dignity of the bardic office.

The characteristics of words as terms, the proportions of words of Romance and Latinate origin as measured by the Romance-Latinate breakdown, the etymological and formative categories and patterns of use brought together in the spectrum of diction, the proportion of verbs to the rest of the parts of speech, the stative and dynamic characteristics of words, meanings, and syntax—these are the aspects of language that I found it helpful to talk about in carrying out stylistic studies of Frost, Stevens, and Moore. I hope that my consideration of them does not seem to imply a method of stylistic analysis, in the sense of a set procedure. To the extent that each important style is unique, an investigation into its working calls for special tools. At least one feature of language that I found it necessary to explore in detail in these studies—the extended complex noun phrase—is, I imagine, of interest for the study of the poetry of Marianne Moore and that alone.

A valid style is a going concern, a sort of economic or ecological system in which many expressive *forces* are simultaneously active, each having its source in some aspect of verbal *form*. Each aspect of verbal form, in turn, represents one way of realizing the potentialities of language where there are others: one kind of term, word, syntactic pattern among many. What the critic of style wants to get at is not the various aspects of form taken singly, but the system in which each is at work. And the best way for him to proceed is to start with something about the language of the text that seems to him to be significant, that makes a measurable contribution to the distinctive quality and power of the work in which it appears. Let him take hold of this clue, whatever it may be, and follow it, rather than carrying out some preconceived plan. A comprehensive description of an author's style, if indeed we could ever arrive at one, would surely not further our understanding at every point. And what is the use of comprehensiveness if understanding is not furthered thereby?

To speak of one way of realizing the potentialities of language where others exist is to come close to the well-known conception of style as resulting from choices made by the poet among alternatives. This formulation does imply an important and never-to-be-forgotten truth: that the poem, as a human product, is contingent, that it could have been other than it is. But no poet, however self-conscious, makes choices among alternatives in isolation from one another. If he chooses to write in a certain diction, for example, that choice will exert a continuous pressure on syntax; if he chooses to write in a certain meter, that choice will rule out certain word-combinations, and so on. What the poet does choose to do is to bring into existence the poem he has envisioned beforehand as possible, and to make this actual poem as much like that preconceived poem as he can. The poem finally crystallizes or precipitates out, in ways beyond the poet's conscious control, as a polyvalent construct, made manifest in a language each aspect of which both determines and is determined by the rest.

The potentialities of language are inherited by succeeding generations; its powers must be created anew. The style of each poet represents a selection from the available resources, concentrated and given dramatic significance in relation to a unique vision of human experience. How that was done, in the poetry of Frost, Stevens, and Moore, is the question I have undertaken to answer in this book.

ONE   WORDS, LANGUAGE, AND FORM

The critic of style begins by listening to the voice of the poet. That is, he begins as a reader. As a critic, he is concerned with what happens to language at the poet's hands—with the distinctive form imposed upon language in the poem and collection of poems. On this much, perhaps all can agree. But then what is form, and in what sense is it imposed on language? These questions are answered in various ways in the chapters that follow; for the moment, it will suffice to exhibit the relationship between language and form in specimen passages. Here are the openings of three poems, one by Robert Frost, one by Wallace Stevens, and one by Marianne Moore—not necessarily in that order.

> The west was getting out of gold,
> The breath of air had died of cold,
> When shoeing home across the white,
> I thought I saw a bird alight.

> On an old shore, the vulgar ocean rolls
> Noiselessly, noiselessly, resembling a thin bird,
> That thinks of settling, yet never settles, on a nest;

> Rapidly cruising or lying on the air there is a bird
>   that realizes Rasselas's friend's project
>   of wings uniting levity with strength.

I take it that the reader who knows the work of these poets, whether or not he has read or can remember the poems in question, will recognize the author of each (the first is from Frost's "Looking for a Sunset Bird in Winter," the second from Stevens's "Somnambulisma," the third from Moore's "The Frigate Pelican").[1] What is more, he will do so in the very act of reading, without stopping to think about language, form, or the relationship between the two. He will apprehend as an indivisible whole what the critic must undertake to describe and analyze into its component parts.

Much that is distinctive and recognizable in the three passages clearly comes under the heading of "language" as such. For one thing, each is made up of certain kinds of words, and as a result its language has certain qualities as diction.[2] In this respect, the Stevens and Moore passages resemble each other and differ from the Frost passage. Both Stevens and Moore use words of a sort that we do not expect to find in Frost's pastoral lyrics: *vulgar,* meaning "common" or "universal" (with perhaps a hint of its philological sense, as in "Vulgar Latin"); *resembling* as an alternative to *like; rapidly* as an alternative to *quickly* or *speedily;*

realizes, meaning "achieves, makes actual"; *levity,* meaning "lightness, buoyancy" (with implications also of gaiety and wit). These are words that we are likely to encounter more often on the printed page than in everyday talk; their presence, among words of neutral coloring, marks the diction of the Stevens and Moore passages as formal. The Frost passage, in contrast, is made up of words we have heard as often as we have read them. To that extent, its diction is not formal but common, though it does contain one phrase that smacks more of the spoken than of the written language ("to be getting out of," as in "getting out of flour" or, more pertinently, "out of breath"), and it alludes to two others (cf. "There wasn't a breath of air" and "I almost died of the cold"). Described comparatively in terms of perceptible qualities, the diction of the Stevens and Moore passages is ornate, that of the Frost passage is simple.

The Frost passage is also simpler in syntax than the Stevens and Moore passages. It can be divided into two complete sentences, and it contains four finite verbs, whereas the Stevens and Moore passages, which are only slightly shorter, are syntactically indivisible, and contain three and two finite verbs, respectively. And the structure of the verb phrase or clause in the Frost passage is itself simple. There is no compounding of verbal forms, as there is in the Stevens and Moore passages ("thinks of settling, yet never settles," "cruising or lying"), and no premodification of nouns (as in "old shore," "vulgar ocean," "thin bird," "Rasselas's friend's project"). And both the Stevens passage and the Moore passage contain a lexical adverb ("noiselessly," "rapidly"); the Frost passage does not.

The qualities of syntactic structures, like the qualities of words as diction, derive from the history of our encounters with them in the language. Compound predicates, nouns with premodifiers, and lexical adverbs appear together as recurrent features in written language of the more elaborate sort, and our response to the syntax of the Stevens and Moore passages, whether we realize it or not, is conditioned by our experience of such language. As regards the Moore passage, it is possible to point out a more specific association. "Rasselas's friend's project / of wings uniting levity with strength" is an extended complex noun phrase, a phrase in which the governing noun is both preceded and followed by descriptive material. This structure is especially characteristic of language designed to convey information, as in the treatise, textbook, or encyclopedia entry. The Frost passage, too, contains a syntactic feature distinguished by purpose and genre. The *when*-clause that forms the last two lines of the stanza differs from the more usual sort of *when*-clause, as in "I started out for home when I saw it was getting dark": its content is not subordinate in significance, but revelatory or climactic. Such clauses are a hallmark of the language of storytelling, both spoken and written; the device might be called "narrative *when*."[3]

This discussion of the "language" of the three passages is by no means exhaustive, though I do not wish to prolong it much further. It could be supplemented by detailed analysis of patterns of meter and rhyme (most obvious in Frost, nonexistent in Moore), and of incidental alliteration (as in *getting, gold*) and assonance (as in *old, rolls*): Each passage could also be examined for the presence or absence of rhetorical schemes, in which case the Stevens passage, with its "noiselessly, noiselessly" and "thinks of settling, yet never settles" would stand out as distinctive. And the Stevens passage, in its opening iambic pentameter line, exhibits inversions of the normal word order such as we are accustomed to in poetry (compare "The vulgar ocean rolls on an old shore"); the other passages do not.

Language as such, in all these senses, clearly helps to give each of the three passages the distinctive form that enables us to guess its author correctly. But each passage also has a distinctive form of a kind that we see not so much in language as through it. Thus the Frost passage presents details of a scene, an agent in that scene (who is also the speaker), and an unfolding event (the speaker thinks he sees something, but whether he really does is not yet clear). This sequence makes up what may be called a narrative "paradigm." The Stevens passage describes the action of an inanimate entity in terms of its resemblance to the action of an animate being. This may be called a paradigm of description by analogy. The Moore passage distinguishes one kind of creature from other similar creatures in terms of its performance of a physical feat. This may be called a paradigm of specification or definition. In each of these paradigms, as in diction and other aspects of language, we can recognize the hand of the author: a Frost who speaks as an agent in a rural scene; a Stevens who describes the qualities of motion by analogy; a Moore who draws to our attention the accomplishments distinguishing this or that species of bird or animal from other species.

Word, structure, pattern, paradigm: however these aspects of the distinctive form assumed by language may differ, they are all the same kind of thing. They are all "features" presented by the text. The critic, as his interests dictate, may turn his attention to one or another of them, describe it in its proper terminology, and point out examples of it along the way. All such descriptions taken together will give us an account of the "form" of passage or poem as a totality, a composite. And we can say that criticism is stylistic insofar as the aspects of form it concerns itself with are features of language as such.[4]

But the critic will have read the poem before beginning the work of criticism, and form as I have just defined it cannot be form as the reader perceives it, for that is an indivisible entity, grasped without taking thought or making distinctions. What, if not a composite of simultaneously present sets of features, is "form" in the sense in which it is the object of the reader's apprehension?

My answer, an old but still useful one, is that the text not only presents but represents, and that what it represents is an act of human speech which calls for a response from its readers as human beings. Let me try to describe the form of each of the three passages in these terms. In Frost, we see that the story being told is "true" in the sense that it could have happened in the world as we know it. The scene in which it takes place is familiar to us, whether at first or second hand, and can easily be visualized. The manner of the telling is not realistic (the poem does not sound like a tape-recorded anecdote); meter and rhyme aside, it is too clear and concise for that. Yet the details of the narrative are presented in a simple, down-to-earth manner, by a speaker who does not set himself apart from us. And his account is objective, devoid of judgment and interpretation. The beauty of the scene, for example, though evident (and important in governing our response to the action of the poem) remains implicit. In the Stevens passage, we see that the content of the description is visionary. The scene is "an old shore," but this shore has no geographical identity, and the "vulgar ocean" rolling on it is nameless. Together, shore and ocean constitute a symbolic version of the world of process in which human beings live their lives. The speaker who describes them is not someone like ourselves, but a kind of priestly bard or bardic priest, one who has access to the repository of myth and legend, and participates in their creation as well as their transmission. In the Moore passage, we see that the content of the description is factual knowledge of the sort typically acquired by reading books and magazines; the frigate bird is a real bird, but neither it nor its habitat is familiar to us. The speaker sounds like an author or lecturer, and the incidental allusion to *Rasselas* heightens this impression.

As the representation of a human action, each passage, and the poem into which it leads us, makes a bid for our attention, tacitly claiming human importance, or, at the very least, human interest. The Frost poem shows us a man acting in accordance with a basic and profound truth: men long, in a beautiful world, for something above and beyond the natural order of things, a sign that the limits of actuality as we know it are not hard and fast. Though the presence in winter of the bird that had sung "sweet and swift" in summer is unlikely, if not impossible, the speaker goes around the tree twice before accepting the fact that it is not there. Yet as the poem ends, we see him calmly and appreciatively observing the scene as it is, including the onset of darkness presaged by the first star. The Stevens poem has the time-honored importance of myth itself. It tells us, in effect, that the mutable world must constantly be rendered into symbols; otherwise, it would be a "geography of the dead," lacking the vital consciousness, the mind of the poet-scholar "separately dwelling," from which all myths proceed. The Moore poem shows us a mind pleasurably animated by factual knowledge, contemplating with interest and admiration the idea of a creature that performs remarkable feats, and making connections, at least to its own satisfaction, between the behavior of this creature and, *inter alia*, a Samuel Johnson novel, the story of Hansel and Gretel, and the life of the composer Handel.

The act of speech as represented by the words on the page, distinguishable from other such acts by our sense of the sort of person who is speaking, his manner, his state of consciousness, and, where relevant, his experience or situation—this is the unitary object of the reader's apprehension. It is the dramatic form of the passage and of the poem. In it, the several "features" presented in and through language coalesce and disappear. Yet they are no less there, as indispensable contributory causes; if they are changed, dramatic form changes accordingly.

Looking at a given feature of language retrospectively, from the point of view of dramatic form, we can see it as having in context a particular significance or force, a "point" that it might not have elsewhere. In relation to the plot of the Frost poem, for example, simplicity of diction and syntax works as understatement does (when recognized as such) to intensify the import of what has been said, giving it, in the words of Edwin Arlington Robinson, "a mighty meaning of a kind / That tells the more the more it is not told." And simplicity in the Frost poem takes on moral significance as well. It implies an unpretentiousness and objectivity that are in keeping with the speaker's final act: the acceptance of a reality unmodified by his personal desires. These values are revealed by an experimental "translation" of the first stanza of the poem into more ornate language:

> As sunset's golden splendor faded
> And deepening chill transfixed the air,
> I seemed to see a bird descending
> To light in branches black and bare.

The revised version, of course, omits some important information relayed by the original: that the speaker is on snowshoes making his way home. But apart from this, its language marks the act of speech as having its source in one different and distant from ourselves, a bardic presence whose experience belongs to a higher than ordinary plane and has high cultural importance. The difference in dramatic form between the two versions is crucial.

In the Stevens and Moore passages, formal diction and syntax, manifested to some extent in identical features, have two quite different kinds of point, helping to portray the solemn manner and hierophantic role of the speaker in one, the book learning and didacticism of the speaker in the other. Other features in the two passages are slanted in like fashion. Reiteration in the Stevens passage is felt to be solemn, not simply emphatic as in everyday speech. In the Moore passage, the extended complex noun phrase, because its content has an identifying or categorizing function, becomes an additional sign of the affinities of Moore's language with that of the essay or treatise. It thus has a dramatic importance or "saliency" that the same grammatical structure in the Stevens passage ("a thin bird, / That thinks of settling, yet never settles, on a nest") does not have.

As elements of dramatic form, the features of language coexist in a field of expressive force which energizes them and gives them direction, like iron filings in the neighborhood of a magnetic pole. It is in these "vectors" of dramatic significance, these reinforcements and resultant saliencies, that form in poetry appears at its most distinctive and characteristic. If we describe its various aspects in terms of what they are, without also saying how they work, our account will have little to do with the reader's experience as he apprehends the poem.

9

The features that coalesce for the reader can be isolated and treated separately by the critic, as if they existed in the text independently of each other. But do they? Insofar as language provides synonymous "alternatives," having different qualities as diction, which can be substituted for this or that word in a given statement, insofar as syntactic structures can be changed without substituting different words ("wings that unite" vs. "wings uniting"), insofar as the narrative content of a passage can be rendered in more or less ornate terms, it would seem that they do. But the more one tinkers with this or that aspect of language, the more abundantly clear it becomes that the composite of features presented by the text, entirely apart from the reader's grasp of it as a dramatic representation, is not a mosaic but a synthetic whole. And not only are the features of language as such tied together in a knot intrinsicate; they are tied in turn to the meanings signified by language. Consider again the opening line of the Frost poem, "The west was getting out of gold." We can, to be sure, express the meaning of the verb phrase it contains in more formal diction, but only by changing the syntax of the sentence as well. If we rewrite it in some such fashion as "The west's supply of gold was diminishing," a new element of lexical meaning is introduced: the abstract noun *supply,* which now becomes the subject of the sentence. Statements can rarely be recast for diction without changes in syntax. And the same holds true for syntactic revisions as well. If, for example, the recurrence of premodifying elements is a feature of syntactically ornate language, as it surely is, then this means that attributes are signified which in simpler language would either remain tacit or appear as predicates in additional sentences; thus the phrase "in branches black and bare," with its compound postmodifying phrase, inveigled itself into my recasting of the Frost stanza. And ornate syntax, like ornate diction, pushes meaning toward abstraction; thus "golden splendor" suggested itself as a substitute for Frost's "gold," adding a qualitative nuance to the factual content of the original in the process.

Meaning—to be precise, the sequence of lexical meanings that makes up the content of a given passage—has been largely ignored in the foregoing discussion. Yet meaning is an indispensable element, not only in the reader's apprehension of the verbally portrayed act of speech, but in our recognition of the qualities of language as such. We perceive *realizes* as a formal word in the opening of "The Frigate Pelican" because we know it means "achieves, makes actual." In the sentence "I think he realizes now that it was a mistake," its value is not formal but common. It is easy to overlook lexical meaning as an element of form, partly, no doubt, because we tend to identify it with content—that which form is not. I hope to show, in the remainder of this chapter, that meaning and content in language are separable and must be treated as such, and that the inclusion of meaning among the elements of distinctive form can lead to a fuller understanding of the concept of literary style.

As a first step, it is necessary to reinvoke the classic concept of an ideational disjunction between words and things, to affirm that words do not, in any useful

10

sense of meaning, "mean" things; rather they mean categories, which are ideas, in application to things.[5] For the purposes of such a theory of language, the word *meaning* is restricted to the denotation of categories. The word-thing relationship, in which meaning may, but need not, serve as an intermediary, will here be called *reference;* the things to which words are related will be called *subjects of reference*—collectively, *subject matter.* The distinction between meaning and reference is too obvious to require extended discussion. It may be demonstrated by such a simple exercise as citing pairs of words, different in meaning in the narrow sense, which might be used to describe or call attention to the same subject, action, or attribute: *man, doctor,* with reference to the same person; *go, drive,* with reference to the same trip; *vivid, scarlet,* with reference to the same color; *heavy, overweight,* or *gross,* with reference to the same poundage; *agree, shake hands,* with reference to the same outcome of negotiations. As an apt designator for words in their denotative-referential capacity, serving to hold this aspect of language separate for purposes of analysis, I propose the word *term.*

But once meaning has been distinguished from reference, it is immediately necessary to put the two together again. Comprehension of the status of a word as a term, that is, of its denotative meaning, depends on our perception of, or assumption concerning, a subject to which it refers. It has been said that no one can understand the word *cheese* unless he has a nonlinguistic acquaintance with cheese. The observation applies a fortiori to those words, and they are legion, having two or more different meanings. A speaker who knows all the dictionary definitions of a word must still know to what it is being applied in order to know which definition is operative. The word *doctor* means one thing with reference to the early Christian writers, another when we are ill; the word *eye* means one thing in a hurricane forecast, another in an ophthalmologist's waiting room. And so on. In that the word *doctor* has two denotative values with reference to two different subjects, it may be said to function in the language as two different terms. Pairs of words like *doctor* and *ophthalmologist* differ as terms in application to a single subject. Given that a word functions as a term only in reference to a known or assumed subject, the possibility of synonymy in language becomes easier to envisage. Two terms may be synonymous—may denote the same category—in the same verbal or situational context (*doctor* and *physician, ophthalmologist* and *eye doctor*), though two words are never or rarely synonymous in the sense of having the same full range of denotative values.

Comparing synonymous terms, we encounter striking and important expressive differences, including those usually treated under the heading of diction. *Doctor* and *physician* illustrate such a difference, as do *eye doctor* and *ophthalmologist;* or, more startlingly, the colloquial metaphor *headshrinker,* or its reduction *shrink,* and *psychoanalyst;* or again, *doctor* and *healer* (in, say, the phrase "the healer's art"), or *doctor* and *leech.* Here we have to do, as I should like to put it, with comparisons not between words as *terms* but between words as *tags,* that is, between words considered as transactional "counters" without regard to meaning. *Physician* and *ophthalmologist* are more learned or formal, as tags, than *doctor* and *eye doctor;* *headshrinker* and *shrink* are more colloquial than *psychoanalyst; healer* is more literary and high-flown than *doctor; leech* is an archaism. These attributes derive not so much from the relation between a given word and the subjects of reference to which it has been applied as from the sorts of occasion with which the word is associated. The concept of "occasion" is taken to include level of formality, an aspect of language that will be considered in detail in later chapters.

If we consider the range of values a word may have as a term together with its qualities as a tag, it is evident that the latter tend to vary with the former. *Leech* is an archaism when used with reference to a man in his professional capacity, but not when used with reference to a bloodsucking worm. More important, the quality of any word as a tag changes when it is used creatively as a metaphor, that is, when one of its values as a term undergoes an intelligible transmutation in a different sphere of reference. A word so used has an enhanced vividness if only because it is startling in its new context. An established metaphor, on the other hand, has qualities as a tag deriving from the contexts with which it has been associated; the word *physician* in the sense of "one who can heal love-sickness," as used by Chaucer, belongs to the poetic diction of his time.

We may sum up by saying that the expressive value of a word in context, as defined so far, consists of its denotational significance as a *term* and its qualities as a *tag.* A third kind of expressive value, of especial importance in the language of poetry, derives from the characteristics of a word as a *thing;* its phonetic shape as made up of syllables and sounds, its audible intensity or degree of stress, even, in certain cases, its appearance or position on the printed page.

Language consists not of words as items but of words syntactically connected in statements, questions, pleas, apostrophes, and so on, which in turn are linked in patterns of reiteration, exposition, argument, description, narrative, and the like. If we consider the part played by syntactic structures in conferring expressive values upon words in sequence, it becomes apparent that these structures play a double role, having conceptual aspects analogous to denotative meanings, and associative or stylistic aspects analogous to the qualities of words as tags. Conceptually, syntactic structures superimpose on the meanings of single words a complex of elaborative meanings expressing such relationships as agency, time, and attribution, as also do the "closed-system items" or "function words," such as conjunctions and prepositions, which are not "terms" as here defined. Consider the following sentence: "The doctor saw him this morning and told me not to worry." Here a set of conceptual relationships among the terms *doctor, see, morning,* etc., is signified by syntax and function words; these relationships would be altered if the sentence were changed to "He saw the doctor this morning and told me not to worry." But another sort of syntactic change, to "The doctor, having seen him this morning, told me not to worry," not only tightens slightly the signified logical connection between the actions of seeing and telling, but gives the first part of the sentence a more formal ring. In fact, there is now an awkwardness resulting from a strain between the formal quality of the participial construction and the everyday diction and grammar of the rest of the sentence. "The doctor, having seen the patient this morning, reports that his condition is good," would be more all of a piece. This wording sounds like an official announcement or news bulletin rather than a statement made in informal talk. Space does not allow detailed consideration of this point, but it is clear that there is a "diction" of syntactic structures, deriving from use on different kinds of occasion as do the qualities of individual words, and differing from the conceptual values of syntax in the same way that the values of words as tags differ from the values of words as terms.

And term differs from any other (synonyms aside) as one denoted idea differs from another denoted idea: the term *chalk* differs from the term *cheese* as do chalk and cheese themselves. But there are certain respects in which terms signifying different ideas may nonetheless be alike. *Doctor* and *ophthalmologist* differ from each other as do *cheese* and *cheddar*, or *book* and *anthology*, or *implement* and *scalpel*, and the members of these pairs resemble each other in that the first is comparatively general, the second specific. "They agreed on the bargain" and "They shook hands on the bargain" signify the same event in different language, that is, in different terms; here the difference is between abstract and concrete—the event in the latter formulation, we may say, is expressed *in terms of* physical action. So too with "He assented" and "He nodded his head," or "He took a newspaper and paid for it" and "He took a newspaper and put a dime down on the counter." Two other classes of terms, qualitative and sensory, may be mentioned briefly. Qualitative terms introduce an explicit component of emotion or judgment above and beyond the factual content of language; sensory terms denote aspects of experience limited to a single sense, such as colors, textures, odors. The statement "The doctor deftly drew a sample of blood" contains a qualitative term of praise which might be replaced by objective language, as in "The doctor drew a sample of blood quickly and without causing the patient pain." "The doctor, in his freshly starched hospital coat, bent over the patient" and "The doctor's white coat rustled faintly as he bent over the patient," represent alternative descriptions in nonsensory and sensory terms.

It should be noted that the same word may have different characteristics as a term in different meanings. A concrete term will, if used with frequency, tend to develop one or more metaphorical meanings that are abstract, for example, *eye* in the phrase "the mind's eye" or "with an eye to." This process is reversed when an abstract term takes on a concrete meaning, for example, *transmission* (in an automobile), *notions* (in a department store). *Fair* is a qualitative term of praise (and a poetic word) in the meaning "lovely"; it is a qualitative term of disapproval (but not a poetic word) in the meaning "mediocre"; it is an objective term in the meaning "sunny, clear" (whether or not we approve of fair weather, the word *fair* in a weather report is purely factual).

It follows from what has been said that the language of a passage may be analyzed from two theoretically distinct points of view. It presents itself on the one hand as a series of terms, each having in context its own primary or "operative" meaning, upon which a set of elaborative meanings has been imposed by syntactic structures. Aside from the particular meaning of each, these terms will have characteristics of a general nature, such as specificity, concreteness, qualitativeness, and so on, which may be salient in particular passages or recurrent as features. To analyze language in this sense is to direct attention toward what is shared between a given passage and a literal translation of that passage in a language having a grammatical system much like that of the original—a passage in English translated, say, into French, German, or another modern language of Indo-European descent. But this same passage, in the original version, is also a series of words having qualities as tags and as things. As tags, the words composing it will be formal or colloquial, common or rare, archaic or current; as things, they may participate in patterns of meter, rhyme, alliteration, and assonance, and they will be more or less dramatically expressive or "sound-symbolic" in relation to subject matter and mood. Moreover, any word in a passage, by virtue of its *range* of values as a term in the original language, may participate in ambiguities, puns, and allusions that will have to be sacrificed in translation.

To analyze the shared aspects of an original and a literal translation in a closely related language is to concern oneself with the ideas signified by syntactically joined words and the subject matter to which those ideas are applied. Such an analysis represents one abstractive step away from the language of the text in its full particularity. So too with synonyms having different qualities as diction. A writer's use of, say, *begin* rather than *commence,* or *doctor* rather than *physician,* or *repose* rather than *rest,* may be thought of as concretizing, giving phonetic shape to, the idea signified by both words of any of the pairs. The relationship between the choice of a meaning and the choice of a word need not be thought of as involving a succession in time, though one may occasionally be conscious, as a speaker or writer, of hesitating between synonyms at the brink of utterance. I shall have more to say on this point later.

How do the characteristics of terms manifest themselves in an author's style? Of the three poets who are the subject of this study, it is Marianne Moore in whose language specificity is most clearly a distinctive feature. This is evident in the very titles of a number of her poems—"The Plumet Basilisk," "The Frigate Pelican," "Smooth Gnarled Crape Myrtle," and "The Paper Nautilus"—and in poems like "The Buffalo" and "He 'Digesteth Harde Yron,'" in which one kind of creature is distinguished from others closely related to it, the Indian buffalo from other bovines, the ostrich from other large flightless birds.

Moore's language affords many instances of what might be called "simple" specificity—terms for which other more general terms could be substituted on a word-for-word basis. A striking example appears in the opening of the second stanza of "Virginia Britannia":

> A *fritillary* zigzags
> toward the chancel-shaded resting-place
> of this unusual man and sinner.

A reader lacking entomological expertise may be forgiven for wondering "Why not just *butterfly?*" Elsewhere, "The whirlwind fife-and-drum of the storm bends the *salt marsh grass*" (p. 5), church columns are "made / modester by *whitewash*" (p. 7), the frigate pelican "flies to . . . the *mangrove* / swamp to sleep" and thus "wastes the moon" (p. 26); a cat in the zoo is described as "a Gilgamesh among the hairy *carnivora*" (p. 40); three baby mockingbirds stand "below / the *pussy-willow* tree" (p. 105); and the workings of human consciousness are likened to "the glaze on a / *katydid*-wing" (p. 134). The distinctive attributes of the particular thing named in such passages are usually significant in the context of the poem: salt marsh grass grows on the seashore, where the storm is taking place; a mangrove thicket is not a place from which one can easily see the moon; a heroic Gilgamesh-figure stands out among other warlike meat-eaters; whitewash is an especially "modest" kind of white paint—and so on. Even the fritillary, being a spotted butterfly, adds an additional touch of variegation to the diversity of Virginian flora and fauna which is stressed throughout the poem.[6]

Elsewhere, specificity is "periphrastic"; that is, lists of specific terms are given for which one more general term might be substituted. In "Four Quartz Crystal Clocks," a poem whose theme is the importance of "punctuality" or exactitude, Moore says,

> The lemur-student can see
> that an aye-aye is not
>
> an angwan-tíbo, potto, or loris.

If she had said that a lemur-student can tell one kind of lemur from another, she would have made much the same statement, but her own words have a colorfulness that is important in the dramatic "economy" of the poem. Similar substitutions can be made for series like "banyan, frangipani, or jack-fruit trees" (p. 6, i.e., "tropical plants"), "wild parsnip- sunflower- or / morning-glory seed" (p. 17, i.e., "a variety of seeds"), "hemp, / rye, flax, horses, platinum, timber, and fur" (p. 40, i.e., "the cargoes of sunken ships"), "prop or hand or broom or ax" (p. 118, i.e., "a number of different tools"), " 'We'll / never hate black, white, red, yellow, Jew, / Gentile, Untouchable' " (p. 137, i.e., "people of other races, creeds and castes"), and "chinchillas, otters, water-rats, and beavers" (p. 193, i.e., "fur-bearing animals"). Each such translation has less of the sort of interest and vividness we look for in Moore's poetic language.

If it is specificity that seems most significant in Moore's descriptive style, it is concreteness that seems most significant in Frost. The setting of Frost's pastoral lyrics is of course the New England farm and surrounding countryside; in them, we see the speaker-farmer at work, or observing the local scene. But the literal action invariably takes on an aura of symbolic meaning; Frost's down-to-earth stories must be read as parables.[7] However the published interpretations of a given poem may differ, they will be alike in one respect: they will be expressed largely in abstract terms. Frost's parables, like other examples of the genre, can thus be said in a very broad sense to represent the abstract in terms of the concrete. But there is more to concreteness in Frost than this; it manifests itself in the handling of the symbolic narrative as well—that is, in the descriptive content in terms of which the gist of the poem is elaborated. A case in point, among many others that would serve equally well, is "After Apple-Picking." Rendered in the manner of a parable in the New Testament, the story might run thus: "When a man who owns a great orchard sees that the time of harvest has come, he will do his utmost to gather in all the fruit and to see that not a single apple is lost. But when the time of harvest is over, he will turn away from his labors to sleep." In Frost's poem, this basic content is "concretized" partly by the inclusion of a number of stage props: details which are not, strictly speaking, necessary to the telling of the story. These include the *ladder,* the *tree* on which it leans, the *barrel,* the *bough,* the drinking *trough,* the *pane* of ice, the *instep arch* of the speaker, the *ladder-round,* the *load* on *load* of fruit filling the cellar *bin,* the *hand* of the picker, the *earth* and its *stubble,* the *cider* made from the bruised fruit, and finally, the *woodchuck.* The harvested *apples* are, of course, a part of the plot of the poem rather than its presentation, but Frost invents two additional "appearances" for them: the speaker smells "the scent of apples" on the air, and looks forward to a dream in which "magnified apples" will "appear and disappear, / Stem end and blossom end, / And every fleck of russet showing clear." And the word *apple* is used more often than it needs to be. It could be omitted from certain passages as redundant, if concrete redundancy of this sort were a fault in such a poem:

> . . . there may be two or three
> Apples I didn't pick upon some bough.
> But I am done *with apple-picking* now.
> . . . .
> And I keep hearing from the cellar bin
> The rumbling sound
> Of load on load *of apples* coming in.
> For I have had too much
> *Of apple-picking . . . .*

16

Finally, the terminology of the poem is "concrete" in that a number of words having both concrete and abstract values in the language are used as concrete terms: *end* in "stem end and blossom end," *arch* in "instep arch," *round* in "ladder-round," and of course *harvest* itself.

The most important abstract term in the poem, *sleep* (it is used four times in the last five lines, and is the last word of all), is equally revealing of Frost's descriptive strategy. For one thing, sleep is a part of the parable, and not of its meaning. The comparison between "human sleep" and the deeper sleep of hibernation points in turn toward a still deeper sleep that is excluded from the manifest content of the speaker's thoughts. The questions raised about the literal sleep he feels coming on are not answered. In the sense in which he raises them, of course, they cannot be answered, since the woodchuck is gone and in any case cannot talk. But even if we give them the answers the poem itself provides—the speaker's sleep will be dream-ridden and restless, unlike hibernation, and what will "trouble" it will be the sort of dream in which the task of the day is endlessly repeated—the answers themselves require further interpretation. The central problem is the meaning of the "harvest" itself, whether as the act of labor or as the fruit of labor. The answer to this question cannot be expressed in concrete terms, act for act or object for object; it must be abstract.[8]

The questions explicitly raised at the end of "After Apple-Picking" are in part playful, in part distracting; the poem ends by emphasizing its own portentousness rather than by explaining itself. The real interface between concrete and abstract, the one place where language points directly toward a dimension of meaning not expressed in the poem, is the indirect question in "One can see *what will trouble* this sleep of mine, whatever sleep it is." The interrogative pronoun *what* nicely straddles the fence: "what will trouble" the speaker's sleep is, in context, the "magnified apples" of the predicted dream; the critic may feel that it is weariness, or regret, or failed responsibility, or thwarted aspiration. Elsewhere, Frost found the indefinite pronoun a useful device for intensifying purport by avoiding commitment to a specific meaning, and we find one or another variety of it in some of his best-known lines.

> Anything more than the truth would have seemed too weak
> To the earnest love that laid the swale in rows.
>
> (p. 17)

> Something there is that doesn't love a wall.
>
> (p. 33)

> The question that he frames in all but words
> Is what to make of a diminished thing.
>
> (p. 119)

17

What was that whiteness?
Truth? A pebble of quartz? For once, then, something.
(p. 225)

What but design of darkness to appall?—
If design govern in a thing so small.
(p. 302)

May something go always unharvested!
(p. 304)

"Take Something Like a Star"
(p. 403)

Abstraction was for Stevens, as we know, an essential part of the process whereby consciousness keeps re-imagining the world—that is, of the writing of poetry. But the complement of abstraction in Stevens is not concreteness, as it is in Frost; it is sensory perception. The plots of many of the poems include a moment of change, an access of inner vitality felt as refreshment in a world grown stale. Such moments are often marked by the appearance for the first time in a poem's language of sensory, that is, sense-specific, terms. "Metaphors of a Magnifico" illustrates the pattern on a conveniently small scale.[9] As the poem opens, the speaker is thinking about an event, formulating it in simple and concrete terms: "Twenty men crossing a bridge, / Into a village." The formula is then varied in accordance with certain unspoken assumptions about the nature of human experience. Since the consciousness of each human being is unique and encapsulated, there are in a sense twenty bridges and twenty villages. But the twenty men are acting in concert (the poem is dated 1918, and they are wearing boots, so they are probably a detachment of infantry); they are in that sense "one man." The sentence that contains these variations is a logical proposition, with to be as link-verb or copula; it is cast in what used to be called in grammar the "declarative mode." Yet the event, so formulated, "will not declare itself": it remains unclear, imaginatively unrealized. A fresh attempt at "clarification" follows, couched in the same terms but founded now on the unassailable truth that the event is what it is: "Twenty men crossing a bridge, / Into a village, / Are twenty men crossing a bridge into a village." But this too fails; the event still "will not declare itself," though it "is as certain as meaning." But how certain is that? There is no lack of "meaning" in the propositions that have made up the poem so far. What is lacking is the all-important "sense" of the event. Though the terms in which it has been envisaged are "concrete," they are nonetheless "abstract" as all denotative meaning is abstract. They signify fixed categories, definitional essentials independent of any particular experience of perception.

Now comes the moment of change, conveyed by several mutually corroborative changes in the poem's language.

18

> The boots of the men clump
> On the boards of the bridge.
> The first white wall of the village
> Rises through fruit-trees.

The verb *clump* has saliency here for several reasons. It is a sensory term, the first such term in the poem. It happens to be a sound-symbolic word, one of a large and strategically important repertoire of such words in Stevens's poetry, to be discussed in a later chapter. And it is a finite verb of "dynamic" force in the grammatical sense, signifying not a characteristic action but an action in process.[10] It is the first such verb in the poem, its predecessors having been two forms of *to be* and one instance of the auxiliary *will*. The sound symbolism initiated by *clump* is continued by the alliteration on *b* in *boots, boards,* and *bridge* in the next line. In the sentence that follows, there appears another sensory term, *white*. The verb *rises*, like *clump*, is dynamic, and it also implies an apparent change in the relative positions of fruit trees and wall as the men approach (compare "The first white wall of the village / *Stands* among fruit-trees"). Though *fruit-trees* is not a sensory term, fruit trees themselves are associated with experiences of smelling and tasting.

In this fresh version of the event, the "thinking" implied by juggling with terms in declarative propositions that fail to declare is forgotten. "Meaning" escapes, and is succeeded by a vicarious experience that gives pleasure. In the final stage of the meditation, the structure of the declarative proposition itself disintegrates as sentences give way to sentence fragments trailing off in ellipsis points. I take these to imply that the speaker has willingly abandoned syntax in his absorption in the imagined details of the scene. If I am right, the poem enacts in little the succession of tenets that gives the three sections of "Notes toward a Supreme Fiction" their titles: "It Must Be Abstract," "It Must Change," and "It Must Give Pleasure."

We see sensory terms emerging into consciousness, with similar significance, in other poems. The speaker of "The Man on the Dump," describing "the purifying change" that occurs in this setting, says,

> That's the moment when the moon creeps up
> To the bubbling of bassoons. That's the time
> One looks at the elephant-colorings of tires.

When the second of the two interlocutors in "On the Road Home" acknowledges that " 'There are many truths, / But they are not parts of a truth,' "

> Then the tree, at night, began to change,
>
> Smoking through green and smoking blue.

19

And in the programmatic statement that concludes "Description without Place," the speaker insists that

> what we say of the future must portend,

> Be alive with its own seemings, seeming to be
> Like rubies reddened by rubies reddening.

There remains the distinction between qualitative terms and objective terms. Of the three poets under consideration here, it is Stevens, in whose poetry an activity of affirmation and repudiation is incessantly taking place, who uses qualitative terms most conspicuously and systematically. His doctrine of perpetual self-renewal is presented in an adversary framework: anything may be "good" or "bad," according as it hinders or furthers imaginative vitality. Like every other aspect of his language, Stevens's stock of qualitative terms is rich and various; every reader will recognize affirmative ones like *brilliant, dauntless, fragrant, holy, illustrious, immaculate, magnificent, majestic, opulent,* and *precious,* and negative ones like *banal, boorish, evil, fake, insipid, monotonous, stale, tedious, vapid,* and *wrong.* (For the sake of simplicity, I am restricting my examples to adjectives, though words belonging to the other major form-classes may also have qualitative values, e.g., *fragrance, junk, evilly, slop* v.) A number of words having both qualitative and objective values in the language at large regularly have their qualitative values in Stevens: *great, high, strong, warm; empty, old, small, stale.* Some terms are ironic, such as *pretty* in "Connoisseur of Chaos," III, and elsewhere. Some are ambivalent; to be human is good in "Before we were human and knew ourselves" (p. 317), bad in "Less and Less Human, O Savage Spirit." And some are idiosyncratic, to be understood as expressing praise or disparagement according as their meanings are associated for Stevens with imaginative "health" or its opposite: *bulging, milky, lewd, swarming,* vs. *blank, lank, motionless, thin.*

Stevens regularly draws on his store of qualitative terms to build intensity in his "hymns" and "jubilas." They do not always work; lines like

> the heraldic-ho
> Of the clear sovereign that is reality,

> Of the clearest reality that is sovereign
> (p. 307)

sound forced, though a similar rhetoric works well in the invocation, in "The Man with the Blue Guitar," to "the shadow of Chocorua"

> aloft,
> Alone, lord of the land and lord

> Of the men that live in the land, high lord.
> (p. 176)

20

But it is in giving a resonant finality to the endings of poems that qualitative language in Stevens comes into its own, whether in clusters, as in

> The venerable song falls from your fiery wings.
> The song of the great space of your age pierces
> The fresh night,
>
> (p. 285)

or in the single, strategically chosen word:

> Hear what he says,
> The dauntless master, as he starts the human tale.
> (p. 456)

Let me now return to my earlier statement that the analysis of words as terms and as elements of syntax differs from the analysis of words as tags and as things by one degree of abstraction from the language of the text in its full particularity. To put it another way, words as tags and as things can be thought of as "realizing" or giving perceptible shape to the underlying conceptual values of words as terms and of the syntactic structures that bind them together. But if this is true, it is also true that terminology and syntax give perceptible shape to the content of the "paradigms" or small-scale units of discourse that appear seriatim in the poem. We can compare alternative formulations of these as we can compare the actual words of a passage with the words used in a literal translation of that passage into a kindred language. One and the same action can be referred to "in terms of" men crossing a bridge or the sound made by their steps on that same bridge; apples may or may not be explicitly mentioned at certain points in reminiscences of apple-picking; kinds of lemurs may or may not be enumerated in a statement defining the expertise of the lemur-student.

One must conclude that there is no single form-content opposition in language; rather, there are various "levels" of form at which the critic may engage the literary text, from the most local and particular to the most broad and general.[11] Though I hold no brief for any set number or nomenclature, I have found it useful for purposes of theory to identify four such levels: verbalization, formulation, development, and conception. Of these, the first two represent complementary aspects of the language of the text as such; the third and fourth are related to each other as an account of the detailed working out and ordering into phases of the verbally portrayed act of speech is related to a summary description of that same act.[12] Regardless of their formulation or verbalization, the statement about lemur-students in "Four Quartz Crystal Clocks," the reflexive comment in the second stanza of "Metaphors of a Magnifico" ("This is old song / That will not declare itself"), and the speaker's description of the ladder at the beginning of "After Apple-Picking," are aspects of form as "development" in the poems in which they appear. Each may be thought of as a feature characteristic of its author: in Frost, the concrete object not essential to the plot; in Stevens, the subjective interpolation in a narrative or descriptive passage; in Moore, the general truth or aphorism not directly connected with anything else in the poem.

Features at the level of development, like those at the levels of formulation and verbalization, are activated—or better, interactivated—as elements of dramatic form, taking on particular significance in relation to the portrayed act of speech. The point of the statement about lemur-students in "Four Quartz Crystal Clocks" is partly that different species of odd little creatures deserve to be distinguished from one another with a "punctiliousness" that is another form of "punctuality." Paraphrasing the end of the poem, one might say that "getting the names of lemurs right is not a crime." The ladder in "After Apple-Picking" becomes a symbol of human aspiration, aligning itself in significance with the manual labor of apple-picking which chiefly occupies the speaker's thoughts. And the shift from objective to subjective in "Metaphors of a Magnifico" is a sign that what the speaker of the poem is really concerned with is not the actions of a group of men, but the quality of thought itself.

To describe the dramatic significance of features of development is to point toward the "conception" of the portrayed act of speech implicit in the poem as a whole. Here too, in "the kinds of poems" that Frost, Stevens, and Moore write, we see form as distinctive and characteristic: in Frost's pastoral parables, Stevens's endless refashionings of the human tale, Moore's informative expositions with their quasi-scientific, quasi-moralistic coloring. And here at last we can set form against the "materials" on which form is imposed by the artist: the language he uses, with all its expressive potentialities; the poetic and other cultural traditions he inherits; and the experiences making up his life.[13]

In what sense, then, is the critic of style concerned with the distinctive forms of language in the literary text? One answer suggests itself immediately: the study of style is the study of distinctive form as it is presented to us in the features of language as such, that is, in features at the levels of verbalization and formulation, including the characteristics of words as terms. But insofar as the critic of style is concerned with *dramatic* form—as he surely is—another, broader definition seems inescapable: the study of style is the study of form at any and all levels as it reflects the creative individuality of the poet.

I began this chapter by noting some of the immediately perceptible qualities of words in passages representative of the language of Frost, Stevens, and Moore. I want now to return to that aspect of form in language, with a view to seeing what sorts of dramatic potentialities are vested in words by the prior history of their use in the language, without regard to meaning or kinds of meaning. And I shall begin with "simplicity" in the language of Robert Frost.

TWO

ROBERT FROST'S NEW TESTAMENT THE USES OF SIMPLICITY

Nothing about the language of Robert Frost has been more often remarked on than its simplicity, a quality doubtless more striking in the earlier than the later poems, yet nonetheless integral to our ideas of Frost and his style.[1] I propose to consider this quality, as manifested specifically in diction or choices among words, in some well-known poems taken mainly from Frost's first three volumes, *A Boy's Will* (1913), *North of Boston* (1914), and *Mountain Interval* (1916); I shall explore some of its observable, factual implications and go on to show how these bear on broader questions of dramatic strategy and structure. The insights thus gained can usefully be applied to later poems of Frost's in which the language is not so simple, as I hope to demonstrate in a concluding analysis of an important and notably difficult late poem, "Directive."

The most obvious objective correlative of "simplicity" in language is word length—the frequency, for instance, of lines made up wholly of monosyllables, and a corresponding infrequency of words of three syllables or more. This can conveniently be illustrated from two passages on the theme of moral transiency, the former from "The Lesson for Today," one of Frost's Horatian, discursive pieces, the latter from the perceptibly "simpler" lyric "The Strong Are Saying Nothing":

> There is a limit to our time extension.
> We all are doomed to broken-off careers,
> And so's the nation, so's the total race.
> The earth itself is liable to the fate
> Of meaninglessly being broken off.
> (And hence so many literary tears
> At which my inclination is to scoff.)
>
> (p. 355)

> Wind goes from farm to farm in wave on wave,
> But carries no cry of what is hoped to be.
> There may be little or much beyond the grave,
> But the strong are saying nothing until they see.
>
> (p. 300)

A more interesting factual reflection of "simplicity" or "difficulty" in language may be found in word origins. Compared with the second passage just quoted, the first four lines of the first poem contain twice as many words belonging to two etymological categories, roughly equivalent to "derived from French" and "derived from Latin," which I shall call "Romance" and "Latinate"; more significantly, the first four lines of the first poem contain five Latinate words, the second none.[2] Samplings of texts from the sixteenth century to the present, representing the widest possible range of subjects and genres, indicate that successive Romance-Latinate percentiles of below 10, counting every word seriatim in 100-word sequences, represent the "low" extreme for English style. I have never found a 100-word sequence containing no Romance or Latinate elements at all, except, of course, where an author has deliberately excluded them as Joyce did at the beginning of his philological tour-de-force in the "Oxen of the Sun" episode of *Ulysses*, or as Edna St. Vincent Millay did in *The King's Henchman*. Percentiles of under 5 are rare even in markedly "low" styles, and percentiles below 10 regularly correlate with an impression of plainness and simplicity such as we associate with Frost (though in some styles, for example, that of E. E. Cummings, odd collocations of words or eccentric syntax may produce an "overlay" of opacity.)

The statistically low extreme in Frost as regards Romance and Latinate diction seems to be represented by "Mending Wall," and I should like to begin my investigation of the relation between language and dramatic structure with this poem.[3] Here a disclaimer is perhaps in order. It is not my view that tabulations of linguistic detail will of themselves yield an understanding of the all-important relationship between what a poem expresses and how it is expressed. But given the critic's initial grasp of what is going on in a poem—its "meaning" in the fullest sense of that term—he can both enlarge his understanding and enhance his sense of the poem as an object by paying some attention to the verbal materials of which it is made, coming to see more clearly "within the illumined large, / The veritable small," and discovering how a certain kind of verbal material can itself be an important determinant of poetic form.[4]

The plot of "Mending Wall" is of course concerned with the opposed attitudes of the speaker and his unnamed "neighbor ... beyond the hill" toward the annual task of mending the stone wall between their adjoining farms, which is damaged every spring when the thawing earth heaves beneath it. The speaker views with humorous detachment the set procedure whereby each moves along his side of the wall putting back whatever stones have fallen into his field; the neighbor, however, takes it wholly seriously. The speaker is thus in sympathy with the force working from within the ground which "doesn't love a wall"; this attitude is also the poet's, and the reader is invited to share in it.[5] But there is a second agency damaging to walls which the speaker is careful to distinguish as quite "another thing": the efforts of the hunters to "please the yelping dogs" by pulling apart the stones behind which a rabbit has taken refuge. This anti-wall agency is characterized by the bearing of weapons and the intention of destroying life (an explicit statement of the disapproval which remains implicit here appears in "The Rabbit Hunter," p. 360). It is thus to be associated with the image of the pro-wall neighbor as he looms in sight toward the end of the poem, "bringing a stone grasped firmly by the top / In each hand, like an old-stone savage armed." The natural gaps made in the wall each spring are large enough so that "two can pass abreast" through them; the image suggests friends or lovers sharing an excursion, as in "Two Look at Two." This sort of companionship is quite "another thing" from that of the speaker and his neighbor, who keep the wall between them as they go. An opening reference to the "spilling" of boulders "in the sun" carries implications of warmth and wastefulness, a sort of spring delight in disorder. The season also brings rising spirits, a groundswell of inner exuberance. "Spring is the mischief in me," the speaker says, and his association with the natural source of the gaps in the wall is thereby reinforced, for later in the poem he considers telling his neighbor they are the work of elves. He himself at one point essays a bit of puckish humor ("My apple trees will never get across / And eat the cones under his pines, I tell him"), but this brings forth no response. The solemn progress down the wall of the two neighbors is, to be sure, likened to a "game," but even here there is a hint of conflict: *side* in "one on a side" means, in the context of the figure, not only "direction in space" but "opposing faction." The line "to each the boulders that have fallen to each" expresses a sort of talion, an Old Testament–like law of equal remuneration, while the use of "spells" to make the replaced stones stay where they are evokes a superstitious past. So, too, the "darkness . . . / Not of woods only and the shade of trees" in which the neighbor's figure is finally seen implies, in context, a benighted primitive era prior to the establishment of amicable social bonds.

By the end of the poem, there has emerged a constellation of related elements: warmth, exuberance, playfulness, humor—and, in opposition to the violence and hostility implicit in the acts of the hunters and in the image of the neighbor as an armed savage, the further and central values of sympathy, harmony, and reconciliation. The literal wall comes to stand for all antagonistic or mistrustful barriers dividing man from man (as well as from other creatures); that which does not love such a wall is, most important, the recurrent human impulse to reach out in sympathy toward other human beings, an impulse identified with the force which thaws the ground in spring.[6] (One thinks of other poems by Frost, such as "A Prayer in Spring" and "Putting in the Seed," where the equation of love on human and natural levels is explicit.) The wall-destroying process is seen as a working from within the earth, gathering upward and spilling out; a widening movement antithetical in character to the verbatim repetition of a cautionary saying from one generation to the next.[7] The poem ends in further repetition, unable to go beyond the saying just as its speaker is unable to get his idea across, either literally or figuratively, to his neighbor. The form of the ending enacts the walling in (or out) which is the negatively viewed component of the theme. But we must distinguish between what the speaker is trying to convey and what he wants to do. It is obvious from his reference to having "made repair" after the visitations of the rabbit hunters that he has no intention of literally allowing the wall to fall apart. The story told in the poem is not about a one-man rebellion against wall mending but about an attempt to communicate. The impulse to communicate and the content of the message itself are integrally related; as his means of communication, the speaker eschews direct statement in favor of appeals to the imagination and sense of humor. The action dramatized in the poem inevitably merges into the act of the poet in writing it.

I said earlier that "Mending Wall" seems to represent a low extreme for Frost in Romance-Latinate content. The poem is 398 words long; of these, 14 are Romance (*pass, rabbit, please, mending, line, use, balance, stay, turned, mischief, firmly, savage, armed, moves*) and 8 are Latinate (*repair, just, cones, fences, notion, offense, exactly, fences*). The percentiles for the four successive 100-word sequences (counting the last 98 words as 100) are 5, 6, 5, and 6.[8] The question arising from this set of facts may be put in terms of either causes or effects. On the one hand, what motives or tendencies operate to keep the Romance-Latinate level so low? On the other hand, what dramatic significance or effectiveness does this sort of language have in the poem?

In answering the first question, it is necessary to admit at once the importance of "subject matter," understanding by this, however, not the plot or conception of the poetic drama, but the successive descriptive details through which this plot is developed. Of the concrete terms denoting persons and things belonging to the scene, not only *wall* but *ground, boulders, hunters, stone, dogs, neighbor, hill, pine, apple, orchard, trees, cows,* and *woods* are native; only *rabbits, fences,* and *cones* are Romance or Latinate. The names of country things in English are, for good cultural-historical reasons, for the most part of native derivation; it seems doubtful whether a poet representing in concrete detail an urban world of business offices, cocktail parties, and traffic jams could write poems with Romance-Latinate counts as low as this of Frost's. So far, then, subject matter might be said to "compel" the use of a certain kind of language. But we should observe that the words in "Mending Wall" denoting things referred to in similes and metaphors—things not properly part of the subject matter of the poem— also show a discernible bias toward native origins. The speaker describes the mysterious anti-wall force as a *groundswell* rather than a *surge;* he calls the differently shaped stones *loaves* and *balls* rather than *ovals* and *spheres;* wondering what to say to his neighbor, he thinks of *elves* but not of *fairies, goblins,* or *spirits.* The only such word not of native origin is *savage,* and as if to balance this, there occurs immediately preceding it a striking "translation" of Latinate *paleolithic* into native *old-stone.*

The argument from subject matter is always treacherous, for any subject can be treated in English, etymologically speaking, in more than one kind of language. It is amusing and instructive to think of equivalents for lines and passages of Frost's simple style, substituting as many Romance and Latinate words as possible while keeping the whole coherent. A student of mine once suggested, as an alternative for the opening of "Mending Wall," "There exists an antipathy toward barriers." One could continue by saying that this antipathy "causes an upward surge in the ground which creates apertures sufficiently large so that two people can pass through them simultaneously," and so on.[9] The opening of "The Oven Bird" might similarly be rendered as: "There exists a species of bird, familiar to all, whose piercing note, sounding deep in the forest at the mid-point of the summer season, reverberates from the solid tree-trunks." The well-known conclusion of "Hyla Brook," "We love the things we love for what they are," could be turned into "Our love of the object of love is based upon its nature in reality." The effect of all such translations is, needless to say, bathetic, if only because the music of the original lines is lost. But aside from this, the substitute versions throw into relief a perceptible stylistic quality of the originals which may be put under the heading of "manner" as opposed to "matter." As has often been noted, the speaker of Frost's poems gives the impression of talking or thinking spontaneously, rather than of uttering a prefabricated discourse which by its very form lays implicit claim to cultural importance. The revamped versions of "Mending Wall" and "The Oven Bird" sound, by contrast, like excerpts from texts on geology and ornithology, and the conclusion of "Hyla Brook" might be a key tenet in a treatise on ethics.

In addition to expressing a certain descriptive subject matter and implying a certain manner, Frost's plain and simple language is functional in a third, less obvious way. This can be demonstrated by comparing "Mending Wall" itself with such an explicit statement of the poem's theme as I presented earlier in this study. Among the more important words used to express the conceptual content latent in action and descriptive detail, *life, love, mistrustful, playfulness,* and *warmth* are native, but *antagonistic barriers, destruction, disorder, exuberance, force, harmony, hostility, human, humor, impulse, lavishness, natur(al), reconciliation, sympathy, violence,* and *wastefulness* are Romance or Latinate. Of these, all except *barriers, force, lavishness,* and *wastefulness* are Latinate. Of the words listed, only *love* occurs in the poem. As in "After Apple-Picking," the abstract terms that inevitably appear in an interpretation of the poem are absent from the poem itself. They are implied by factual statements ("We keep the wall between us as we go") or offhand comparisons ("Oh, just another kind of outdoor game, / One on a side"). When the speaker finds it necessary to point verbally toward the invisible forces and moral qualities which are in a sense the real subject of the poem, he takes refuge in the indefinite pronoun, as explained earlier, or in negative statement ("He moves in darkness... *not* of woods *only*"). "I could say 'Elves' to him," he thinks, "but it's *not* elves *exactly,* and I'd rather/He said it for himself." The poet, clearly, prefers that his reader should do the same.

We have observed that a translation of the simple language of "Mending Wall" and other poems of Frost's into heavily Romance-Latinate English produces an effect of prefabricated discourse, whereas the language of the originals sounds like spontaneous talk or thought. The reason for this is to be found in the history of the English language—or, more exactly, in the historical processes responsible for the transmission of the English language, as of any other, from one period to the next. In order that words may descend, they must be learned anew by successive generations of speakers, and different words are learned on different sorts of occasions—on different levels of use. Any educated man has in his vocabulary certain words which he may never have spoken, or heard spoken, on everyday occasions—words which he has learned from books or other formal modes of discourse, and which he uses, if he uses them at all, as an author or lecturer. These are "distinctively formal" words, transmitted in the language exclusively or mainly at the literary level of use. At the other extreme, there are words which we learn by hearing them used in everyday speech, and which we are not likely to meet in books except as the language of fictional forms mirrors the language of everyday. These are "distinctively colloquial" words, transmitted exclusively or mainly at the colloquial level or in an author's simulation of it. Between these two extremes lies the "common" level to which most words belong.[10] Such words are "common to" literary and colloquial use alike, as well as "common" in the less technical sense of being frequently used and hence well known. They are generally lacking in distinctive stylistic qualities; this is because such qualities depend upon restrictions in range of use over a period of time. They are chameleon-like, standing out neither as conspicuously folksy or talky in literary contexts nor as conspicuously pretentious in colloquial contexts.

Now the formal word belongs to the public domain of cultural importance, including not only literature in all its forms, but government, law, religion, and other social institutions. The body of Romance loan words in English is, in the main, associated with the dominance of the Norman French and their Anglo-French descendants, during the Middle English period, in government and in the cultural establishment generally. The Latinate loan-word group consists of words borrowed from literary, chiefly classical, Latin during and after the Middle English period, by French and English writers who had learned them from books long after classical Latin had parted company with the popular spoken Latin which was to evolve into the Romance vernaculars (see n. 2 to this chapter). It is these aspects of cultural history which are responsible for the correlation between elevated stylistic quality in English words and Romance and, especially, Latinate origin. And it is this correlation, in turn, which gives the etymological analysis of passages of English text its potential value for the study of style.[11] A further correlation, that between Latinate origin and abstractness of meaning, is illustrated by the above list of words significant in a thematic explication of "Mending Wall." In this respect, too, the expressive powers of words are determined in the course of time by the contexts in which they are used and the levels at which they are transmitted. The definition and discussion of abstract concepts are associated primarily with "the public realm of cultural importance," notably in such of its branches as science, religion, and philosophy. In contrast, the distinctively colloquial level of language grows out of, and reflects back upon, the world of everyday existence, a practically oriented world of physical activities directed toward concrete objects.

To sum up: through etymological breakdowns, we may corroborate our impression that a number of Frost's best-known early lyrics are made of a language from which distinctively formal words are largely excluded. But it is equally true and important—although for this, etymological breakdowns cannot provide objective corroboration—that the language of these poems is lacking in words and expressions of distinctively colloquial quality. If Frost does not say "There exists an antipathy toward barriers," neither does he say "Seems like there's something that's down on walls." He says that the annual mending of the wall "comes to" little more than a game, not that it "doesn't amount to" much more. (We should note that in this instance the general correlation between word origin and stylistic quality does not hold, the Romance word *amount* as used here being more, rather than less, colloquial than native *come;* see n. 3 to this chapter.) The poem does contain a few of the contracted phrases which are more characteristic of the colloquial than of the formal level of language ("doesn't," "isn't," "I'd," "it's"), but the number of corresponding full forms it contains is larger ("I have," "they have," "no one has," "do not," "he is," "spring is," "will not"). What is true of "Mending Wall" we find true elsewhere in Frost. The regionalisms so paradoxically lacking in poems so thoroughly regional are but one subclass of the distinctively colloquial elements of the English vocabulary which, with the distinctively literary elements, are by and large excluded. Frost's elected norm of discourse here, and the key to his verbal artistry, is the common level of style, which represents a selection from the spoken language rather than a reproduction of it. (One is reminded of Wordsworth's claim, in the preface to the 1800 edition of *Lyrical Ballads,* that he used "*a selection of* the real language of men" [emphasis added].) At the common level, the associations of words with both literary and colloquial realms are strongly maintained in the life of the language. Such words are forever ascending and descending the Jacob's ladder that connects the concrete and abstract dimensions of meaning. They are "common," too, in the more general sense; they seem simple because we know them so well, and they carry with them into abstract meanings something of the solidity of the world of everyday. Readily understood in context as a short form of *stone wall,* the word *wall* has the power of signifying a particular thing, familiar in structure and appearance. Through its equally familiar figurative uses in such expressions as "tariff wall" or "wall of indifference," it can lend itself to the process whereby the

29

literally signified object takes on moral and emotional significance. The end product is not verbal but conceptual; not metaphor but symbol.

Stylistic effects, it must always be remembered, depend on the cooperation of many features as contributory causes. The characteristic diction of "Mending Wall" and other similar poems is one important aspect of a seemingly realistic style in which features of syntax, word order, and sentence structure drawn mainly from the common level also play their parts. In this style, too, the meanings of words and the content of successive statements are readily intelligible, even though the thematic interrelationships and implications of the statements may be subject to dispute. Nothing on the verbal surface is eccentric, illogical, or cryptic; there are no difficult metaphors or sophisticated plays on words: the references to stones as *loaves* and *balls* and the metonymy "He is all pine and I am apple orchard" are immediately understood because they are the sort of figures of speech we ourselves might use in conversation. All these aspects of style combine in an artful simulation of straightforward thought or speech which has at the same time a preternatural lucidity. Quite dissimilar effects have been produced by other poets using the same diction—by Housman in "Loveliest of trees, the cherry now / Is hung with bloom along the bough," by Cummings in "anyone lived in a pretty how town / (with up so floating many bells down)," by Thomas in "Time held me green and dying / Though I sang in my chains like the sea."

If diction is only one element of style, it is equally true that style is only one element of the poem. The artistry which made "Mending Wall" famous includes, it goes without saying, the power to compose sequences of lines which seem to speak themselves, lines in which dramatically expressive patterns of phrasing, intonation, and stress coexist miraculously with metrical form. Frost set great store by what he called his "sentence sounds," and indeed seems to have considered the ability to create them the one indispensable poetic gift.[12] Yet the verbal power of a poet of Frost's stature is less than the architectonic power through which details of scene and action are made to assume dramatic force, so that the literal story, told with the utmost simplicity, gathers meaning as it unfolds without ever seeming staged. At such moments as that when the stone-bearing neighbor, approaching in darkness on the far side of the wall, metamorphoses in the speaker's thought into a caveman, the shaping hand of the artist disappears from view entirely, and we are struck as if by the portentousness of an event in real life.

I have so far discussed "Mending Wall" and other poems as if the style in which they are written never departed from the common level. In fact, Frost skillfully exploits the potentialities of the common style as a staging area for excursions upward or downward: pitched between literary and colloquial levels, it can be modulated either way without an obtrusive break. In Frost's hands, it dips occasionally to the distinctively colloquial level of everyday talk, as in the remark "Spring is *the mischief* in me" in "Mending Wall" or the pregnant question "what to *make of* a diminished thing" in "The Oven Bird." It is embellished with an occasional poetic or biblical archaism of native derivation (*o'er night* and *hence-forth* in "The Tuft of Flowers," *ere* in "Putting in the Seed"), or archaic construction ("knew not" in "Mowing") or inversion of word order ("Something there is" in "Mending Wall"). But more significant than these for the thematic structure of Frost's poems is the exploitation of a body of words of native origin belonging to the common level of English diction, which have traditionally Christian associations, particularly with the Authorized Version of the Bible. An early sign that we may expect allusiveness of this sort in "Mending Wall" is the echo in line 7 of Matthew 24:2 (cf. Mark 13:2, Luke 21:6), "There shall not be left here one stone upon another." I have suggested that the line "to each the boulders that have fallen to each" expresses a sort of talion or Old Testament law of exact retaliation, and, in fact, the values of sympathy and reconcilement symbolically asserted in the poem are related to the prudential values of wall-maintaining much as, in Christian thought, the New Testament ethic of love is held to be related to the Old Testament ethic of justice, not so much superseding as broadening and deepening it. In such a setting the Christian connotations of certain salient words, given the reader's conscious or unconscious memory of them, are set vibrating. The *darkness* in which the neighbor is said to appear carries a suggestion of the spiritual state signified by that word in such texts as Matthew 4:16: "The people which sat in darkness" (cf. Luke 1:79); and John 1:5: "And the light shineth in darkness; and the darkness comprehended it not." Of major importance are the associations with the Christian ethic of the word *neighbor,* notably in the parable of the Good Samaritan with its final question, "Which . . . was neighbor unto him that fell among the thieves?" (Luke 10:36); and, of course, in the second of the two great commandments given by Christ in Matthew 22:37–39 (see also Mark 12:29–31; Luke 10:27): "Thou shalt love thy neighbor as thyself." The allusiveness of its final word gives to the concluding "saying" an additional dimension of ironic force.

The Christian religion is of course a part of "the public domain of cultural importance" which is also the domain of the distinctively formal in language. In its Christian allusiveness, Frost's language thus takes on a formality marked not by Romance and Latinate words but by words of native origin. And in so doing, it associates itself with what may be called the "high formal" tradition, marked out within the formal tradition generally by solemnity of tone. "High formality," in language as in other aspects of social behavior, serves to perpetuate time-honored cultural values by imputing dignity to the subject matter it treats; in some writers, it serves to confer authority on a new vision. High formality in language cuts across genres; it is found consistently in the language of religion; it is present uniformly or sporadically in the language of the law, of government, and of public oratory; it is what we know as the "high style" in the classical canon of English poetry. Much high formal language in English contains high percentiles of Romance and Latinate diction. Stevens, who of my three poets most consistently writes in the high formal style, is a case in point, as the tabulations for his poems in Appendix A make clear. But there is a branch of high formal language in English that is characterized by extremely low Romance-Latinate percentiles, and such language also tends to have the biblical allusiveness I have pointed out in certain passages of "Mending Wall." The tradition exemplified by these passages is Christian in origin and significance; its arch-exemplar for us is the Authorized Version of the Bible, and we find it also in Herbert's *The Temple,* Bunyan's *Pilgrim's Progress,* and Blake's *Songs of Innocence.* It complements and contrasts with the high formal tradition characterized by elaborate diction and syntax. Each of the two traditions is exemplified in certain texts in comparatively "pure" form: Donne's sermons and devotional prose are consistently elaborate in style, while *Pilgrim's Progress,* as noted, is consistently simple. But they may also be combined, as they are in *Paradise Lost,* where Milton modulates with unfailing mastery between the extremes of simplicity and elaboration.[13]

I have traced out some of the implications of "simplicity" in Frost in terms of a statistically verifiable generalization, namely, that the language of certain poems has an extremely low Romance-Latinate content. One cause of this is the descriptive subject matter of the poems, a series of details referring to country things which tend to be designated by words of native origin. If we now turn from Romance-Latinate diction statistically considered to an examination of the particular Romance and Latinate words used—a complementary procedure essential for a full interpretation of the statistical results themselves—we find something more. In certain poems, such words play a distinct part in the thematic dramatization of the poet's world, having a "saliency" which outweighs their importance as "items" (cf. n. 4 to this chapter). A particularly striking case is "Mowing."

If we read this poem with attention to the stylistic qualities of its language, we note a fluctuation in lines 9–12:

> Anything more than the truth would have seemed too weak
> To the earnest love that laid the swale in rows,
> Not without feeble-pointed spikes of flowers
> (Pale orchises), and scared a bright green snake.
>
> (p. 17)

The diction of these lines departs in two directions from Frost's norm of the common and familiar. *Swale,* here a shortened form of *swale hay* or *swale grass,* would seem to be a local farmers' term;[14] it implies the marshy ground on which both pale orchises and snakes are likely to thrive. *Orchises* is a learned word, whose collocation with *pale* results in an image that is, for Frost, unwontedly "poetic." We note also that the native word *weak* in line 9 is succeeded by its slightly more literary synonym *feeble,* of Romance origin, in line 11. Statistics alone, though they overstate the case, might have drawn our attention to the passage; six words out of nine in the little description of the orchises are Romance

32

or Latinate, almost as many as occur in the first 100 words of the poem (see Appendix A). The elevated quality of the language here is thrown into relief by the language preceding and following it. *Scare,* in the reference to the snake, is more colloquial than *frighten* (which is also of native origin) and has the additional value of a specific association with wild animals in the sense "cause to take flight (by startling)."

What is especially interesting about the cluster of Romance-Latinate elements in lines 11–12 is its relation to what is happening in the poem. Its appearance corresponds to the perception of something irrelevant to the task in which the speaker is engaged, something of aesthetic rather than economic value. Yet the inclusion of this perception in the meaning of the task is insisted on. The "earnest love" that wields the scythe repudiates mere wishful thinking, fairy-tale dreams of idleness and "easy gold," but it includes the orchises and the bright green snake. They, too, are implicitly part of the facts that labor knows and, hence, part also of the love and the sweetness of labor's self-fulfilling dream. In portraying a widening out of strictly practical into imaginative values, "Mowing" turns out to be reminiscent of "Mending Wall," and it suggests the other poem too in the speaker's wish to leave the message tacit, "whispered" but not spoken. Here again, what the speaker is shown as thinking or saying merges into the poet's act in writing the poem. The verb *to make* has long-standing associations in English with the writing of poetry, translating as it does the Greek verb which is the basis of the word *poetry* itself. At the end of the poem, the hay is left "to make" in the technical sense of becoming fit for stacking as a result of the drying action of the sun (see *OED* s.v. "make," v.¹, sense 38). The drying grass is a "fact" in the Latin sense of "something done"; both it and the poem itself remain as tangible, non-discursive legacies of the farmer-poet's love of his double task.

Close examination of language here leads to an insight into dramatic form which, tested out on other poems, proves valid for them as well. The central figure of these poems is shown at work on the farm he himself owns and maintains. His dutiful performance of an economically necessary task in a "workaday world" is the *donnée* of the poetic drama, but the performance of the task yields an unanticipated return in the form of an "earned" enhancement of experience—the perception of something having a beauty or meaning irrelevant in practical terms. The two—labor and its imaginative reward—are interdependent. Without the moment of perception, the task would be stultifying, but it is the carrying out of the task which makes the moment of perception possible. The swale must be mowed in order for the pale orchises and bright green snake to appear.

In "The Tuft of Flowers," a second character is incorporated into a similar plot: the change in the speaker's thought follows from his sympathetic understanding of the experience of the laborer who has preceded him in the field. The role of aesthetically or disinterestedly perceived object is taken over by the butterfly and, in turn, by the spared tuft of flowers, a "leaping tongue of bloom" which, like a

Pentecostal tongue of flame, communicates the message made explicit in the poem's conclusion. So, too, in "Putting in the Seed," the "white / Soft petals fallen from the apple tree" are part of the speaker's experience, along with the peas and beans he is planting. (It is significant for our purposes that *seed, pea,* and *bean* are native words, while *petals* is Latinate.) The petals are irrelevant in practical terms; they are not seeds, although he is "burying" them (thus actually experiencing the "softness" of which he speaks). Yet neither are they "barren"; on the contrary, they are an inseparable part of that "springtime passion for the earth" which "burns through" the prosaic motions of the task.

The tragic story told in "Out, Out—," a poem Frost never would read aloud because it was "too cruel,"[15] is predicated on the denial of this process whereby labor becomes one with love. The narrow viewpoint of the adults, the "they" for whom the boy is working, is implied from the beginning in the speaker's description of the scene:

> And from there those that lifted eyes could count
> Five mountain ranges one behind the other
> Under the sunset far into Vermont.

Here the phrase "lifted eyes" ("raised their eyes" would have been equally satisfactory metrically, and perhaps more idiomatic) is reminiscent of Psalm 121:1, "I will lift up mine eyes unto the hills." The point is that "they" do not lift their eyes; the sunset is ignored. The boy is not allowed that extra "half-hour" at the end of the day that would have meant so much, and it is during this enforced continuation of work that the accident occurs which maims him and then ends his life. "They" are thus responsible; it is significant that the boy appeals not to "them," but to his sister, to save his hand when the doctor comes. The loss of the hand is obviously ironic in that it renders the boy useless for work: "No more to build on there." He now sees "all spoiled," but all is spoiled at the outset in a world dominated by so rigid a work ethic; life in such a world is indeed, in the Shakespearean phrase alluded to by the title, "a tale . . . signifying nothing." At the end of the poem, the speaker, far from indicating approval of "their" stoical acceptance of bereavement, dismisses them with contempt as they turn to their "affairs."

We have found basic to the dramatic structure of several of Frost's best-known early poems a process whereby the "economic and imaginative dimensions of experience," as we may somewhat pretentiously term them, are made one, the latter growing out of and depending on the former. The sequence of events in "Out, Out—" can be viewed as a thwarting of this process fraught with tragic consequences for an innocent party. Here, the separation between economic and imaginative dimensions is willfully imposed; in other poems it is more deeply founded—necessitated, it would seem, by the conditions of human life itself. In what is probably Frost's most famous poem, "Stopping by Woods on a Snowy Evening," the pressure of distant responsibilities, referred to in abstract terms, prevents the speaker from lingering to contemplate a sensuously appealing landscape near at hand. In his longing for the darkness and sleep represented by the "lovely" woods, swept by "easy wind and downy flake," he seems to look forward, as also in "After Apple-Picking," to the final rest that succeeds all engagements with reality.[16]

Elsewhere, these same thematic relationships are made explicit. Thus, in "The Investment," a married couple is seen as trying to unite "potatoes" with "piano and new paint," in order to "get some color and music out of life." In "Two Tramps in Mud Time," the speaker's happiness consists in the uniting of the task of chopping wood (certified as practically necessary by the thought of frosty nights yet to come) with a perceptive look at a bluebird and a sensuous delight in the limber play of his own muscles. Toward the end of the poem there is a burst of moralizing leading off with a manifesto couched in heavily Latinate and abstract language:

> But yield who will to their separation,
> My object in living is to unite
> My avocation and my vocation.

In this final stanza, the two dimensions are named outright as *avocation* and *vocation, love* and *need, play* and *work,* "Heaven and the future's sakes."

In "The Investment" and "Two Tramps in Mud Time," the saliency against the native backdrop of certain Romance and Latinate elements of diction—*extravagance, impulse, color,* and *music* in the former, *separation, object, unite, avocation,* and *vocation* in the latter—may well seem too obvious, their thematic role too pat to be interesting. Such words operate more subtly and satisfactorily in other poems to highlight an aesthetic or meditative turn in the speaker's train of thought: for example, *pale orchises* in "Mowing," *petals* and *passion* in "Putting in the Seed," *scented, stuff,* and the disregarded *mountain ranges* of "Out, Out—," and, in "Two Tramps" itself, *tenderly, plume, crystal,* and *vernal.*[17] In responding to their particular expressiveness, most clearly perceptible where a native synonym (*love, rows* [of mountains], *softly, spring*) is available for comparison, the reader gains a heightened sense of the verbal texture of the poem.

Once the thematic pattern I have described is identified, it becomes possible to see a closely related pattern in what might be called "poems of observation" as opposed to the previously discussed "poems of the task." The "task" now takes the form of disciplined observation itself, a long close look at the object free of philosophical or emotional preconceptions, while the "imaginative dimension" appears as a moment of insight or understanding validated by the process of which it is the culmination.[18] The two groups of poems have in common a single structural paradigm: a dramatized movement in which some saving grace of widening awareness at once builds on and transcends, in New Testament fashion, the limitations of an original point of view.

An adequate discussion of this related group of poems is not possible within the limits of this essay, but a few brief comments may serve to indicate the direction such a discussion would take. In "Hyla Brook," a scrupulously unsentimental account of how the farmer-poet's brook goes dry and drab in summer yields an insight into the nature of love, which, to be worthy of the name, must (as my earlier paraphrase had it) be based on the nature of the object in reality. In "The Oven Bird," the refusal to sentimentalize either the bird or the late summer season is equally insistent. Here the positive significance of the ending, despite the fact that it is phrased as a question, depends on an implicit identification of the the dramatized train of thought with the act of writing poetry. Again, as in "Mowing," the associations of the verb *make* with the word *poetry* and its cognates are called into play. We note, too, that the question "what to make of a diminished thing" is *framed* by the bird, rather than merely *put* or *posed*—that is, he builds something around it. As with the bird, so with the poet, who is also traditionally a "singer." For him, the answer to the question is the poem itself. In "The Wood-Pile," too, despite the melancholy final cadence ending on the word *decay,* the motion of the plot is basically expansive and outward-reaching. The speaker's quest carries him from his initial consciousness of an oppressive, prison-like scene ("the view was all in lines / Straight up and down") to an act of imaginative identification with an unknown other man whose self-forgetfulness he sympathetically admires. The poem is a later version of "The Tuft of Flowers" in minor key.

The language of these poems has the same extremely low Romance-Latinate content that was found earlier in the "poems of the task," and the dramatic significance of this feature remains the same: in addition to expressing a descriptive subject matter drawn from country life, the diction implies a casual, unpretentious manner and a reluctance to perceive the subject in abstractive or qualitative terms. A significant proportion of the Romance-Latinate elements themselves, as in the earlier group, can be seen as "symptomatic" of a turn toward the analytical or aesthetic in the speaker's thought: *remember* in "Hyla Brook," *question* and *diminished in* "The Oven Bird," *paused, view, lines* in "The Wood-Pile." Some serve less obvious purposes; in "The Wood-Pile," *cord* (signifying a precise quantity), *measured,* and *clematis* add a nuance of "scientific" accuracy to the speaker's observations; in "Hyla Brook" the cluster *flourished, jewel* (in *jewel-weed*), and *foliage* functions ironically to imply qualities not actually present in the main subject, the brook. And some—*June, paper* in "Hyla Brook," *trunk, sound, past* in "The Oven Bird," *save, place, pile, carry* in "The Wood-Pile"—have no particular saliency, simply merging as additional items into the level of common diction represented by the native words which constitute over 90 percent of the poems.

The Uses of Simplicity

In Frost's later volumes there occurs a perceptible shift toward a more elaborate and literary language, due in part to an increase in the number of poems in the satiric and discursive modes. Statistically, the Romance-Latinate component of Frost's later language falls less often to the low extreme represented by "Mending Wall" and others. But the insight into dramatic structure yielded by a study of the simple language of the early poems remains useful, if only as something that can be tried on to see if it will fit, and the "causes" or "significance" of the heavier load of Romance-Latinate language furnishes in itself a topic of potential interest. I must limit myself here to a discussion of one poem, "Directive" (originally published in *Steeple Bush* in 1947). "Directive" is notoriously opaque even as regards its verbal surface, while its deeper meaning has been the occasion of almost as much disagreement as discussion.[19] The comparatively literary diction of the poem is reflected by successive Romance-Latinate percentiles, for the first 500 words, of 11, 20 (lines 12–24), 10, 7, and 15 (lines 48–59). (The poem contains 524 words in all.) It is also reflected by the perceptibly elevated quality of such words as *monolithic, serial ordeal, village cultures,* and *Grail.* Despite its enigmatic character and certain flaws of tone which I shall touch on in due course, "Directive" may well be, in Reuben Brower's words, "the major poem of Frost's later years."

Reading the opening sentence, we are immediately struck by its syntactic and rhetorical elaboration. The main clause is delayed until line 5, and is both preceded and followed by parallel constructions. In mode, the opening is literary rather than anecdotal, the first five lines being an expansion of the "once upon a time" or "long ago" formula used by tellers of old stories in invoking the dark backward and abysm of time. But it also contains a contradiction which may easily escape us on a first reading, for it says, not that long ago there *was,* but that long ago there *is.* Other contradictions follow as, in a series of riddling paradoxes, we are told of "a house that is no more a house / Upon a farm that is no more a farm / And in a town that is no more a town." The speaker now explicitly introduces himself as "a guide," one who, again paradoxically, "only has at heart your getting lost." As he proceeds to describe the landscape through which his directive is to take us, and especially as he dictates our actions after we have arrived, it becomes increasingly apparent that he has much in common with the narrators of the old epics and romances, poets who were not mere tale-tellers but repositories of historical knowledge and transmitters of ethical ideals. Any solemnity implied by such a role, however, is undercut by his casual manner and jocular tone. His remark "And there's a story in a book about it" (I take the "story" to be the account of the glacier which follows, as the colon at the end of the line would imply) might have assumed some such more pretentious form as "There exists a published account of the geological history of the locality." (According to *ODEE,* the words *story* and *history* are both Latinate, deriving ultimately from *historia,* but the more extensive phonetic change visible in *story* is a sign of its more colloquial status, earlier as now.) The monolithic ledges on the mountainside are humorously compared to bare knees sticking out of torn or worn pants left unmended, and the treatment of the personified Glacier, who, as he wielded his chisel, "braced his feet against the Arctic Pole," is whimsical.

If we take the riddling and contradictory character of the opening as a sign that it is a kind of test imposed on the reader by the poet, we will not be surprised to find that the journey in store for him is also a test—an initiation rite designed to elicit proof of courage—in which the "guide," while pretending to reassure, actually gives more and more cause for alarm. There is menace and a suggestion of the uncanny in the "coolness" that "haunts" the quarry-like road. The very name *Panther Mountain* implies the mountain lions that once inhabited the New England wilderness.[20] The reader is told that he will be "watched" as if by hidden eyes, that there will be sudden "light rustle rushes" in the leaves. He is encouraged to make himself up "a cheering song"—that is, to whistle in the dark—but the comfortable notion that this was once "someone's road home from work" turns suddenly into the unsettling possibility of an apparition on the road just ahead. The speaker in these lines reminds us of Robert Frost the man in his irritating aspect of professional tease—the teacher who liked to challenge his students to figure out whether he was serious or "fooling."[21] But the teasing manner is dropped once the reader arrives at the lost farm and prepares to receive the enlightenment traditionally following upon the ordeal of initiation. Any expectations of explicit moral counsel he may have, however, are disappointed. Rather, he is instructed in the enactment of a ritual: he must drink from "a brook that was the water of the house" from "a broken drinking goblet" stolen by his guide from "the children's house of make believe, / Some shattered dishes underneath a pine."

The meaning of this ritual must be inferred in part from a series of images, present throughout the poem, in which natural processes of attrition and obliteration—including, on a grand scale, the geological processes embodied in the glacier—are seen as working against, and eventually defeating, man's efforts to maintain life in an inhospitable setting—a favorite subject of Frost's. The first such image is that of the gravestone sculpture "burned, dissolved, and broken off" by time and the weather. The distant past, which is the subject of the comparison, is called "a time made simple by the loss / Of detail," and here, too, the poet has planted a hidden meaning which can easily escape us. Ostensibly, he is making the standard comparison between the hyper-complexity of the present ("all this now too much for us," where *now* serves at once as adverb and noun) and the simplicity of a primitive past. But the past was not simple in the past; it has been "made simple" by the distance which separates us from it.[22] The poem restores the lost details dissolved by this distant perspective, and these—the iron wagon wheels moving over rocky roads, the fields and apple orchards cleared in woods, the cellar holes and the houses built over them, the creaking buggy-loads of grain, together with the firkins, harness galls, and rising dough gratuitously invoked in comparisons—collectively represent the labor of establishing and maintaining a foothold in the wilderness: the hardships of the economic dimension of life and the courage and strength required to endure them. "This was no playhouse but a house in earnest." For this earnestness, the cold water of the brook that once supplied the house is an apt symbol.

But we have learned to look in Frost for the imaginative dimension without which labor is stultifying and for this another symbol is close at hand: the medicinal waters of the brook cannot be drunk except from the hidden goblet. Through its association with "the playhouse of the children," the goblet is linked with the imagination (understated by Frost as "make believe") and a joy transcending harsh reality to which we are told we must sympathetically respond ("Weep for what little things could make them glad"). The two together—necessity and imagination, earnestness and joy, the water and the goblet containing it—make up the integrity or "wholeness" which the act of drinking is said to bestow.

If, in the light of this interpretation, we look again at the language of the poem, it becomes clear that the comparatively high Romance-Latinate component of certain passages has its significance in relation to the character of the speaker, as compared with the speaker of "Mending Wall" and other early poems. Such words function to suggest, in a basically understated and casual style, the historical knowledge, the intellectual overview appropriate to the traditional bard-figure of poetic narrative. They include *sculpture, monolithic, enormous, Glacier, Arctic Pole, serial, inexperience,* and *cultures*—all Latinate except for *Glacier* (Romance) and *monolithic* (a French borrowing from Greek). To these should be added a group of words whose presence in the poem has frequently been noted, and which associate the speaker specifically with the narrators of the chivalric romances: *adventure, goblet, haunt,* and *Grail,* all Romance. (*Spell* and *ordeal,* which serve the same purpose, are of native derivation.)

But there is also a sort of allusiveness in the language of the poem which involves native rather than Romance or Latinate diction, and in recognizing this we are brought face to face with the problem posed by the speaker's explicit reference to the Gospel of Mark in the concluding lines. The passage in question, as identified by Frost himself,[23] is Mark 4:11–12, two verses which immediately follow the parable of the sowing of the seed on thorny and good ground:

And he said unto them, Unto you it is given to know the mystery of the kingdom of God: but unto them that are without, all these things are done in parables:
That seeing they may see, and not perceive; and hearing they may hear, and not understand; lest at any time they should be converted, and their sins should be forgiven them.

39

In addition to this overt reference, there are other more or less obvious allusions to the New Testament. The line "And if you're lost enough to find yourself" unmistakably (if colloquially) echoes Matthew 10:39: "He that findeth his life shall lose it: and he that loseth his life for my sake shall find it" (cf. Luke 17:33). Several critics have seen a connection between the importance of the children's playhouse in the concluding ritual and the emphasis in the gospels upon becoming as a little child, for example, in Matthew 18:3: "Except ye . . . become as little children, ye shall not enter into the kingdom of heaven" (cf. 19:14). Frost does not speak of "*little* children," but the Christian connotations of the adjective, as well as the paradoxical importance in Christian doctrine of the trivial and humble, seem implicitly present in the instruction to "weep for what little things could make them glad." (It is perhaps worth noting that references to "little ones" and "a cup of cold water" are found side by side in Matthew 10:42.) The word *water*, of course, has important associations in the New Testament with both physical and spiritual healing, that is, salvation, as in John 5:1–13 and Revelation 21:6; and so too does the word *whole* (Matthew 9:21–22, 14:36, etc.). These words form the same sort of allusive network I noted earlier in "Mending Wall"; they function similarly to elevate the style of certain passages of the poem, and they associate the speaker with the Christian tradition as well as with traditions of secular literature and learning.[24]

The passage in Mark identifying the "wrong ones," those who will not be able to find the goblet, makes it clear that the salvation promised at the end of the poem is available only to those who understand what is said in "parables." If by a parable we mean a story in which things and actions are to be interpreted symbolically, differing from allegory not so much in the formal relationship between literal and symbolic as in the homely and everyday character of its subject matter and its emphasis upon the moral qualities of human action, then poems like "Mending Wall," "Mowing," "Hyla Brook," and others discussed above are, precisely, parables.[25] So too is the conclusion of "Directive." Only if we understand the symbolic significance of the ritual will we receive its saving moral message: only in the imagination capable of understanding these symbols is the "good ground" on which the message will bear fruit. Yet the message itself, it must be insisted, is not Christian. The revelation the poem brings is moral rather than supernatural; its source is not a divine incarnation but a secular figure, the poet, who, although his garments may resemble the priest's, belongs to the realm of human experience and memory. Despite his exploitation of the Christian tradition in the structure, symbolism, and language of his poems, the supreme bearer of spiritual enlightenment in our time, for Frost, was poetry itself. The last line of "Directive," as S. P. C. Duvall has pointed out, is reminiscent of the poet's famous definition of poetry as "a momentary stay against confusion."[26]

In setting himself up as the exclusive "guide" ("And put a sign up CLOSED to all but me") to a truth he has hedged about with verbal and symbolic obscurities, and in proceeding to imply that only those who can interpret this poetically mediated truth are worthy to be saved, Frost, one may well think, has his nerve. The teasing and testing, the archness and complacent whimsy, will always alienate a certain number of readers, and long familiarity will not render them any less irritating. But though "Directive" is flawed in part by the arch-avuncular pose of the elderly Frost, it is not seriously damaged. The ideal it upholds—the encompassing of Puritanical grimness and strength by a saving joy and imagination—is powerful and viable in this as in the other poems which make up Frost's New Testament. And, in "Directive" particularly, we must admire the brilliance with which so great a range of resources—rural Americana, American-style humorous under-statement, legend, history and fairy tale, the literary past, the chivalric and Chris-tian traditions—has been drawn upon and forged into a stylistic whole. Here, as in all Frost's best poems, what is literary and elevated seems not to impose itself upon, but to rise naturally from, basic simplicity—the everyday things of country life, lucidly and concretely rendered in common language—which is Frost's primary and most memorable poetic world.

THREE # WALLACE STEVENS'S WORLD OF WORDS
THE USES OF DICTION

It is a world of words to the end of it,
In which nothing solid is its solid self.
—Stevens, *Description without Place*

As with the elephant encountered by four blind men in the fable, the impression given by the verbal exterior of the poetry of Wallace Stevens depends on where it is touched. Even if we set aside the clearly individuated and consistently maintained substyles of such longer poems as "The Comedian as the Letter C," "Sunday Morning," "Like Decorations in a Nigger Cemetery," and "The Man with the Blue Guitar," the *Collected Poems* provides ample material for a display of passages in which different kinds of words, among other things, make for different qualities of style.[1] We find the discursive, difficult language of

> The major abstraction is the idea of man
> And major man is its exponent, abler
> In the abstract than in his singular,
>
> More fecund as principle than particle;
> (p. 388)[2]

the solemn simplicity of

> He was more than an external majesty,
> Beyond the sleep of those that did not know,
> More than a spokesman of the night to say
> Now, time stands still. He came from out of sleep.
> He rose because men wanted him to be;
> (p. 299)

the elevated rhetoric of

> It is the visible rock, the audible,
> The brilliant mercy of a sure repose,
> On this present ground, the vividest repose,
> Things certain sustaining us in certainty;
> (p. 375)

the eccentricities of

We enjoy the ithy oonts and long-haired
Plomets, as the Herr Gott
Enjoys his comets;

(p. 349)

the colloquial phrasing of

For myself, I live by leaves
So that corridors of clouds,
Corridors of cloudy thoughts,
Seem pretty much one:
I don't know what.

(p. 134)

Stevens's use of all sorts of notes to compose his verbal music can be demonstrated equally well within the smaller compass of the single passage, line, or phrase. Nothing is more characteristic of his style than the odd or quirky combination of words. The oddness in question is not merely a matter of unaccustomed "collocations," that is, of bringing together words not usually found in each others' neighborhoods. Nor is it a matter of incompatible meanings such as resolve themselves into metaphors, as in "corridors of clouds," above. It arises rather from the contrasting characteristics of words as "tags"—their qualities as diction and their phonetic-rhythmic shapes.[3] Dissonances of this sort give an unmistakably Stevensian ring to passages like

a syllable,
Out of these gawky flitterings,
Intones its single emptiness;

(p. 294)

or

addicts
To blotches, angular anonymids,
Gulping for shape among the reeds;

(p. 371)

to lines like "The commonplace became a rumpling of blazons" (p. 483) or "The honky-tonk out of the somnolent grasses" (p. 489), to adjective-noun linkings like "oh beau caboose" (p. 347) or "puissant flick" (p. 517).

It is a natural guess, and a correct one, that the peculiarity of these sequences—their "much-mottled" character, to borrow an apposite bit of Stevensian diction—has something to do with diversity of source. *Emptiness, shape, reeds, became,* and *grasses* are of Old English origin; *flitterings* and probably *gawky* have stems derived from Old Norse; *caboose* and *rumpling* are Dutch; *single, commonplace, blazons,* and *puissant* are Romance; *syllable, addicts, angular,* and *somnolent* are Latinate. *Blotch* is apparently a blend of earlier *blot* and

43

botch, perhaps owing something also to an obsolete word *plotch;* the origin of the Americanism *honky-tonk* is unknown.[4] Several words take us beyond the bounds of the established vocabulary of the language; *anonymids* is a Stevensian derivative of *anonymous,* itself Latinate, with the Latinate suffix *-id*—used here, as in zoology, to designate a class of living creatures: "things without names." *Beau,* in its adjectival role, is a Gallicism. Of special interest are two words, *flick* and *gulp,* for which the lexicographer's hypothesis of "imitative origin" is confirmed by a seeming appropriateness of sound to sense. With these, whatever their linguistic affiliations, we must surely class *blotch, gawky,* and *flitterings* as sound symbolic in present-day "motivation" if not in historical "derivation."[5] And *honky-tonk* seems to belong to this group as well. In the line "The honky-tonk out of the somnolent grasses," Stevens clearly has in mind for the word some such meaning as "loud, jazzy music," in which its sound-symbolic force is especially striking; it is also a metaphor, referring not to "music" but to the strident clamor of locusts and crickets in August.[6]

As regards the stylistic effect of Stevens's odd assortments of words, a preliminary observation may be made at once. Words differing conspicuously from one another as tags become, in consequence, more visible; they interpose themselves between the reader and the discursive sequence of a text much as materials of differing textures in a collage attract the eye and thus compete for attention with the design.[7] *Honky-tonk* and *blotches* contrast phonetically with *somnolent grasses* and *angular anonymids,* respectively, in ways that enhance their sound-symbolic force; the chivalric connotations of *blazons* and the elegance of *beau* are emphasized by the adjoining homeliness of *rumpling* and *caboose.* This literally "arresting," and hence opaque, quality of language is programmatic in Stevens, for all his conviction that "it is life that we are trying to get in poetry" (*O.P.,* p. 158). The anonymous "X" of "The Creations of Sound" must be bluntly informed that speech, meaning poetic speech,

> is not dirty silence
> Clarified. It is silence made still dirtier.
> (p. 311)

Needless to say, Stevens is not the only twentieth-century poet to have devised sequences of words that resist the intelligence almost successfully, or even wholly so. But the verbal obscurity of Stevens is not the obscurity of Eliot or Pound, or Hart Crane or E. E. Cummings. The particular dramatic purposes served by the self-signalizing juxtapositions of different kinds of words in his poems remain to be explored.

Verbal motley may, of course, be donned for comic effect. A phrase like "oh beau caboose," whatever it may mean, is surely rather funny (we might note that the elevated apostrophe prefixed to "beau caboose" reinforces the bathos).[8] But "funny," equally surely, is not exactly the right word for the quality of these lines and passages in general, even if we sense the accents of "fat Jocundus" in them here and there. Their net effect seems rather to result from a process of undercutting or deflation whereby the less respectable words—the etymological wild oats—work against the more dignified ones.[9] Declamation is "clipped" or cut down, as Stevens thought might happen in the relating of any man's fiction (witness the ending of "The Comedian as the Letter C"). This dampening of eloquence, observed on the surface level of verbalization, reflects certain dramatic tendencies operative at the deeper levels of development and conception,[10] especially in the longer poems, where again and again we find bravura giving way to sobriety or cynicism, exuberance to restraint, exaltation to uncertainty, even fear. The scope of vision narrows; an assertion toward which a series of reflections has seemed to be moving, if and when it finally does emerge, is qualified or distanced almost to the vanishing point. The confidently predicted dance of turbulent sun worshipers in "Sunday Morning" is succeeded by darkness and the ambiguous flicker of descending wings; "Like Decorations in a Nigger Cemetery" begins with its immortal fire-bearded Whitman chanting apocalypse but ends with an anonymous "wise man" silently building his city in snow; resonant "Credences of Summer" give way to the falling apart of "a complex of emotions . . . / In an abandoned spot" (p. 377) and the introduction of characters who, as Helen Vendler says, are mere "marionettes," distantly manipulated, seen as free only for a moment.[11] The opening of "Notes toward a Supreme Fiction" shows us teacher and ephebe embarking on an ambitious curriculum presumably leading to a master's degree in poetry, but the course is never completed. In the final sections, a single leaf spins its "eccentric measure," and the solitary "I," walking home from a lecture, awaits a "flick" of feeling that may "one day" enable him to call the world by name (pp. 406–7). "The Auroras of Autumn," which contains the most opulently rendered cosmic panoramas in all Stevens, modulates at last to logic-chopping and obscurely expressed intimations of "the full of fortune and the full of fate," and leaves us with a cryptic reference to a scolding "harridan" against the backdrop of a seemingly trivial "haggling of wind and weather" (pp. 420–21).

If we wish to move beyond intuitive recognition and insight toward a more informed understanding of Stevens's exploitation of the resources of English diction, it will be helpful to have an account of these resources, one in which the various kinds of words available to the poet to use in their established values, or modify as his creative bias directs, are systematically described. I spelled out in chapter 2 the factual implications of a well-known aspect of the relationship between word choice and English style, the readily observed correlation between statistically "high" proportions of words of Romance and Latinate origin (properly so called) and effects of ornate or elaborate elevation.[12] The statistical measurement involved here is carried out uniformly for all verbal sequences alike, taking into account neither the a priori qualities of particular words nor how these qualities are altered in context. Even so crude a method as this yields results of interest when brought to bear on extensive samplings of Stevens's poetic language. It becomes apparent that no one statistical level can be judged typical or "emblematic" of his style; an average figure for all samples analyzed would in his case have remarkably little bearing on any one passage.[13] Again, it is true that other poets have written in different "modalities," differing consistently, among other things, in the proportion of Romance and Latinate words each tends to contain—as Frost's discursive and satirical poems, for instance, differ from his simpler lyrics and poetic narratives. But statistical variation in Stevens is so much greater in range—one might say, so much more consistent—that it comes to seem a difference in kind. And the protean diversity of his diction, viewed in terms of the stylistic values of particular words, transcends any statistical tool, as indeed it transcends any systematic account of the kinds of words making up the language that W. H. Auden, in "The Cave of Making," called "good mongrel barbarian English."

In speaking with confidence of the stylistic values of particular words, we may seem to be forsaking the solid ground of verifiable facts for the quicksands of impressionism. But in stylistic as in grammatical studies, an appeal can be made to the "competence" of a properly qualified informant—his sense, for one thing, of the affinities of a given cast of statement with formal or colloquial contexts. By "formal contexts," I mean all elaborated verbal structures designed for publication and some degree of permanence, including, therefore, not only literary works, both imaginative and expository, but other genres such as laws, ceremonial recitations of a secular as well as a religious nature, and legal and business documents. By "colloquial contexts," I mean episodes in the life of language as it is used on everyday occasions; such use, though it has its own "formalities" in the rather different sense of stereotyped and predictable expressions (more properly called "formulas"), and though it may be published and preserved for special purposes, is essentially private and fugitive. Words, idioms, patterns of word order and syntax, and other identifiable features of language are "distinctively formal" or "distinctively colloquial" to the degree that they are used in one sort of context and—an essential point—excluded from the other sort. (I disregard for the moment the phenomenon of "allusion," which is dealt with below.) Words and other linguistic features not subject to such exclusion are called "common." It must be added that the difference between formal and colloquial contexts, or "occasions," is in fact one of degree. Conversations taking place during television panels and interviews, for example, may be witnessed by a large impersonal public and may generate statements on issues of social importance which are recorded and repeated intact; such occasions are to that extent "formal." Conversely, some "verbal structures," such as folktales and jokes, are in part traditional in form, in part fluid and spontaneous; they therefore have affinities with the colloquial uses of language. Literature may of course imitate everyday life (or it may not), as in the mimetic genres and certain types of essay. And the personal letter identifies itself with one realm or the other in accordance with the qualifications and intentions of its author.[14]

The range of our experience of the language on many kinds of occasion enables us, without stopping to identify particular features, to make instinctive judgments as to the formal or colloquial character of a given sequence of words. Thus a "competent" reader may be expected to feel that, as between "he had not previously seen his assailant" and "he had never laid eyes before on the man that hit him," the first looks like an official writeup or newspaper account of an incident, the second like a paraphrase in the third person of the words of someone talking about it. And the same reader may be expected to recognize in each the presence of certain distinguishing features or "markers," the words *previously* and *assailant* being characteristic of the more formal, the expression "laid eyes on" of the more colloquial version.

As regards the stylistic qualities of particular words, we can call on this same competence by borrowing from grammatical studies the commonly used device of the "test frame" containing a blank or slot: an informant is asked whether a given alternative does or does not seem to fit.[15] The differing networks of phrasal combinations and syntactic patterns that bind words together, without our realizing it, in formal and colloquial discourse make it hard to invent versatile frames and limit the practicality of the method. But the point at issue, that stylistic values are a class of verifiable fact, remains unaffected. Thus we should expect from our competent informant the judgment, for instance, that *somnolent* does not fit the slot in "I'm starting to feel ———; I guess I'll turn in," whereas *sleepy* does, and contrariwise, that *turn in* does not fit the slot in "weary with toil, I haste[n] to ———," whereas *seek repose* or *lay me down* does. (I have changed Shakespeare's "haste me to my bed" to allow a grammatical parallel and have supplied the variants *haste* and *hasten* for the sake of the meter.) The frames must of course contain formal or colloquial markers, and they must specify the subject to which the inserted word is to refer; this is important, for different stylistic values tend to be associated, for a given word, with different subject matters; witness the elevated, common, and colloquial status, respectively, of *seat* in "the ——— of power," "a ———at the theatre," and "the ——— of his pants."

The values we ascribe to words and phrases in such judgments, though they seem inherent and inevitable, are in fact fortuitous, dependent on customs perpetuated by successive generations of speakers. Quite simply, a word or any other feature of language seems appropriate for formal contexts if it has regularly been encountered in such contexts and inappropriate if it has not. But in the life of language, history is not destiny. Tests such as I am referring to are valid only to the extent that language is thought always to be used straightforwardly, and to assume this is to disregard the power of the not merely competent but accomplished or resourceful speaker to shift words from their preordained roles. Such speakers, even or perhaps especially in casual and familiar talk, habitually draw on the language of literature and learning for playful, emphatic, and otherwise express- ive effects, while literary prose for its part may be inspired to yank a word out of the colloquial idiom now and then. Such "allusive" incorporation into either sort of context of an element of diction conventionally barred from it complements in the realm of style the vital activity of metaphorical innovation, in colloquial and literary language alike, which occurs continuously in the realm of meaning. A word newly made a metaphor undergoes a sea change; its quality as a word becomes richer and stranger, if only because we find it startling in its new milieu. When Stevens says of the light of the evening star that it "shines / From the sleepy bosom of the real" (p. 481), *sleepy* is not the same sort of word it is in the sentence "I'm starting to feel sleepy." As Stevens uses it, it is twice metaphorical, first because it signifies the state of a "bosom" rather than of a person, second because the bosom in question belongs not to a person but to an idea: reality. Yet the original flavor of the word as diction remains as part of its total effect; if *somnolent* were substituted in the line, a valuable quantum of homeliness and immediacy would be lost.

Though the spectrum of diction in English can be described and schematized without reference to any one area of meaning, it will be helpful as we approach it to have a body of illustrative material in mind. Such material can easily be accumulated by compiling lists, small thesauruses of verbal alternatives for the expression of a given subject matter, ranging from the distinctively formal to the distinctively colloquial. I shall present two such lists here. Their subjects (let them for the moment remain unverbalized) were arbitrarily chosen, though it seemed appropriate, in a discussion having as its ultimate concern the language of poetry, that they should be drawn from the realm of human emotion—our comic or tragic responses to the fortune that lies, as Stevens says, under the clouds and over the frost.

Such lists need not, of course, be restricted to single words; they can and should include phrasal combinations. And as we attempt to determine the stylistic status of individual items on the lists, considerations of syntax and sentence structure will prove relevant as well. We have already had occasion to note that both formal discourse and everyday speech are seamless fabrics, woven together at the verbal surface and beneath it by conventions and laws that defy efforts at exhaus- tive analysis. The qualities of individual words are important in determining the qualities of language, and due attention must be paid them. But language is not modular—the elements it is composed of do not vary independently. If we start with the test frame "I'm starting to feel ———; I guess I'll turn in," the word *somnolent* will not be "generated" in the mind of an informant as an appropriate filler. If, on the other hand, we start with the word *somnolent* and ask for a sentence, the sort of structure exemplified by the original test frame will not be generated. (Cf. the subject compounded of two gerunds in "fasting and watching had made him more than usually somnolent," one of the citations given for *somnolent,* in the meaning in question, in *OED;* in everyday speech, this statement would take some such form as "he had gone without food and sleep for so long that he was much sleepier than usual.") Everyday speech and formal discourse simply do not set about saying things in the same way.

Any area of meaning shades off into others in various directions, and its limits must be arbitrarily defined. In the discussions that follow, I have cast my net wide enough to obtain examples of all the categories of words making up the spectrum of diction in English, without attempting an exhaustive list under either heading. I have not given definitions, or made distinctions among similar meanings, except where meaning is related to stylistic status, and I have let a number of fine points of usage go unremarked, lest this section of the essay grow to disproportionate length. Nor, since the stylistic qualities I am chiefly concerned with are shared by words of all four of the main parts of speech, have I felt it necessary to present the examples under separate grammatical headings.

In relation to my first subject, the words *laugh* and *laughing* come immediately to mind. Both belong to the common level of diction; they are freely used, and felt to be appropriate, in formal and colloquial contexts alike. With the related words *laughter* and *laughable,* we have already moved a notch in the direction of the distinctively formal. The word *laughter* is less at home on the colloquial level than *laugh* or *laughing* because we tend in spontaneous talk to describe behavior in terms of nouns signifying persons and verbs signifying their actions, rather than nouns signifying actions or events. We say "I love to hear him laugh," and "my sides ached from laughing so hard," in preference to "I love to hear his laughter," and "my sides ached from so much laughter." But on those few occasions when the spoken language concerns itself with the action in general—in references to "canned laughter" on television, for example, or a proverb like "Laughter is the best medicine"—the word falls naturally into place.[16]

With regard to the stylistic status of the adjective *laughable* (and its related adverb), we must take note of an aspect of meaning which involves a distinction among kinds of terms. *Laughable* is used in everyday speech largely as a qualitative term, passing judgment rather than simply conveying information. This becomes clear if we compare Dryden's comment on Persius, "He was not a laughable writer" *(OED)* with some such statement of colloquial cast as "you could hardly hear the poor man in the second row—it was laughable," and note the differences in intonation and stress associated with the two kinds of use. *Ridiculous* has the same qualitative function as *laughable* in everyday speech and would seem to be the more widely current of the two. It is also used descriptively, in speech as well as in writing, to mean "causing laughter," and in that meaning may be assigned, along with *laugh* and *laughing,* to the common level of diction.

As we move from *ridiculous* to *ridicule,* we encounter for the first time the sort of distinctively formal word that seems bookish, standing out as high flown in a colloquial frame in comparison with a synonym of common status: "All the kids used to (*laugh at/ridicule*) him behind his back." Continuing with formal examples in this same vein, we think of *ludicrous, hilarious* (in the sense "disposed to laugh") and *hilarity.* Of these, *ludicrous* and *hilarious* have some currency at the colloquial level, resembling *laughable* and *ridiculous* in meaning and tone, while having a more self-consciously "allusive" aura. (*Ridiculous* itself must once have seemed high flown in ordinary speech and must have changed in stylistic quality as a result of continued allusive use; it is a Latin loan word, first recorded in the language in 1550.) Going on to *risibility* and *risible,* we observe a distinction within the formal level; these are true "hard words," encountered at a more advanced stage of education, and thus known to fewer speakers, than *ridicule, ludicrous,* and *hilarious/hilarity.* (An exception should be made for the expression "to tickle someone's risibilities," a formula of allusive and humorous character occasionally heard in everyday speech.) The most learned words of all in this area of meaning, and the least likely to turn up in colloquial contexts, are *cachinnate* and *cachinnation;* the latter appears in Stevens's "Mozart, 1935" in a request to the "poet" to play the "envious cachinnation" of the present on the piano. Another group of words of distinctively formal quality includes *mirth, merry,* and their cognates *mirthful, merrily,* and *merriment;* these words are associated for us rather with literature than with learning, as is true also of the formula "to laugh to scorn."

Looking now in the direction of the colloquial, we think of the word *funny.* Beyond this, the examples that come to mind are, significantly, not colloquial words, but colloquial meanings of words which in other meanings belong to the common level of diction: *killing, a scream, a howl,* and the verbs *howl* and *roar.* These are metaphorical and also hyperbolical in character; each must at some time have been used innovatively in the everyday language with reference to laughter and have become established in such use by repetition. Similar meanings are expressed by another group of words, including *hysterical, hysterics,* and *convulsions,* and such related phrases as "to have hysterics," "to be convulsed." As Latin borrowings of originally learned and formal quality, these words further illustrate the allusive propensities of language at the colloquial level (cf. the expression "excruciatingly funny"). The same metaphoric and hyperbolic tendencies are shown by a group of colloquialisms of compound form, for example, *belly laugh, horselaugh, laugh (laff) riot, laugh fest,* and *sidesplitting,* as well as by formulas such as "to die laughing," "to split one's sides," "to be in stitches." The word *laugh* also figures in certain colloquial expressions: "to (just) laugh and laugh," "that's a laugh," and "So-and-so is a lot of laughs," that is, "a very funny person." (The last two are instances not of metaphor but of metonymy, the word signifying laughter being used for the thing or person that causes laughter.)

My remaining examples belong for the most part to two specific formative categories and present special problems of tone and stylistic status. There is, first, a group of frequentatives: verbs (and nouns derived from them) which have in modern English the suffixes -er and -le and which denote repetitive or continuous actions, usually on a small scale.[17] The relevant examples are *chortle, chuckle, giggle, snicker, snigger,* and *titter.* All are sound symbolic in force, as is true of this class generally.[18] Some frequentatives seem to have been formed from existing stems; a case in point here is *chuckle.* Others, like *giggle, snicker* (of which *snigger* is a modification), and *titter* are words without pedigree, having their source in the anonymous expressive activities of the spoken language. *Chortle,* a blend of *chuckle* and *snort,* was of course created by Lewis Carroll, but is no less "of imitative origin" for having a known author.

A second group is the iteratives: two-part compound words of which the elements are related as phonetic variants of a stem, and whose meanings, like those of the frequentatives, involve an element of "iteration" or repetition.[19] The iteratives signifying various kinds of laughter are *ha ha* and its dialect variant *haw haw, he-he, tehee,* and the recent American slang coinage *yuk-yuk,* which is listed in *Webster's 3d* but not in *Webster's 2d.*[20] Most of these started out as interjections; some have acquired a limited range of use in other grammatical roles. Like the frequentatives, the iteratives are regularly sound symbolic in expressive force.[21] There are three subtypes, of which the reduplicative is exemplified above by *ha ha,* the rhyming by *tehee.* The third subtype, richly represented in the language at large, though not, as it happens, in the area of meaning we are canvassing at the moment, exhibits gradation, or repetition of a consonant frame with a change of vowel (usually, though not invariably, from short *i* to short *a* or short *o*); random examples are *chitchat, zigzag, ding-dong,* and *flip-flop.* Iteratives may be extended in form (*hanky-panky, higgledy-piggledy*), and are sometimes made up of frequentatives (*pitter-patter, tittle-tattle*).

To complete the roster of sound-symbolic words relevant to the action of laughing, we should add *guffaw,*[22] and should note that the iterative *yuk-yuk* is based on an interjection *yuk,* imitative of a sarcastic laugh (see n. 30 below).

The stylistic status of the frequentatives and iteratives, like that of many other words of sound-symbolic origin, cannot be adequately described in terms of a distinction between formal contexts and colloquial contexts generally. We must ask not merely whether such words appear in literary works as well as in everyday speech, but what sorts of literary works they appear in and to what effect. In this connection, it is necessary to consider their expressive values as terms. They have of course a sensory vividness deriving from the mutually reinforcing relationship between phonetic shape and meaning. More important, many of them have qualitative meanings tending to inhibit their use in discursive prose and literary works belonging to the high formal tradition. The iteratives as a class are playful, tinged with familiarity and often with more or less gentle ridicule. And the same is true of those frequentatives whose subject matter is human behavior.[23] Under the heading of laughter, the actions denoted by the words listed above are stigmatized as foolish or trivial (*tehee, giggle, titter*), crude or coarse (*haw haw, yuk, yuk-yuk,* and, less emphatically, *guffaw*), malicious, gloating, or lewd (*he-he, snicker, snigger*). We do not find them in the Bible or religious ritual, or in laws or political oratory; they appear rarely or never in Spenser, Milton, Wordsworth, and Arnold.[24] Phonetically self-signalizing and qualitatively charged, they lack the simplicity and potential dignity of words like *laugh* and *laughter*. And they lack also the conscious or unconscious associations for us of such words with the sententious and the sacred. "A time to laugh"; "Laugh and the world laughs with you"; "I am tired of tears and laughter, / And men that laugh and weep"; to substitute *ha ha* or *chuckle* or *titter* in any of these would bring about stylistic collapse. Yet the more colorful words have dramatic potentialities of their own, as poets have not failed to recognize. *Tehee* was immortalized in *The Miller's Tale* (its earliest recorded use in English), and we remember the melancholy yet vivid words of J. Alfred Prufrock, who had seen the eternal Footman hold his coat, and snicker. The peculiar derogatory force of the frequentative is exploited, too, by Stevens in the concluding lines of "The Dwarf," where "the final dwarf of you" is pictured as

> Sitting beside your lamp, there citron to nibble
> And coffee dribble . . . Frost is in the stubble.
>
> (p. 208)

Stubble, in origin a diminutive formation, enhances the "belittling" effect of the frequentative verbs *nibble* and *dribble,* and the three words rhyme together in a kind of inane singsong befitting the dramatized *reductio ad absurdum.*

The examples relative to the second of my two subjects can be presented more briefly, as they fall into corresponding groups to which much the same generalizations apply. *Cry, crying,* and *tears* come first to mind as "common" words comparable in value with *laugh* and *laughing. Lament, lamentable,* and *lamentation* are distinctively formal; of these, *lament* and *lamentable* are most susceptible of emphatic allusive use among educated speakers, though neither has gained the currency of *hilarious* or *ludicrous. Lachrymose, lachrymal,* and *lachrymation* correspond to *risible, risibility,* and *cachinnate/cachinnation* as learned words, less widely known than *lament* and its cognates. *Weep, weeping, tearful,* and the compound word *teardrops* (used largely as a metrical variant of tears) resemble *mirth, merry,* and their cognates in seeming not so much learned as literary or poetic words. The language also possesses an alliterating formula of traditionally literary quality, "to weep and wail."

Looking next for colloquial examples, we think of the metaphors *bawl* and *howl;* the latter, as noted earlier, also has a colloquial meaning, "to laugh loudly." *Hysterics* and *hysterical,* like *howl,* have colloquial meanings with reference to weeping, as well as laughter, which presumably developed as a result of allusive use. Another adjective of colloquial status is *weepy;* so too is the noun *cry,* as distinct from the verb. *Crybaby, crying jag,* and *tearjerker* correspond to *laugh fest* and its ilk as colloquial words of compound form and metaphoric-hyperbolic meaning; colloquial formulas of similar quality include "to cry one's eyes out," "to weep one's heart out," and "to weep buckets." The relevant frequentatives are *blubber, sniffle, snivel,* and *whimper;* the iterative class is represented only by *boo-hoo,* which belongs to the rhyming subtype. All these have the vividness and derogatory tone of the frequentatives discussed under the heading of laughter, and have been subject to the same sorts of limitations in range of use. But the word *sob,* though of sound-symbolic origin, is free of trivial and derogatory implications and may be assigned to the common level of diction as equally suitable for use in the spoken language of everyday and the most serious of literary narratives.

The general account of the spectrum of diction in English that follows will be illustrated so far as possible from the two preceding lists. It posits a range of stylistic values between formal and colloquial extremes, divided into the three levels of the formal, the colloquial, and the common. These levels are seen as correlating with certain categories of origin and formation in the realm of language per se, such that the words belonging to a given category will tend to inhabit a given level—though, as with all correlations, general rules do not guarantee the accuracy of predictive judgments. The range of stylistic values and the relevant linguistic categories are seen in turn in relation to the range of frequency of use in the language, between the extremes of common words and rare.

The basic correlation, referred to early in this chapter, between statistically high proportions of words of Romance and Latinate origin and distinctively formal stylistic qualities, was described as holding true for passages of English text, that is, for sequences of words of which a majority will, inevitably, be native. A similar correlation is presupposed for words taken singly; such a correlation implies that, as between Romance or Latinate and native alternatives within a given area of meaning, the Romance and Latinate words will tend to seem more formal than the native ones. If we look first at the specifically Romance component of the language, as opposed to both Latinate French and Latin, we find this tendency most clearly operative in areas of meaning involving distinctions of social class or degrees of refinement—which is to say that formal stylistic status in Romance words is to a significant degree "subject-matter bound." Neither of the two lists compiled above, in fact, contains a Romance alternative of distinctively formal quality: the verb *cry,* which is Romance, belongs to the common level equally with native *tears.* But we may note that *cry* is distinctively formal in the meaning it shares with native *call* (*out*), and to that extent follows the rule. Relevant topics which will be familiar to students of the history of the language include food and clothing; thus native *meal, food,* and *eat* belong to the common level of diction, whereas Romance *banquet, feast, viands,* and *dine* are formal. Native *clothes* and *clothing* differ similarly from Romance *dress* (in its general meaning), *apparel, attire, garb, garments,* and *raiment.* (The "apposite ritual" projected by Stevens for the ripened melon in "The Comedian as the Letter C" is to be "performed in verd *apparel*" [p. 39]; we might note also the more specifically described "complacencies of the *peignoir*" [p. 66] of "Sunday Morning.") The fact that the Romance words tend to add some such qualification as "sumptuous" or "elegant" to the basic meaning of each group does not invalidate them as alternatives of expression; rather, it reminds us that formality is a social as well as a stylistic mode of behavior (see n. 14 to this chapter). Even in areas of meaning such as these there are counterinstances, for example, *dress* (in the sense "woman's garment"), *coat, dinner, supper,* and others, all of which belong to the common level of diction and show how thoroughly it has been infiltrated by the Romance component of the language since the Norman Conquest.

The correlation between etymology and stylistic value is stronger for Latinate (including Latinate French) words than for Romance words and is illustrated in a wider range of meanings. Within the lists compiled above, it is exemplified by *ludicrous, hilarity, lament,* and their cognates. At the formal level of diction, Latinate origin is most predictable in words that strike us as learned or difficult; *risible, cachinnation,* and *lachrymose,* among others cited earlier, are cases in point. Here again a cultural specification is involved: the technical vocabularies of both humanistic and scientific learning, for obvious historical reasons, are predominantly Latinate, though recent exceptions like *string* and *kernel* in transformational grammar, *black hole* in astronomy, and the delightful *quark,* borrowed from *Finnegans Wake* by the atomic physicist Murray Gell-Mann, may be cited as exceptions to the rule which perhaps indicate a trend.[25]

If "qualities of ornate or learned elevation" in passages of English text are conferred on them by the Romance and Latinate words they contain, it would seem to follow that words of native origin are in general lacking in such qualities. Native words do, in fact, tend to occupy the common level of diction; that is to say, they have been handed down in literary and colloquial contexts alike. Passages having statistically high proportions of words of native origin (defining "high" precisely, as "over 90 percent") will, barring eccentricities of grammar or unusual phrasal linkages, seem simple and lucid. Purged of distinctively colloquial elements, such language may take on a biblical loftiness of tone:

> Was heaven where you thought? It must be there.
> It must be where you think it is, in the light
> On bed-clothes, in an apple on a plate.
> It is the honey-comb of the seeing man.
> It is the leaf the bird brings back to the boat.

(p. 217)

Of the above forty-nine words from Stevens's gospel of the everyday, only *plate* (Romance in the sense "shallow dish") is of non-native origin; the dramatic significance of the references to honeycomb[26] and the return of the dove to the ark is enhanced by the poet's choice of diction.

Such suggestive powers are most strikingly present in an important group of words within the native stock to which we must now turn our attention. These words once belonged to the common level of diction: they were used in the early sixteenth-century translations of the Bible associated with the coming of Protestantism to England and in the poetry of that century as well. They became obsolete in the spoken language but continued in use in the inherited language of literature and religion, where they have remained familiar to us to this day. The processes whereby these words were confined to the formal level of diction were under way well before the publication in 1611 of the linguistically conservative King James or Authorized Version of the Bible, which no longer reflected the common idiom of its time.[27] The resultant body of archaisms naturally acquired a sacred and solemn aura; it was drawn on by Milton and others in the seventeenth century and, later, by the Romantics and post-Romantics, from Blake through Frost and Stevens, in a still viable tradition of high formality in English.[28] The words *merry, mirth, weep,* and others cited as examples of formal diction in the two lists compiled above, belong to this special biblical-poetic vocabulary, which includes a host of words in all areas of meaning. It also includes a number of words in particular senses which otherwise belong to the common level (e.g., *tongue* "language," *fowl* "small birds," *whole* "healed," and *cast* "throw"); a set of verb forms, inflectional endings, prepositions, and conjunctions (e.g., *spake* "spoke," *builded* "built," *increaseth* "increases," *be not* "do not be," *unto* "to," and *or ever* "before"); and certain phrasal combinations (e.g., *called his name* "called him," *take heed* "pay attention," *bow down* "bow").[29] Lines in Stevens such as *"Thou art* not August unless I make *thee* so" (p. 251), *"Behold* the men in helmets *borne* on steel" (p. 259), and "We make a *dwelling* in the evening air" (p. 524), derive part of their power from this source.

If we look for an etymological category comparable with Romance or Latinate origin that correlates positively, at the other end of the spectrum of diction, with distinctively colloquial status, we find it, paradoxically, in lack of etymology—in the sort of word history that is obscure or, at most, conjectural. The significance of this category becomes clearer when we have recognized a distinction in lexicography between two senses of origin: a genealogical sense (as in "native origin," "French origin") and a psychological or motivational sense (as in "imitative origin"). All words, if we trace their ancestry back far enough, are "of unknown origin." For the etymologist, the origin of a word is unknown in terms of a chosen time standpoint, a period prior to which evidence is lacking. If an Old English or Old French word is the ancestor of a modern word, we say that the origin of the modern word is known. But the origin of the Old English or Old French word may itself be obscure. A word is said to be of unknown origin in modern English if it is first documented in the language after the Old English period, has no known Old English cognates, and cannot be explained as a foreign borrowing.

The stylistic implications of lack of documentary evidence for the history of a word depend partly on the fact that the written records from which our knowledge of earlier phases of the language is derived are limited both in quantity and in kind. They probably do not give us a complete picture of the vocabulary of Old English at any level; in addition, their nature is such as largely to exclude diction of a lively and familiar sort. Aside from the poetry, which is uniformly composed in a solemn and dignified traditional style, they consist largely of legal documents and discursive prose dealing with religious and other weighty subjects. (The lists of native equivalents of Latin words in the surviving glossaries are an important exception and contain a goodly number of Old English words we would otherwise not have seen.) The stylistic scope of the written language becomes larger in Middle English. Many words which now make their first appearance must have existed earlier on the colloquial level—this, we assume, has always had its characteristic fecundity and vigor—but gained no entree into lexicographical history until they served the expressive purposes of a particular author whose works happen to be known to us. The frequentative verbs are a case in point: though few are found in the written records, cognates in other Germanic languages provide clear evidence for the existence in Old English of a considerable number of formations of this type, both inherited and new. Further evidence is supplied by the appearance of what we must assume to be descendant forms in Middle English and by cognates belonging to other parts of speech. Thus, the Old English verb *scymrian* "to shimmer" (originally *scimrian*, related to a stem *scim-*) is not recorded until late in the period but has cognates in Old Frisian, Middle Dutch, and Middle Low German which indicate that it may well have been part of the common Germanic inheritance. A verb presupposing an Old English form *wrǣstlian* "to wrestle" is found in Lawman's *Brut*; *wrǣstlian* is further implied by the recorded nouns *wrǣstlunge*, *wrǣstlere*, and *wrǣstlinde* (see *OED*, s.v. *shimmer* v.[1], *wrestle* v., and the general discussions s.v. *-le suffix*, 3, and *-er*, suffix[5]).

It is not in the least surprising that many words "of unknown origin" in English in the historical sense are of sound-symbolic origin in the motivational sense. Such words might be described as "anonymous" or "popular" in derivation, and they have marked affinities of a dramatic nature with the language of everyday. The spontaneous coinage of new sound-symbolic words, which we can observe taking place around us,[30] is merely a more striking manifestation of the imitative handling of the sounds of words in which all or most of us engage in lively talk, prolonging *long* for emphasis, saying *cold* with an expressive shiver, sounding the *s* and *g* of *disgusting* with more sibilant and velar force than the same letters in *guest* or *gossamer*. And the sound-symbolic vocabulary of the language (in which the frequentatives and the iteratives must in general be included) reflects too the tonal coloring of everyday speech: its earthiness, its humor and exaggeration, its affectionate or hostile raillery—qualities tending to inhibit the use of this vocabulary in literary contexts.

The available historical data on the sound-symbolic words listed above under the headings of laughter and tears are such as we might expect. Except for *ha ha* (which happens to be mentioned in Aelfric's *Grammar*, along with *he he*, as "betokening laughter in Latin and English"), none is recorded within the Old English period. *Blubber* and *tehee* make their first appearance in Middle English, *tehee* in *The Miller's Tale*, as already noted, *boohoo* in Skelton (ca. 1525). Of the remaining frequentatives—*chortle, chuckle, giggle, snicker, sniffle, snigger, snivel, titter,* and *whimper*—the earliest citation given in *OED* is that for *giggle* (1509).

In considering the stylistic implications of "unknown" and "sound-symbolic origin," we must again remind ourselves that we are dealing with correlations which may not be reflected in particular cases. Some sound-symbolic words were apparently in common use in Old English, and are well documented; of these, a few have venerable pedigrees indeed, for example, *spīwan* or *spīōwian* "to spew," thought to be cognate with Latin *spuere* and thus to go back to Indo-European. And some words of unknown origin in the sense discussed here belong rather to the literary than the common or colloquial level of diction today, such as *gaze*, recorded earliest in Chaucer's *Clerk's Tale* in its original derogatory meaning "to look vacantly . . . about," and perhaps related to the now obsolete and clearly sound-symbolic verb *gaw* "to gape" (see *OED*, s.v. *gaze* v. and *gaw* v.; cf. *gawk* a. and v. and *gawky* a. and sb.).

If we now look at diction from the point of view of the range of frequencies of occurrence, rather than the range from formal to colloquial, a few hypothetical generalizations suggest themselves. It seems clear that those words which are common in terms of level of diction are also most commonly in use, or, to put the idea in reverse, that lack of restriction in range of use makes for frequency of occurrence. This generalization would seem equally plausible whether we are thinking of "use" in terms of alternatives relative to a given area of meaning or absolutely, in the language at large: the word *laugh,* we assume, occurs more commonly than either *hilarity* or *giggle* in all references to laughter; the vocabulary of the common level of diction occurs more commonly than that of the formal or colloquial level on all occasions taken together, in relation to all subjects (see Appendix B). At either level, further limitations in range of use will confer more specific stylistic values. Formal language will be restricted primarily in terms of kinds of literary works or formal genres associated with specific areas of culture, and colloquial language primarily in terms of socially or otherwise defined groups of speakers. Thus, words encountered in literary contexts only at advanced levels

57

of learning are a subgroup of the formal words encountered in literary contexts generally, while the use of poetic diction and the "biblical" diction of sermons and prayers (as well as the Bible itself) is restricted in terms of genre. The "technical terms" of particular branches of learning, insofar as the distinctions and categories they signify are "subject-matter bound," are not true alternatives of diction in the sense in which *cry* and *lament,* or *laugh* and *giggle,* or *sickness* and *malady* (frequent in Stevens) are alternatives. But in allusive use, translated out of their proper contexts, technical terms become an aspect of descriptive style, of what I wish to call the terminological level of form. In this connection, we think of Stevens's sporadic appropriation of words from the language of philosophy; relevant examples are *absolute* sb. (p. 263), *apperception* (p. 440), *ding an sich* (p. 29), and *premise* (p. 489), among others, while *major* (pp. 334, 340, 404, etc.) doubtless owes something to "major premise." Within the colloquial level, range of use may be further restricted geographically, or in terms of age, class, educational background, or occupation. And areas of practical expertise such as farming and seafaring, whose primary mode of expression is the spoken language, will develop technical vocabularies of their own which remain nonetheless essentially colloquial when written down in manuals of instruction and the like.

As we approach, at either level, the extreme of the "rare" or unfamiliar word, an element of the personal or of chance inevitably intrudes itself: unfamiliar to whom? A word, literary or colloquial, that has never been encountered by one person may happen to be well known to another. At this point an additional consideration must be brought into play: the tendency of a seldom or newly encountered word, by virtue of its assumed meaning in context, its phonetic shape, and its recognized or guessed-at linguistic affiliations, to assimilate itself to groups of words of established stylistic status. Both the unusual word and the true nonce word or neologism are conspicuous ingredients in Stevens's verbal peddler's pie, and his innovative language runs the gamut of stylistic values from the most high-flown Latinity to the most homely and vivid sound symbolism. Words that a given reader may encounter in English for the first time in Stevens's poetry include, on the one hand, *curule* (p. 363), *degustations* (p. 181), *lacustrine* (p. 24), and *perihelion* (p. 490) and, on the other hand, *chirr* (p. 80), *gawks* sb. (p. 460) *rucks* (p. 31), and *scraggy* (p. 393), all duly listed in *Webster's Eighth Collegiate Dictionary*. They also include new Latinate borrowings and formations like *epitaphium* (p. 364), *fulgor* (p. 495), *spissantly* (p. 133, from Latin *spissare* "to thicken," used here in the sense "increasingly," or perhaps "in increasingly large numbers"), and *vocalissimus* (p. 113); new sound-symbolic words like *whirroos* (p. 442) and *glubbal glub,* with a sideswipe at *global* (p. 301), new frequentatives like *chantering* (p. 277), *clickering* (p. 28), and *skritter* (p. 160), and new iteratives like *dizzle-dazzle* (p. 530), *fuddle-fiddling* (p. 260), *lol-lolling* (p. 458), *parl-parled* (p. 268), and *shiddow-shaddow* (p. 279), not to mention importations from the modern European languages such as *roy* (p. 302), *phantomerei* (p. 459), *niño* (p. 248), and *scienza* (p. 248).

A few observations about the nature of the dictional repertoire at distinctively formal and distinctively colloquial levels remain to be made. A major difference between the two is that the formal level has a sizable vocabulary of its own, consisting to a large extent of Romance and Latinate loan words which entered the language in literary use. Some of these have changed their status from formal to common, coming into favor in the spoken as well as the written language, with or without new developments in meaning. Another component of the formal vocabulary consists of words that have changed their status by restriction, starting out as common but falling into disuse in speech while continuing to be transmitted in written texts. This group is largely of native origin, but includes a number of Romance words and some Latinate words as well (see n. 29 below). The colloquial level also has a small vocabulary peculiar to itself, including words of sound-symbolic origin, frequentatives, iteratives, and fanciful or parodic coinages. But the colloquial idiom consists to a much greater extent of special meanings and uses of words that are otherwise of common status. All these elements reflect the dramatizing and emphatic tendencies of familiar speech; their metaphorical and hyperbolical character is striking, though vividness may become dulled in particular cases by routine use. Of the common words which have developed colloquial meanings, most are of course of native origin; fewer are Romance, still fewer are Latinate.

We should also note in passing a difference between the two levels with respect to terminology: an abundance of abstract terms in formal language complemented by an abundance of concrete and sensory terms in colloquial language. The historical reasons for this are obvious; abstract concepts are dealt with far more in the various literary genres than in familiar speech, which is preoccupied most of the time with the practical problems and noncognitive experience of everyday life. And there is another sense in which the vocabulary of the formal level of language is abstract. To the extent that the colloquial level has names for abstract concepts as such, these tend to be metaphors based on concrete and sensory terms: *guts* meaning "courage," *the blues* meaning "melancholy," *shakedown* meaning "extortion." Such words bring their experiential immediacy into the realm of the abstract. The more formal Romance and Latinate alternatives are usually metaphors themselves, but the sources of these metaphors (the heart in *courage*, the black in *melancholy*, the twist in *extortion*) are rarely thought of as such in ordinary use.

The essentials of the above discussion of the spectrum of diction in English are set forth in figure 1. It must be remembered that double vertical rules stand for correlations or tendencies rather than for rigid rules of correspondence.

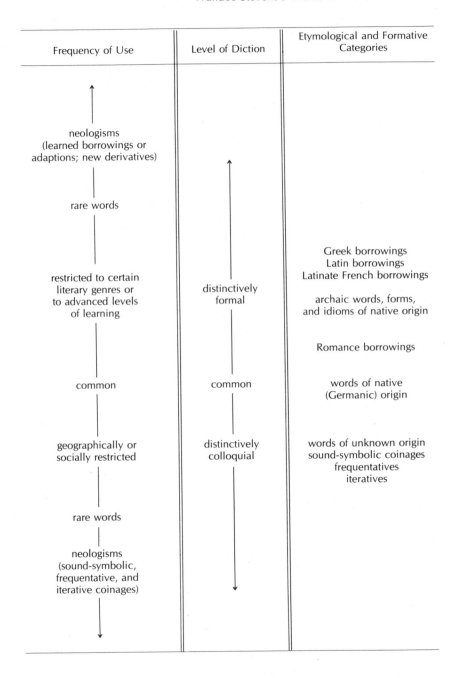

Fig. 1. The spectrum of diction in English

FOUR

WALLACE STEVENS'S WORLD OF WORDS
AN ALWAYS INCIPIENT COSMOS

The exact repetition in the present of the verbal and other forms of behavior used on ceremonial occasions in the past has always been an important means of inducing or perpetuating reverence for authority. Despite Wallace Stevens's insistent and sometimes rude repudiations of the cultural establishment, including the academies and their old descriptions of the world, the first thing to be noted here is his consistent and thorough exploitation of the inherited resources of high formal language. These of course include elevated diction (sporadically undercut, as we have observed, by eccentric word combinations); they also, less obviously, include a repertoire of grammatical constructions, ways of putting together and connecting phrases, clauses, and sentences whose expressive power consists in our conscious or unconscious identification of them with certain kinds of formal context. Two areas of culture and the literary genres connected with them are of especial importance for Stevens. We find them reflected in a scholarly or discursive and a sacred or hierophantic strain, respectively, in his idiosyncratic version of the high style.

The scholar in Stevens's poetry (more narrowly, the philosopher) expounds and excogitates in a language whose forms and patterns suggest the treatise, the textbook, or the classroom lecture. This discursive voice sounds sporadically in single lines and short line sequences; it is most conspicuously audible in whole poems or sections of poems explicitly dramatized as philosophic essays—for example, "Study of Two Pears" (an "opusculum paedagogum"), "The Glass of Water," "Connoisseur of Chaos," "Description without Place," and parts of "Notes toward a Supreme Fiction" and "An Ordinary Evening in New Haven."

In such passages and poems, terminology and syntax are characterized by the preponderance of nominal over verbal and adjectival elements; abstract nouns of course occur frequently, as does the verb *to be* in its role of copula.

> If seeming is description without place,
> The spirit's universe, then a summer's day,
> Even the seeming of a summer's day,
> Is description without place;
>
> (p. 343)

> The freshness of transformation is
>
> The freshness of a world. It is our own,
> It is ourselves, the freshness of ourselves,
> And that necessity and that presentation
>
> Are rubbings of a glass in which we peer.
>
> (p. 398)

> The poem is the cry of its occasion,
> Part of the res itself and not about it.
>
> (p. 473)

Another feature of importance in these examples is the reiteration of key words and phrases. The effect is didactic; the pace of exposition seems to be deliberately held back while thought is elaborated and qualified, as if by a careful teacher. With regard to larger grammatical structures, Stevens's poetry of course presents us with a host of examples of the patterns traditionally used in formal discourse and excluded, by and large, from spontaneous utterance—multiple subordinations, compoundings of subordinate and independent clauses, participial or infinitive constructions where everyday speech would prefer a finite verb. But sentence structure in Stevens's discursive language may go to the opposite extreme, with a brevity and simplicity as remote from ordinary speech as the conventional elaborations and complications of formal syntax.

> The pears are not viols,
> Nudes or bottles.
> They resemble nothing else . . .
>
> The shadows of the pears
> Are blobs on the green cloth.
> The pears are not seen
> As the observer wills.
>
> (pp. 196–97)

> Ideas are men. The mass of meaning and
> The mass of men are one. Chaos is not
>
> The mass of meaning. It is three or four
> Ideas or, say, five men or, possibly, six.
>
> (p. 255)

Again we note the reiteration of key words and phrases; again there is an effect of didactic emphasis and retardation of pace. A minor feature of similar import is the sequence of numbers or letters conventionally serving to mark off the divisions of a text or the points of an argument—the Roman numerals preceding the stanzas of "Study of Two Pears," the "A" and "B" propositions and "Projections" of "Connoisseur of Chaos" and "So-and-So Reclining on Her Couch," the numbered descriptive "exfoliations" of "Someone Puts a Pineapple Together," part III.

A second important realm from which Stevens draws traditionally formal features of language is the sacred or hierophantic, and, in looking to this source, we must recognize that the formal language of religion cannot be fully distinguished from that of poetry itself. Much of the most important poetry of the earlier periods of English, as of other European literatures, is explicitly Christian. And those later poets who found Christianity inadequate or rejected it entirely have themselves tended to assume the role of nondenominational or secular priest, proselytizing in the very accents of religious authority. Stevens himself is a notable case in point. Though he is capable of lashing out ironically against major articles of the Christian faith, of calling the resurrected Jesus a "three-days' personage" (p. 97) and the crucifixion a "glamorous hanging" (p. 192), his poetry from first to last uses Christian imagery for its own purposes with utmost seriousness, having its "dove, alighting" (p. 357), its "communion" (p. 253), its "Candle a Saint" (p. 223), its "chants" of "final peace" (p. 258), its "pastoral nun" whose final vision identifies poetry with apotheosis (p. 378), even its "sudarium" (p. 188) and "wounds" transfigured into roses (p. 318). Genres and modes of discourse associated with the sacred—invocation, prayer, prophecy, hymn, litany, parable—frequently give form to single lines and short passages and, on a larger scale, to poems and sections of long poems; "To the One of Fictive Music," "The Idea of Order at Key West," "Chocorua to Its Neighbor," "The Owl in the Sarcophagus," and parts of "Esthetique du Mal," "Notes," and "An Ordinary Evening" are important examples.[1]

Terminology and syntax are here characterized by the predominance of nominal *and* adjectival over verbal elements, with heavy reliance on qualitative terms of solemnizing or celebratory import, some venerable, some innovative:

> The brilliant height
> And hollow of him by its brilliance calmed,
> Its brightness burned the way good solace seethes.
>
> This was peace after death, the brother of sleep, . . .
>
> Adorned with cryptic stones and sliding shines,
> An immaculate personage in nothingness.
>
> (p. 434)

We find inversions of word order of the time-honored poetic sort ("Green is the night" [p. 223], "In his poems we find peace" [p. 251], "By one caterpillar is great Africa devoured" [p. 456]); the negative qualifications and logical connections among clauses characteristic of the discursive mode give way to appositives and series of nouns and adjectives (also, strikingly, of finite verbs). These may accumulate with a rhythmic continuity furthered by the use of linking conjunctions that eliminate pauses and with an intensity enhanced by traditionally "rhetorical" repetitions of meanings, words, and sounds:

> There was
> Only the great height of the rock
> And the two of them standing still to rest.
>
> There was the cold wind and the sound
> It made, away from the muck of the land
> That they had left, heroic sound
> Joyous and jubilant and sure.
>
> (p. 126)

> And I walked and talked
> Again, and lived and was again, and breathed again
> And moved again and flashed again, time flashed again.
>
> (p. 238)

When the discursive content itself of Stevens's poetry takes on a solemn aura, as it frequently does, the propounding and sanctifying voices merge. Thus the sixth section of "Description without Place" moves from its expository opening,

> Description is revelation. It is not
> The thing described, nor false facsimile,

to a climax in which definition and distinctions give way to celebratory variations on the symbolic theme of a "text we should be born that we might read,"

> the book of reconciliation,
> Book of a concept only possible
>
> In description, canon central in itself,
> The thesis of the plentifullest John.
>
> (p. 345)

We see the abstract concept of revelation turning into the Book of Revelation as philosophic statement becomes colored by Christian allusion.

The inherited language of the formal modes of discourse in English is, as we know, associated with elevated diction of the sort tending to give rise to statistically high percentiles of words of Romance and Latinate origin. It is thus to be expected that successive Romance-Latinate percentiles of 20 and over will be found in poems like "Credences of Summer" and others in which the discursive and hierophantic modes predominate.[2] The diction of this and other similar poems is to some degree bound to the subject matters or areas of culture associated with these two modes, as is apparent in the passages quoted above in words like *description, presentation, res, state, concept,* and *thesis,* on the one hand; and *peace, immaculate, revelation, reconciliation,* and *canon,* on the other. But subject matter cannot fully account for the presence in these same passages of other words of Romance and Latinate origin such as *cry, resemble, brilliant, adorned, cryptic, personage, facsimile,* and *central.* These latter must be recognized as

symptoms of the pervasive bias in Stevens's language we noted earlier, its persis-
tent exploitation, for all its flamboyant originality, of the inherited features of high
formal style. An abundance of such features may even make his most opaque
passages *rhetorically* intelligible, directly conveying such qualities as discursive
seriousness or visionary exaltation:

> This is the mirror of the high serious:
> Blue verdured into a damask's lofty symbol,
>
> Gold easings and ouncings and fluctuations of thread
> And beetling of belts and lights of general stones,
> Like blessed beams from out a blessed bush
>
> Or the wasted figurations of the wastes
> Of night, time and the imagination,
> Saved and beholden, in a robe of rays.
>
> (p. 477)

Here the words themselves dazzle not only in the intricacies of their sounds and
rhythms and their qualities as diction but in their unaccustomed combinations
and applications as well, whether or not we grasp their meanings as metaphorical
and symbolic description. The reader of such a passage may well feel that in it
rhetoric has shouldered meaning aside to an extent verging on self-indulgent
display—a vice of style that is perhaps inevitable, given so tremendous a virtuosity.

Stevens's pervasive formal bias, then, manifests itself on the level of diction not
only in learned and allusive language but also in the frequent occurrence of
distinctively formal words of Romance and Latinate origin, tied neither to any
particular area of meaning nor to any particular genre or set of genres, for which
native synonyms belonging to the common level of diction are available. Examples of such "free formal" tags are *desire* versus *want*, *distant* versus *far*, *edifice*
versus *building*, *interior* versus *inner/inside*, *labor* versus *work*, *possess* versus
own, *regard* in the meaning it shares with *look (at)*, and *respond/response* versus
answer.[3] Another such symptom is the use of full, in preference to contracted,
forms of the verb: "*Let us* make hymns" (p. 151), "I *cannot* bring a world quite
round" (p. 165), "*We are* conceived in your conceits" (p. 195), "*It is* how he gives
his light. *It is* how he shines" (p. 205), "*It has not* always had / To find" (p. 239),
"We *do not* say ourselves like that in poems" (p. 311).

While fully exploiting the inherited repertoire of formal Romance and Latinate
diction, Stevens by no means neglects that other traditional means of elevation in
English, described in the preceding chapter, which involves the use of simple words
mostly of native origin, associated since early modern times with poetry and the
Bible. Except in the case of archaisms and archaic forms (e.g., *begat*, *spake*), our
recognition of such associations and our response to the stylistic qualities gener-

ated by them are dependent on the contexts in which the words appear—on relationships among the ideas expressed and on the cooperative presence of other words of similar potential. In this respect, poetic-biblical diction differs from diction of the ornate, elevated variety. The word *argentine,* for instance (used memorably by Stevens in the third part of "Notes"), has its distinctively formal quality regardless of context; the word *silver* belongs to the common level of diction but has certain biblical associations (most notably in connection with the thirty pieces of silver paid to Judas) which might or might not be evoked and form part of its expressive value in a literary work.

To follow this allusive process in operation, let us look at what happens to the word *know,* among others, in "The Hand as a Being." The poem is written in the form of a parable or simple allegorical narrative; its story is located at the outset "in the first canto of the final canticle" and is thereby linked in significance to the similarly allegorical (or at least traditionally allegorized) Song of Songs, also known as Canticles.[4] Like the Song of Songs, "The Hand as a Being" has an ostensibly sexual theme. In it, the beneficent seduction of the central figure by a mythic feminine being symbolizes a change within the mind from confusion to order. Having been "too conscious of too many things at once," "our man" becomes "composed," with a play on the meanings "serene" and "put into form." At the end of the poem, diction modulates to the extreme of simplicity and Romance and Latinate elements all but disappear:

> Her hand took his and drew him near to her.
> Her hair fell on him and the mi-bird flew
>
> To the ruddier bushes at the garden's end.
> Of her, of her alone, at last he knew
> And lay beside her underneath the tree.
>
> (p. 271)

Of the preceding forty-four words, only *garden* is non-native (Romance). (I consider *mi-* to be a sound-symbolic coinage, as it is also in "the thinnest *mi* of falsetto" in "Parochial Theme" [p. 191], and not the Latinate name of the third note of the musical scale.) In context, the potential biblical suggestiveness of the words *garden* and *tree* and, retrospectively, of *naked* in the first stanza of the poem, is realized with specific reference to the fall of man, and "the hand appeared" of stanza 5 may be seen as alluding to the story of Belshazzar's feast. The verb *drew* in the passage quoted has archaic-poetic status in the sense of "pulled," and *lay beside* is reminiscent of the archaic expression *lie with,* designating sexual intercourse. The prediction of the materializing hand, unlike that of the Old Testament story, is favorable; enlightenment does not bring perdition but comes as a saving grace. The play on the modern and biblical senses of *know,* bringing together the concepts of intellectual enlightenment and sexual consummation, epitomizes the basic symbolic equation of the poem.

So far, we have considered formality in Stevens as a means of associating his poetry with the inherited forms, and thus imputing to it the inherited values of literary and cultural tradition. But it serves other purposes as well, and these should at least be mentioned briefly. First, the solemnity of tone reinforced by formal language in much of the poetry is consonant with Stevens's often-expressed belief in the importance and dignity of the imaginative enterprise, in the poet's public role of helping people to lead their lives (N.A., p. 29). Second, learned diction and other features of elevated language serve here as elsewhere (the point is so obvious that we tend to overlook it) as a kind of accreditation, investing the user with a believable authority. Entirely apart from the significance of each in its context, the foreign words and wide-ranging references to persons and places which appear throughout Stevens's poetry are impressive in general as "verbal credentials." We respect the desire to repudiate the past in the man who proves himself thoroughly conversant with it. And there is a heightening of dramatic intensity in the longing of such a man to divest himself of his knowledge, his melancholy conviction that mental nakedness is a condition of imaginative vitality.

> It may be that the ignorant man, alone,
> Has any chance to mate his life with life
> That is the sensual, pearly spouse, the life
> That is fluent in even the wintriest bronze.
>
> (p. 222)

Such lines, paradoxically redolent of erudition, bring to mind the speaker of Yeats's "The Dawn," whose longing to be "ignorant" is tacitly frustrated by the knowledge displayed in the very poem in which the longing is expressed. Third and last, formality in the sense in which I have been using the word is consonant with formality in the different but related sense of dignity or aloofness of manner. The "central man" of Stevens's poetry is not only an erudite scholar and polyglot but also an austere personage who keeps his distance from us and confides nothing, seeming to dismiss as trivial all personal griefs and joys, if not all personal relationships whatsoever. A symptom of his loftiness of tone is his preference for the impersonal pronoun one over a possible I or you: "One has a malady here" (p. 63); "Among the dogs and dung, / One would continue to contend with one's ideas" (p. 198).

To recognize the pervasive formality of Stevens's poetic language is not to say that that formality is unremittingly sustained. Colloquial phraseology was, in fact, exemplified by one of the passages cited at the beginning of the preceding chapter. But such passages are hard to come by in Stevens, and it is surely significant that statements of major importance in his poetry do not sound like anything anyone would actually say. It is instructive to compare him in this respect with Frost, setting such lines as "Home is the place where, when you have to go there, they have to take you in"; "Something has to be left to God"; "We have ideas yet we haven't tried"; and "It's knowing what to do with things that counts" side by side with "The gaiety of language is our seigneur"; "Life consists / Of propositions about life"; "The reason can give nothing at all / Like the response to desire"; and "The sentiment of the fatal is a part / Of filial love." (Though I cannot resist citing a delightful counterinstance, from "Parochial Theme": "Piece the world together, boys, but not with your hands.") Colloquial phrases may appear in the immediate neighborhood of important pronouncements ("That's it: the more than rational distortion, / The fiction that results from feeling. Yes, that" [p. 406]), but they serve as intensifiers of tone rather than as content carriers, conveying the urgency and excitement attendant upon insight rather than insight itself:

> That's it. The lover writes, the believer hears,
> The poet mumbles and the painter sees,
> Each one, his fated eccentricity.
>
> (p. 443)

More typically, the colloquial note is sounded when all is not well—to express a failure of inner vitality ("My old boat goes round on a crutch / And doesn't get under way" [p. 120]) or the speaker's sense of a stale past or an inane present ("Panoramas are not what they used to be" [p. 134]; "The solar chariot is junk" [p. 332]; "All sorts of flowers. That's the sentimentalist" [p. 316]). Beyond this, it serves in a few poems to give a deceptively casual air to symbolic or mythic narration ("Sure enough, the thunder became men" [p. 220]; "So you're home again, Redwood Roamer, and ready / To feast" [pp. 286–87]).

A particularly interesting and significant aspect of Stevens's poetic language, considered in conjunction with its prevailingly formal tenor, is his vocabulary of sound-symbolic words, including frequentatives and iteratives. This vocabulary bulks large in both number of items and frequencies of occurrence; some of the words in it are used a dozen times or more: for example, *flash* (21), *hum* (20), *boom* (13), and the frequentatives *glitter* (31), *dazzle* (14), *flutter* (14), *sparkle* (12), and *tumble* (12). *Flick* and *flicker* (13 total) and *glisten* (16) should also be listed here; the latter, though labeled sound symbolic neither by the *Oxford Dictionary of Etymology* (1966) nor by the *Shorter Oxford English Dictionary* (3d ed., 1973), has obvious affinities of phonetic shape and meaning with *glitter* and the archaic word *glister*. Such words are inherently sensory and specific, with an immediacy that can animate scenic description (the more so in that many of them literally designate some sort of rapid motion or change), or, in startling metaphorical translation, relieve the dryness of abstract discourse:

> Air is air.
> Its vacancy glitters round us everywhere.
>
> (p. 137)

The banners of the nation flutter, burst
On the flag-poles in a red-blue dazzle, whack
At the halyards.

(p. 390)

Then Ozymandias said the spouse, the bride
Is never naked. A fictive covering
Weaves always glistening from the heart and mind.

(p. 396)

The satisfaction underneath the sense,
The conception sparkling in still obstinate thought.

(p. 448)

Substitution of either a simpler or a more elevated word for any of the sound-symbolic words in the passages above (*brightness* or *glory* for *dazzle, shining* or *luminous* for *glistening* or *sparkling*) throws into relief the latter's peculiar expressive force.

Many, if not most, of the sound-symbolic words in Stevens are in fact assigned metaphorical roles. Reviewing the examples amassed in chapter 3 in relation to the topics of laughing and crying, we find that, of the sound-symbolic words listed there, Stevens has *chuckle, guffaw, titter, blubber,* and *sob.*[5] *Guffaw* and *sob* occur once each in their literal meanings (pp. 15, 317), but *blubber, chuckle,* and *titter,* each used once, refer to sounds made by tom-toms, birds, and locusts, respectively (p. 41; *O.P.,* pp. 28, 71), while *sob* denotes the cooing of the turtledove, called "turtle" in biblical fashion (*O.P.,* p. 71), and, with bitter paradoxical force, the sharp intake of breath in "the laughter of evil" (p. 253). The dramatic qualities deriving from the affinities of such words with the spoken language is retained in metaphorical application, while any suggestion of triviality vanishes in strangeness.[6] The shift of reference may be from one physical agency to another, as when frogs boom (p. 17), water makes a blather (p. 22), the blue guitar chatters or buzzes (p. 167), thunder straggles (p. 208), grass dithers (p. 234), roses tinkle (p. 252), fire fidgets (p. 352), wind whimpers (p. 477), and crickets babble (p. 523). A more radical shift is that from the sensory to the abstract, as in "the pitter-patter of archaic freedom" (p. 292), "the hullabaloo of health and have" (p. 292), a "flick" of feeling (p. 407) or "false flick, false form" (p. 385), "a strength that tumbles everywhere" (p. 354), and "form gulping after formlessness" (p. 411). Words are said to make "glistening reference to what is real" (p. 309), and in "apparition" there are "delicate clinkings not explained" (p. 340). Perhaps most characteristically of all, such metaphors figure in an interpenetration of substance and thought, as, for example, in "The Bouquet":

The bouquet stands in a jar, as metaphor, . . .

> [as] a growth
> Of the reality of the eye, an artifice,
> Nothing much, a flitter that reflects itself, . . .

> The bouquet is part of a dithering:
> Cloud's gold, of a whole appearance that stands and is.
>   (pp. 448, 452)

An especially remarkable metaphorical operation is performed on certain sound-symbolic words which, as normally used, designate partly audible or intelligible speech and have some degree of derogatory force, but which in Stevens are applied to fully articulate speech, including the language of poetry itself. In "The Reader," the statement

> Everything
> Falls back to coldness,
> Even the musky muscadines,
> The melons, the vermilion pears
> Of the leafless garden,

emanates from a disembodied voice described as "mumbling" (p. 147), while in "Examination of the Hero in Time of War" the hero is said to glide

> to his meeting like a lover
> Mumbling a secret, passionate message.
>   (p. 276)

In "A Primitive like an Orb," the speaker concludes that

> the lover writes, the believer hears,
> The poet mumbles and the painter sees,
> Each one, his fated eccentricity.
>   (p. 443)

In "An Ordinary Evening in New Haven," cosmic "actors . . . walk in a twilight muttering lines" (p. 497), and "milky [Stevens-ese for "spiritually nourishing"] lines" are muttered by "the philosophers' man" of "Asides on the Oboe" (p. 250). Elsewhere, Stevens refers to hymns that buzz (p. 65), "a crackling of voices" (p. 292), a lecturer who hems and haws a disquisition on "This Beautiful World of Ours" (p. 429), "the tragic prattle of the fates" (O.P., p. 34), and "the poet's hum" (O.P., p. 71).

By all odds, the most significant instance of this sort of metaphorical use is the word *gibberish* in its three occurrences toward the end of the second section, "It Must Change," of "Notes toward a Supreme Fiction":

> The poem goes from the poet's gibberish to
> The gibberish of the vulgate and back again,

and "It is the gibberish of the vulgate that [the poet] seeks" (pp. 396–97). I shall return to this important passage later. Here the point is that *gibberish*, like other sound-symbolic words similarly translated, dramatizes Stevens's paradoxical insistence that poetic language remain partly inarticulate, partly inhuman, that it incorporate within itself something of "the incommunicable mass" (p. 328) of external reality. The "necessary angel of earth," speaking to the countrymen who have welcomed him, tells them and us that

> in my sight, you see the earth again,
>
> Cleared of its stiff and stubborn, man-locked set,
> And, in my hearing, you hear its tragic drone
>
> Rise liquidly in liquid lingerings,
> Like watery words awash; like meanings said
>
> By repetitions of half-meanings.
>
> (p. 497)

The expressive powers of the sound-symbolic word, half meaning, half echo, fit this description with uncanny aptness.

It is now time to return to our starting point: the perceptible diversity of Stevens's poetic language and particularly his use of many different kinds of words. In terms of the variables included in the spectrum of diction, we can now say that, on a scale of levels of formality, his vocabulary runs from common to elevated, while on a scale of frequencies of use it runs from common to rare, transcending the established boundaries of the language with a profusion of innovative borrowings and formations of both learned and popular types. Colloquial elements, save for a sprinkling of contracted verb forms, are almost wholly lacking. Sound-symbolic words are an important expressive resource for Stevens, but the colloquial tendencies of these are modified by their use in metaphorical meanings. As one element of a prevailingly formal style, diction figures in the production of a variety of effects, from a studied simplicity (with or without biblical allusiveness) to elaboration and exoticism. Odd verbal combinations were identified at the beginning of chapter 3 as a hallmark of his style; among these, we can single out one type as especially worthy of note: that in which Latinate (L) and sound-symbolic (s-s) words appear side by side. The examples "A syllable [L], / Out of these gawky [s-s] flitterings [s-s], / Intones [L] its single emptiness"; "addicts [L] / To blotches [s-s], angular [L] anonymids [L], Gulping [s-s] for shape"; and "the honky-tonk [s-s] out of the somnolent [L] grasses," which were cited earlier, may now be supplemented by "the irised [L] hunks [s-s]" (p. 227); "sprinklings [s-s] of bright particulars [L] from the sky" (p. 344); "delicate [L] clinkings [s-s]" (p. 340); "the dazzle [s-s] / Of mica [L], the dithering [s-s] of grass, / The Arachne [L] integument [L] of dead trees" (p. 234); and "Alive with an enigma's [L] flittering [s-s]" (O.P., p.

71

105). Iterative coinages appear in "A shiddow-shaddow [s-s] of lights revolving [L]" (p. 279) and "a destroying spiritual [L] that digs-a-dog" [s-s] (p. 332). Such sequences become the more conspicuous as one's ear is alerted to their peculiar timbre; they are dramatically significant in that they blend abstraction with sense perception, solemnity with familiarity, embodying on the level of diction one kind of "choice [not] / Between, but of" (p. 403).

To understand how diversity of diction in Stevens is dramatically motivated, we need to think of it in terms not of static patterns of contrast but of temporal unfolding. From this point of view, diversity is change, perceived as we read a number of poems or a single long poem—as we pass, say, from "The Idea of Order at Key West" to "The American Sublime" in the *Collected Poems*, or from "Chocorua to Its Neighbor" to "So-and-So Reclining on Her Couch" in *The Palm at the End of the Mind*, or from section IV to section V of "The Bouquet," or from section III to section IV of "Esthetique du Mal." Within such lines as "addicts / To blotches, angular anonymids / Gulping for shape" or "alive with an enigma's flittering," change is kaleidoscopic, the hand of the poet all but deceiving the eye. We may be aware of a pleasant strangeness in the proportion, without knowing exactly wherein that strangeness consists.

What the reader perceives as change, a diversity enacted in successive periods or instants of time, may also be described in terms of the activity of the poet. As everyone knows, the basic concerns and preoccupations of Stevens's poetry remained the same from first to last. His essential theme, the interplay of imagination and reality, may be defined, in terms of the plots dramatized in the poems themselves, as the relationship of a central consciousness to its perceived world. From this relationship real people and the real events and circumstances of the poet's life are almost wholly excluded (an important exception is "To an Old Philosopher in Rome"). Such autobiography as there is remains implicit in the seasonal movement, to summer and then to autumn, of the titles of the successive volumes, and in the long backward perspective of the last poems, as, for example, in the opening of "Long and Sluggish Lines," "It makes so little difference, at so much more / Than seventy, where one looks, one has been there before," and the first section, entitled "Seventy Years Later," of "The Rock." Good and bad fortune consist wholly in the success or failure of the mind in its lifelong attempt to achieve, and simultaneously to find words for, a satisfying apprehension of reality.[7] This activity and the writing of poetry are one and the same; thus Stevens can say that "Poetry is the subject of the poem. / From this the poem issues and / To this returns" (p. 176) and that "Life consists / Of propositions about life" (p. 355). The poems may be seen in their entirety as the record of a "never-ending meditation" (p. 465), so defined, as "makings of [the] self" which are "no less makings of the sun" (p. 532). But vitality is change, "life is motion" (p. 83), no less for the mind than for the world which is the mind's necessary complement. And herein we detect a paradox as dramatically fruitful as it is logically insoluble. Poetic statement is language set into form, sequences of words which are and must remain fixed, so that the mind's attempt to give definitive expression to its sense of an "always incipient cosmos" (*O.P.,* p. 115), is doubly self-defeating. "It must be abstract"; "it must change"; these two equally important dicta regarding the supreme fiction meet each other head-on. The very word *abstract,* it should be noted, is in origin a past participle, designating the result of an action that has already taken place; it properly applies neither to natural nor to mental process. Thus

> There's no such thing as life; or if there is,
>
> It is faster than the weather, faster than
> Any character. It is more than any scene.
>
> (p. 192)

(*Character* here may well mean "written letter" as well as *dramatis persona;* cf. "written in character" [p. 257].) The vital formulation loses vitality in the very moment of utterance, as the iridescent scented rushes gathered by Alice from the boat in *Through the Looking-Glass* became instantly dull. We see language in Stevens straining through time to express instantaneity:

> The breadth of an accelerando moves,
> Captives the being, widens—and was there.
>
> (p. 440)

So too the giant conjured up in the present tense in "Poem Written at Morning" immediately reverts to the past: "Green were the curls upon that head." The mind must constantly discard its own representations. "Goodby, Mrs. Pappadopoulos, and thanks" (p. 296), or, in the more solemn accents of "The Auroras of Autumn," "Farewell to an idea."

Just as we see the Stevens of the *Collected Poems* turning from one metaphor, one analogy, one symbolic setting, person, or event to another, so also we see him turning from one expressive means to another, trying out now this kind of language, now that, now this kind of word, now that, in the incessant attempt to express what remains perpetually "beyond the rhetorician's touch" (p. 431). And in this same restlessness of mind, these same rejections not only of the past but also of the present which has already become the past, we can see a motive for his ransacking of the lexicon, his borrowings from foreign languages, his creation of new metaphorical meanings, the coinages and innovative formations that mark his diction. "It is never the thing but the version of the thing" (p. 332); Stevens's poetic language is diverse, versatile, full of *divertissements,* in the root sense of all those words, knowing that "what it has is what is not" and turning from it "as morning throws off stale moonlight and shabby sleep" (p. 382). These turnings or shiftings at the verbal level are analogous to the changes with which the poems are concerned in their subject matter and descriptive detail—the cycles of day and night and the seasons, the rising and falling of waves or, on a geological time scale, of mountains, the endless transformations of the weather. The world of Stevens's poems may well be described, adopting one of his happiest coinages, as a *tournamonde* (p. 476) in large and in little, from the grandiose "shiddow-shaddow of lights revolving" at the climax of "Examination of the Hero in Time of War" to the single leaf "spinning its eccentric measure" toward the end of "Notes." Cyclical change, despite Stevens's cynical treatment of the theme in "Le Monocle de Mon Oncle," is for him most characteristically a source of pleasure—not the fateful intersecting gyres of a Yeats or the monotonous "birth, copulation, and death" of an Eliot but "The Pleasures of Merely Circulating," repetition felt as "beginning, not resuming" (p. 391), necessity accepted without tragic posturing as "final . . . and therefore, good,"

> the going round
>
> And round and round, the merely going round,
> Until merely going round is a final good,
> The way wine comes at a table in a wood.
>
> (p. 405)

The last line of this passage, to my mind one of the finest touches in "Notes," deserves further comment. From the point of view of the reader, it both signifies and accomplishes the giving of pleasure and so accords with the title of the last section of the poem, to which it belongs. Unanticipated by anything that precedes it and no sooner introduced than dropped, it typifies the prodigality of Stevens's inventiveness, an ever-accruing wealth which need never hoard itself but can be spent at once. As an event in the mind of the speaker of the poem, it represents a refreshment of life following the acceptance of finality, an ending giving way to a new beginning. Such freshness and spontaneity are thematic. If the moment of imaginative satisfaction, resulting as it does from an encounter between two changing entities, is fleeting, it is by that same token unpredictable. "One looks at the sea / As one improvises, on the piano" (p. 233). A poem entitled "The Sense of the Sleight-of-Hand Man" opens with a statement of this theme, leading off characteristically with a series of three alternative images:

> One's grand flights, one's Sunday baths,
> One's tootings at the weddings of the soul
> Occur as they occur.
>
> (p. 222)

The speaker now asks rhetorically, introducing yet another image, "Could you have said the bluejay suddenly / Would swoop to earth?" He continues,

It is a wheel, the rays
Around the sun. The wheel survives the myths.
The fire eye in the clouds survives the gods.
To think of a dove with an eye of grenadine
And pines that are cornets, so it occurs.

These lines make clear that what are called "occurrences" belong both to the external world (the sun with its rays, the red eye of the dove, the sound of wind in the pine trees) and the world within (the metaphors of wheel, eye, grenadine and cornets). To the day-by-day vagaries of wind, weather, and cloud within the framework of seasonal change, the mind responds in accordance with its own fluctuations of vitality and mood, constantly rising to unforeseen occasions. Reality "occurs" independently of our expectations; we say of it what it "occurs" to us to say.

As in the opening lines of "The Sense of the Sleight-of-Hand Man," the grammatical device of the series—whether of words, phrases, or similarly constructed clauses or sentences—lends itself in Stevens to the expression of alternative and equally valid apprehensions. Such sequences dramatize the rapid "play" of thought upon object or idea, and the mind appears in them as "playful" in that its activity is self-sufficing, intrinsically pleasurable without regard to what it accomplishes.

The wind is like a dog that runs away.
But it is like a horse. It is like motion

That lives in space. It is a person at night,
A member of the family, a tie,
An ethereal cousin, another milleman.
(p. 352)

Some of the poems, indeed, consist largely or wholly of lists of appellations amounting to so many descriptive "hypotheses" among which no choice need be made—or, rather, all of which must be chosen. In "Jumbo," for example, the figure named in the title is a tempest, plucking the trees like the "iron bars" of a huge stringed instrument, or as a captive elephant might pluck apart the iron bars of his cage. The speaker's question to himself, "Who was the musician . . . wildly free," is answered in the last three stanzas of the poem:

The companion in nothingness,
Loud, general, large, fat, soft
And wild and free, the secondary man,

Cloud-clown, blue painter, sun as horn,
Hill-scholar, man that never is,
The bad-bespoken lacker,

> Ancestor of Narcissus, prince
> Of the secondary men. There are no rocks
> And stones, only this imager.
>
> (p. 269)

Another grammatical device, the appositive, may similarly express an unanticipated turn of thought, as in the famous manifesto of "Notes":

> the sun
> Must bear no name, gold flourisher, but be.
>
> (p. 381)

"Gold flourisher" is of course a name for the sun, but in appositive use it strikes us
as a designation that occurs to the speaker at this moment, as he thinks about the
necessity of freeing the sun from the designations of the past. The same effect of a
mental occurrence or event is similarly produced in "Two Versions of the Same
Poem," which opens with the lines

> Once more he turned to that which could not be fixed,
> By the sea, insolid rock, stentor.
>
> (p. 353)

Later, the sea is addressed as "Lascar, and water-carcass never named."[8]

If there is something both "shifty" and "makeshift" about the imagination's
endlessly self-destructing output, there is also something tentative. Again and
again, the poet-speaker speaks of what he has achieved so far as "Segmenta" (p.
485), "fragments found in the grass" (p. 515), "patches and pitches" (O.P., p.
114), "edgings and inchings of final form" (p. 488). We remember in this connection that Stevens thought of calling *Harmonium,* his first book, *The Grand Poem:
Preliminary Minutiae* and of calling the *Collected Poems* in turn *The Whole of
Harmonium.* If the full experience of reality resists even momentary expression,
how much more unlikely of accomplishment is the grand poem itself, the supreme fiction in which being will come true and the structure of ideas will be one
with the structure of things. We hear, in Stevens's poems, of total edifices, com-
positions of the whole, summaria in excelsis, but these projects remain forever
"possible"; we do not see them realized. The most important of the long poems,
"Notes toward a Supreme Fiction," "The Auroras of Autumn," and "An Ordinary
Evening in New Haven," lack the architectonic unity, the linear movement toward culmination and resolution or systems of complementary relationships
among parts, of "When Lilacs Last in the Dooryard Bloomed," "The Tower," *Four
Quartets,* or even "The Waste Land"—though each has its own emotional climate, its dramatic succession of moods and modes, its risings and fallings off of
intensity, its thematic repetitions. In a sense, each is a collection of shorter poems,
a set of variations rather than a symphonic movement.[9] When Stevens does
develop a single fictional concept at length, as in "Examination of the Hero in

Time of War," "Chocorua to Its Neighbor," and "The Owl in the Sarcophagus," he is not at his most compelling. Something in him did not love the building of massive monolithic structures.

At the end of "The Owl in the Sarcophagus," Stevens's solemn "mythology of modern death" gives way to a simple and self-deprecatory image:

> It is a child that sings itself to sleep,
> The mind, among the creatures that it makes,
> The people, those by which it lives and dies.
>
> (p. 436)

This conception of the imagination's lifework as child's play is a sign of another happy paradox: the presence, in so austere and abstruse a poet and one who took the poetic vocation so seriously, of so much that does not take itself seriously. Our pleasure in Stevens has its source in the picnics as well as the parades and processions, the clowns as well as the rabbis, the ithy oonts and long-haired plomets as well as the lions and swans, the banjo's twang as well as the reverberations of choirs and bells, the beating of the lard pail as well as the blows of the lyre, the hair ribbons of the child as well as the glittering belts and flashing cloaks of the stars. And then there is the irrepressible gaiety and glitter of the language itself, the embellishments of its verbal music "lol-lolling the endlessness of poetry" (p. 458), its flashes of immediacy amid the most abstract or solemn statements, its "tootings at the weddings of the soul" (p. 222). This strain of unpretentiousness and playfulness finds expression in the *Letters* as well as the poems. "People ought to like poetry," Stevens wrote, "the way a child likes snow" (p. 349); and "Many lines exist because I enjoy their clickety-clack in contrast with the more decorous pom-pom-pom that people expect" (p. 485). From the *Letters,* too, we learn that for a long time Stevens thought of adding other sections to "Notes toward a Supreme Fiction" and "one in particular: *It Must Be Human*" (pp. 863–64).

Toward the end of the second section of "Notes," "It Must Change," there occurs a statement that I quoted earlier in another connection: "The poem goes from the poet's gibberish to / The gibberish of the vulgate and back again." The description of imaginative activity as a dialectic in process leads to a series of questions:

> Does it move to and fro or is it of both
>
> At once? Is it a luminous flittering
> Or the concentration of a cloudy day?
> Is there a poem that never reaches words
>
> And one that chaffers the time away?
> Is the poem both peculiar and general?

As is usually the case in Stevens when the nature of poetry is in question, all these pairs of alternatives apply, even, or rather especially, when they contradict each other (so too, later in the poem, with the Canon Aspirin's mutually exclusive alternatives, thought as thought and fact as fact, both of which must be chosen [p. 403]). This is made clear by the definitive statement at the end of the passage, where it is said of the poet that

> He tries by a peculiar speech to speak
>
> The peculiar potency of the general,
> To compound the imagination's Latin with
> The lingua franca et jocundissima.

Lingua franca, that is, "a mixed language or jargon," is an apt metaphor for the element of "gaiety" in Stevens's diction—his borrowings from modern foreign languages, his sound-symbolic vocabulary, his playful alterations and coinages. Nor is it surprising that the words used in this passage themselves exemplify the opposite extremes which must be fused into a single voice—*flittering* and *chaffers* belonging to the *lingua franca; luminous, concentration,* and others, to the imagination's Latin.

The power to bring about such compoundings remained undiminished in Stevens's last years, and the late poems collected in "The Rock" and *Opus Posthumous* make manifest his continuing delight in "reality as an activity of the most august imagination" (*O.P.,* p. 110).[10] As a final emblem of delight and renewal, we may take the description of the chapel rising from "Terre Ensevelie" beside the ruins of the church in "St. Armorer's Church from the Outside." The church is replaced by the chapel as the past, for him who chooses to remain on the "outside," is perpetually replaced by the present:

> The chapel rises, his own, his period,
> A civilization formed from the outward blank,
> A sacred syllable rising from sacked speech, . . .
>
> Time's given perfections made to seem like less
> Than the need of each generation to be itself,
> The need to be actual and as it is.
>
> St. Armorer's has nothing of this present,
> This *vif,* this dizzle-dazzle of being new
> And of becoming, for which the chapel spreads out
> Its arches in its vivid element,
>
> In the air of newness of that element,
> In an air of freshness, clearness, greenness, blueness,
> That which is always beginning because it is part
> Of that which is always beginning, over and over.

The chapel underneath St. Armorer's walls,
Stands in a light, its natural light and day,
The origin and keep of its health and his own.
And there he walks and does as he lives and likes.

With its high-style rhetoric, its mixture of common native words with elements of the imagination's Latin and of the *lingua franca* (foreign borrowing, sound-symbolic coinage, and all), its play on the ordinary and archaic poetic meanings of *keep,* its succession of equally valid descriptive formulations, its protracted series of nouns and nominal phrases giving way in the last line to a flurry of finite verbs (couched in the simplest of diction), this passage speaks a language such as we find in no other poet—abstract, changing, pleasure giving, and human.

FIVE

MARIANNE MOORE'S PROMOTIONAL PROSE
THE USES
OF SYNTAX

> Nor is it valid
>   to discriminate against "business documents and
>
> school-books"; all these phenomena are important.
>> —*Poetry*

> There's a girl who might
>   have stepped out of the sixteenth century:
> billowing skirt, gai-
>   ly striped apron, tight
>   black bodice. . . .
>   they still dress
> like that in Dalecarlia. In their spotless
>   wooden farmhouses you may
> still see the rare old Biblical
>   wall paintings; you may still
>   hear the whirr
> of the shuttle and watch the housewife deftly
>   weaving her
>   cloth. You can read by electric light
> and call up London by telephone. . . .

If the hand of the illusionist has been successful, the above not only looks but sounds like a stanza from a poem by Marianne Moore. It is not, in fact, by Moore; nor is it a passage from an article in the *National Geographic* or some such periodical counted off by syllables, as a disabused second guess might judge it to be. It is the opening of an advertisement published by the Swedish Travel Bureau in the 28 June 1930 issue of the *Illustrated London News*.[1] I use it as my epigraph to epitomize a major theme of this essay: Marianne Moore's notoriously prosaic poetry[2] owes a debt of deep significance to two kinds of journalistic writing, themselves not wholly distinct, which I shall collectively call promotional prose. They are the newspaper or magazine feature article and the newspaper or magazine advertisement. Not that the poetry itself can properly be called "journalistic," or is likely ever to appeal to large audiences. As poet and literary critic alike, Moore presents for our inspection the most impeccable of high cultural credentials; she was, after all, for several years the editor of an important little magazine. But she was also a devoted reader of newspapers and magazines having a circulation much larger than the *Dial*'s, and it was here that she encountered the more popular forms of prose whose idiom became so oddly important a part of her own.

What sort of thing is the feature article? We know from its name that it "features" or brings into the limelight a subject presumed to be of interest: a person, a place, a species of animal, a competitive sport, an artistic activity, a handicraft or new machine, whatever the traffic will bear. It is not tied to a particular date like the news story (hence it does not date as easily), nor does it provide practical instruction or advice like the "how-to" or public service column, or seek to influence our aesthetic judgments or political opinions like the book or theater review or the editorial. Rather, it gives us, removed from unfolding events, a factual description of its subject. Subject, facts, and presentation alike depend on the intellectual level and preferences of the prospective reader. The feature article is all things to all men; to see it in the form in which it stimulated Marianne Moore's imagination, we must look for it (as the Notes direct us to do) in newspapers like the *New York Times* and the *New York Sun,* and in magazines like the *Illustrated London News,* the *National Geographic,* and *Natural History.*

But the feature article is descriptive prose of a certain kind, with a style all its own. What that style is can be made clear by a comparison with the didactic article or essay properly so called, at the cultural level at which the two genres overlap in subject matter. One can learn a great deal about wild animals, for instance, by reading *Natural History,* but one can also learn a great deal about them, and learn many of the same things, by reading a zoological textbook or consulting an encyclopedia. The difference is basically one of purpose, and it is from this difference that all other differences proceed. Didactic prose sets out to make knowledge available to those who seek it; "casually informative" prose (to call it that for lack of a better name) offers its reader a more or less high-minded form of diversion. One who reads a feature article, say, on pangolins, has not opened a magazine with the expectation of finding out about that particular creature. His attention is attracted by a title and he begins to read, but he is not committed to reading on; he may at any moment turn over the leaf and choose another tale. This freedom to break off relations is crucial; it exerts a pressure, at once positive and negative, on the author. On the one hand, he must do his best to hold the reader captive; on the other hand, he must avoid alienating him whether by plying him with an overabundance of detail or by demanding of him a degree of intellectual effort that he is unwilling, on that sort of occasion, to exert.

The recreational purpose of the feature article must be emphasized because it is crucial in the determination not only of form at all levels but also, within limits, of subject matter itself. Even when the readers of a given periodical can be counted on to favor a certain kind of subject matter, editors choose the topics of feature articles for their attention-getting value. Articles in travel magazines are likely to be devoted to primitive peoples in remote parts of the world, or, closer to home, to foreign countries or native communities whose inhabitants dress or behave "quaintly." Natural history and wildlife magazines feature animals that are freakish in appearance, or behave improbably, or have startling physical capabilities. With more material available on a given subject than can be used in the available space, the writer of the feature article looks for the eye-catching or mind-boggling detail, for strong colors and color contrasts, for the unexpected, the anachronistic, and the incongruous, for mystery, suspense, and excitement. (Since I am speaking with Marianne Moore in mind, I am ignoring the more blatant forms of audience appeal, the sex and violence, often found in feature articles on a low cultural plane, though it is interesting to note that one of Moore's poems, "The Icosasphere," is partly based on a newspaper story about a series of crimes.) The staple of the feature article is "the remarkable" in all its forms; it regales us with accounts of preeminence in performance and endurance, describes the amazing feats of animals, birds, and insects, caters to our curiosity about the genius or champion in every field of human endeavor. And these preoccupations in turn generate the statistics and numerical details with which the feature article abounds in all its manifestations: dates of famous "firsts," all-time records, scores, sizes, speeds, distances, as well as the human interest of ages, heights, and weights. The world as portrayed for us by the feature article is not so much idealized and exalted as it is brightened and heightened, with a kind of "Believe-It-or-Not" vividness surpassing the qualities of everyday experience.

These positive aspects of the descriptive style of the feature article will be familiar to everyone. But it is also important for the purposes of this study to describe the feature article negatively, in terms of what it is not like and does not do. Most obviously, it is not comprehensive; here it differs from the textbook and the reference work, both of which are duty-bound to present a full account (geared to the educational level of the intended reader) of what is known about a given subject at a given time. But if the feature article does not and cannot strive for comprehensiveness, neither does it aspire to profundity. The feature article dwells in the house of fact—the "mere fact," on the one hand, divorced from the ideas that give facts their importance, and the "received fact," on the other hand, unexamined as to meaning and unquestioned as to validity. The more advanced the textbook, the more specialized the reference work, the larger the proportion of space it devotes to problems in the field, while the original scholarly or scientific article begins at the edge of present knowledge or theory and forges on from there. But the feature article stays well within familiar terrain, avoiding the conceptual analysis, logic, statistics, and symbolic calculation which must be brought into play to conquer the "here be dragons" of *terra incognita*. At its more popular levels, the feature article does not hesitate to intersperse information acquired at second hand with what has been directly observed. If by "information," as opposed to "knowledge," we mean facts in separation from theory and experience alike, then we must admit that the feature article is in the business of purveying information, satisfying the sort of intellectual curiosity that asks who, what, when, where, and how in superficial terms, without probing in search of significance. If we look for profundity in the poetry of Marianne Moore, we will not find it in the characteristics her poems share with feature articles about basilisks, ostrich eggs, and pangolins.

The superficiality of the feature article implies another negative characteristic: its lack of pretensions. As a form of journalism, it is by definition of passing interest, disappearing from the scene, more often than not, immediately upon publication. (I speak here, of course, of the article itself as a literary production and not of its subject, which may be of lasting importance: a great painter, an astronomical theory, the recently unearthed cultural remains of an ancient people.) The unpretentiousness of the feature article extends to its author as the expounding "I" through the medium of whose words its content reaches us. This author may tell us about someone who is famous, but we do not expect him to be famous himself; indeed, we pay little if any heed to him as a personality in his own right. To the extent that he draws our attention to his thoughts, emotions, and experiences as an individual, he has gone beyond the conventionally defined limits of the genre. When an eminent scientist, philosopher, or other cultural authority writes in a newspaper or magazine about his work, he becomes for the duration of the article his own journalist, giving us "information" about his ideas rather than developing them as he does in his primary writings. And when a writer of feature articles becomes a focus of attention in himself (as has happened, for example, with Tom Wolfe), his writings move away from topical journalism in the direction of the literary essay.

The advertisement, as it appears side by side with the feature article in newspapers and magazines, is too protean to lend itself to compendious genre-definition.[3] It is perhaps best described as a message, presented in words or pictures or both, having as its purpose the sale of something to the recipient.[4] The purely visual aspects of the advertisement, including typography and layout as well as illustration, are of less obvious significance for a study of Marianne Moore than the verbal aspects.[5] As a verbal construct, the advertisement assumes for strategic purposes a variety of generic masks. Partly for reasons of space and partly for reasons of relevance, I shall limit the discussion that follows to one of these, namely, descriptive prose, disregarding quasi-fictional forms such as anecdote, testimonial letter, dramatic dialogue, and verse. And I shall be concerned chiefly with the discursive body of the advertising text—that is, with sequences of complete statements as opposed to headlines, slogans, and other "disjunctive" elements.[6]

In its descriptive prose guise, the advertisement has all the "positive" characteristics of the feature article, and for obvious reasons. It too must present its subject as "remarkable"; it too must create an imagined world in which things are intensified in quality, charged with vivider-than-life definition and attractive power. (What mail-order customer, however experienced, is not regularly disappointed by the actual article in the package—its drab appearance, even its seeming decrease in size, in comparison with the mental picture conjured up as much by the words as by the pictures in the catalog?) The advertisement, like its less designing cousin, goes in for bright colors, amazing facts (or purported facts), and extraordinary feats; it too likes to associate itself with champions, and it too supports its claim on our interest with an abundance of statistics.

We take it for granted that the expositor of the feature article is interested in his subject; the liveliness of tone which is the corollary of that interest is a virtue in the genre. But in his capacity as a reporter of facts, the author of the feature article must take care not to seem overenthusiastic. The advertisement is a less inhibited genre in this as in other respects. In its "documentary" mode, it confines itself to facts and figures and speaks in objective terms. In its "lyrical" mode, it gives itself over to expressions of personal gratification and praise. In either case, it borrows its stylistic plumage from kindred genres. The documentary advertisement appropriates the descriptive strategies of the feature article; the lyrical advertisement converts to its own ends such poetic devices as apostrophe, rhetorical repetition, simile and metaphor, alliteration and rhyme. Most advertisements, as we know, mix the two modes more or less equally, often informing and extolling in the same breath.

Whatever the stylistic affiliations of the advertisement, we can expect its language to reflect an abiding condition of its existence: the space available to it must be paid for by the inch. The language of the lyrical advertisement has the expressive density of poetic language; that of the documentary advertisement is loaded too, though with a different sort of burden. As will be shown later, feature article prose makes use of certain syntactic patterns that promote a high "fact-to-clause" ratio and thus expedite the conveying of information. The documentary advertisement uses these same patterns but more often and in exaggerated forms, distancing itself from other prose genres in the same direction as the feature article but at a further remove.

What of the connections posited at the outset between the feature article and the advertisement? We have spoken so far as if the feature article were designed to arouse and hold the reader's interest and nothing more, and could thus be differentiated from the advertisement, which is by definition always trying to turn reader into customer. One genre would seem to be contemplative, the other active. But this, of course, is not the whole story. At the very least, the newspaper or magazine in which the feature article appears wants to sell itself, and profits, or at least solvency, depend on the sale of advertising space as well. Advertisers for their part choose their periodicals to attract the attention of the right kind of reader, seeking customers for ocean cruises and foreign hotels in *National Geo-*

graphic, for wilderness tours and African safaris in *National History,* and so on, *mutatis mutandis.* In the most extreme form of symbiosis between the two genres, the advertisement actually disguises itself as a feature article, imitating the host periodical in typography and format.[7] And certain publications inhabit a gray area between the subscription or newsstand-based periodical and the advertising brochure. The regional handbooks published by the American Automobile and similar associations contain short essays on places their members may wish to visit, side by side with advertisements for hotels and restaurants, while articles on Where to Go and What to See in the in-flight magazines given to airline passengers are scarcely distinguishable from advertisements in those same magazines. The feature article shades into the documentary advertisement; in the last analysis, one is as much promotional prose as the other. The poetry of Marianne Moore has important affinities with both, and, as we shall see, with the advertisement in its lyrical mode as well.

In saying that Moore's poetry is like prose, her critics have not meant simply that her lines lack metrical form, or that she avoids "poetic" archaisms and inversions of the natural word order, though these things are true. Rather, such statements purport to describe what we do find in Moore's language: features which have especially strong associations with certain genres of formal prose, and which therefore carry with them into new contexts distinctive stylistic qualities and expressive powers. We will see more clearly what this means as we compare "formality" in Moore with "formality" in Stevens, focusing attention particularly on diction and syntax.

The Romance-Latinate tabulations in Appendix A yield much the same statistical patterns for Moore as for Stevens. Moore's average of 19.9 percent is very slightly higher than Stevens's of 19.7 percent; the median percentile for both is 20. And Moore's range from 33 percent to 9 percent is slightly narrower than Stevens's range from 34 percent to 6 percent. The language of these two poets thus differs sharply from that used by Frost in his pastoral lyrics, with its average of 9 percent, its median of 8 percent, and its range from 18 percent to 4 percent. Most obviously, the figures tell us that there is a good deal of highly ornate language in Stevens and Moore, language representing the high watermark for Romance-Latinate content in English, and comparatively little language of this sort in Frost. Stevens's "Credences of Summer," for example, has an average Romance-Latinate percentile of 23.5; Moore's "Virginia Britannia" averages out to 24.6 percent. It also means that we can expect to find in both Stevens and Moore, *passim,* a number of "free formal tags" of the sort described in chapter 4, words of Romance-Latinate origin for which there are native synonyms belonging to the body of common diction. *Desire, distant, edifice, interior, labor, possess, regard* "look at," and *respond/response* were cited as examples of such tags in Stevens;

almost all of these, as it happens, occur in Moore, although we can expect the vocabulary of each poet to contain a number of similar items lacking in the vocabulary of the other.

But the particular qualities of a formal style depend on its cultural and generic affiliations, and here Moore and Stevens part company. Stevens, as we saw, utilizes the inherited language of philosophy in its metaphysical and phenomenological branches, of the Christian religion, and of the classical canon of English poetry itself in its inherited priestly functions. This "high formal" language works in Stevens, as in other authors, to dignify and exalt the subject matter to which it refers, whatever that subject matter may be. We thus find in Stevens's poetry a Romance-Latinate vocabulary alien to the poetry of Moore, including not only words having specifically philosophical and religious associations but idealizing qualitative terms tied to no particular subject matter—words like *effulgence, embellishment, evocation, illustrious, luminous, majesty, mystical, opulent, sacred, solemn, sonorous, sovereign,* and *venerable*. Of these, Moore has only *majesty (2×* to Stevens's 14×) and *solemn* (2× to Stevens's 10×).[8] Though such diction may strike us as more poetic than prosaic, some of it does in fact occur in such prose genres as political and ceremonial oratory ("illustrious predecessors," "the majesty of the law," "sacred trust," "solemn obligations"). It will not do, then, to say that Moore uses "the language of prose" while Stevens uses "the language of poetry." Rather, the two poets must be distinguished in terms of their relation to the high formal tradition in English, exemplified here in its Romance-Latinate aspect. Stevens draws continuously on the resources of this tradition, its inherited diction and idiom amounting almost to a norm of his style. Moore does not. Her poems speak a prose language that may without redundancy be called "prosaic."

Just as the ornate solemnity of Stevens's diction is largely lacking in Moore, so too, with a few notable exceptions,[9] is the august simplicity, heavy with biblical allusiveness, which makes an equally important contribution to Stevens's version of the high formal style. When Stevens's language is low in Romance-Latinate content, it is usually "simple" in this elevated sense, whereas low percentiles in Moore tend to be found in language that is down-to-earth, even chatty. Contrast the following lines from Moore's "Saint Nicholas,"

> But don't give me, if I can't have the dress,
> a trip to Greenland, or grim
> trip to the moon. The moon should come here,

with the conclusion of Stevens's "Evening without Angels,"

> Where the voice that is in us makes a true response,
> Where the voice that is great within us rises up,
> As we stand gazing at the rounded moon.

86

The Uses of Syntax

Among the prose genres, Moore's most important stylistic affiliations are with journalism, and notably, or so I am insisting here, with the descriptive prose of the feature article and its analogue in the documentary advertisement. Moore's Romance-Latinate diction occasionally seems "journalistic" in the derogatory sense when it strings together polysyllabic words with suffixes that rhyme or jingle, as in the switch from narrative words to Latinate at the close of "Efforts of Affection":

> Thus wholeness—
>
> wholesomeness? best say efforts of affection—
> attain integration too tough for infraction.

She is capable of describing birds building their nests as "working for concavity" and achieving "spherical feats of rare efficiency" (p. 143), and of defining love, in terms reminiscent of the advertisement as well as of the news article, as "vermin-proof and pilfer-proof integration" (p. 147). She uses the word *punctualize* to describe the effect of the clocks in the New York Bell Telephone laboratories on the radio and press (p. 115), and tells us that as a result of the association of Saint Jerome with the lion, the "lionship" of the saint "seems *officialized*" (p. 201). And a "not un-" construction of the sort frowned on by critics of contemporary prose usage finds its way into "The Pangolin," where the form of the creature is said to be "not unchain-like" (p. 118). In all fairness, it must also be said that many lines similarly heavy with Romance and Latinate diction have an elegance reminiscent of the literary essay rather than of the daily paper or business document. Among these, one might single out as especially felicitous "The illustration / is nothing to you without the application" (p. 84), "Ecstasy affords / the occasion and expediency determines the form" (p. 88), and "If tributes cannot / be implicit, // give me diatribes and the fragrance of iodine" (p. 151).

The most idiosyncratic component of Moore's Romance-Latinate vocabulary, with a saliency out of all proportion to its numbers, is a scattering of terms taken over from the natural and social sciences. Many of these, of course, can be explained away in terms of the subjects of the poems. We are not surprised to find *vibrators, laboratory, comparator, prism,* and *electrified,* as well as the above-mentioned *punctualize,* in "Four Quartz Crystal Clocks," or *gizzard, contracting, apertures, aggressive, plantigrade,* and *habitat,* in "The Pangolin." Other words reflect in similar fashion the subject matter of a particular passage: *melanin* and *spinal* in "Saint Nicholas," *apteryx* and *gyroscope* in "The Mind Is an Enchanting Thing," *crustacean, equine,* and *amphibious* (in a single array, referring to seahorse-shaped decorations) in "A Carriage from Sweden." For good and sufficient historical reasons set forth in an earlier chapter, these words are almost all Latinate. The single word of Romance origin among the examples quoted in this paragraph is *gizzard.*

More important than the subjects to which such terms refer are the kinds of mental activity (and thus the attitudes) they imply. The word *aperture,* which came into use in English in the seventeenth century, is a typical case. It found a place in the language, establishing itself at the formal level of diction, not because it denoted a new concept or even a refinement of an old concept; it was and is, in its most common meaning, synonymous with the far older word *opening.* What it distinctively expresses it expresses as a tag; an aperture, one might say, is an opening looked through for scientific purposes (see especially the citations under senses 3 and 4 in *OED*). When a writer calls an opening an aperture we expect, depending on the field of inquiry, to hear about its adaptive value (the protective "contracting nose and eye apertures" of the pangolin), its exact shape and dimensions, its experimental uses, and so on. The vocabularies of the sciences imply not only the systematic observations and precise measurements we think of as essential complements to intuition and deduction in the "scientific method," but the schemes of classification to which these give rise. The word *plantigrade* presupposes a comparative study of posture and mode of locomotion in the various species of animals, the word *habitat* presupposes the branch of natural science we now call ecology, and so on. Such words are alien to the language of everyday in that they are impersonal and analytical; they have the coldness of intellectual detachment. But this same quality makes them equally alien to the high formal style, which is committed to celebrating the values of the past. As high formal language is typified by the archaism, scientific language is typified by the technical term. One exists apart from present reality and derives its potency from that very isolation; the other originates in an investigation of present reality unhindered by reverence and subject to continuing revision. If words like *amphibious,* *apteryx,* and *melanin* are non-colloquial, they are also non-solemn. And they not only lack solemnity themselves, they inhibit the production of solemn effects in the contexts in which they appear. They are, one might say, solemnity-retardant.

These attitudes and habits of mind, at once clinical and inquisitive, are revealed with special clarity by Moore's use of scientific diction where her subject matter does not require it—when, for example, it is used to signify the vehicles of metaphors and similes. Only she, we feel, would have described the horns of the American buffalo as "*hematite*-black" (p. 27), or have said that a woodpecker on a tree trunk goes "up up up like *mercury*" (p. 149), or have likened the straight line over which a dancer keeps his balance to the *axis* of the new moon (p. 169) or the beads on the spinal ridge of the chameleon to *platinum* (p. 196) or an intimidated former "land-grabber" in Manhattan to a *neonate* (p. 230). Similarly distinctive is Moore's use of technical terms when a less technical alternative meaning much the same thing is available in the language; thus the eyes of a cat are said to be *bisected* by its narrowed pupils (p. 43); things dropped in the sea move without *volition* (p. 50); a bird stands in the *semi*-sun (p. 108); affection brings about a wholeness "too tough for *infraction*" (p. 147); a sparrow's song is of "hayseed *magnitude*" (p. 149); the downstroke of a canoe paddle is *vertical*

(p. 169); the three *"arcs* of seeds" in a cross-section of a banana are *equidistant* (p. 170).

The journalistic-technological flavor of Moore's diction is enhanced by an admixture of polysyllabic Latinate words that are more or less unfamiliar to us, including some listed in unabridged dictionaries only, and some not even there. In form, these are *derivatives,* made by adding prefixes or suffixes to previously established words. *Punctualize* and *officialize,* cited above, are cases in point: the former is evidently a coinage; the latter exists but is rare.[10] Many words of this sort in Moore are based on words which are themselves scientific or technical—for example, *chlorophylless* (p. 74), *contractility* (p. 85), *perpendicularity* (p. 83), *unmetronomic* (p. 209). Others—for example, *clandestinely* (p. 25), *unextirpated* (p. 97), *unsolicitude* (p. 100), *unparticularities* (p. 142), and *uncompunctious* (p. 205)—are not, but these too by virtue of their sheer length and Latinity are reminiscent of technological or journalistic prose as it teeters on or topples over the brink of jargon. Formations with *un-,* as the above examples show, are especially frequent. Another noteworthy group is made up of words ending in *-ist,* as in *absolutist, meliorist, opportunist,* which in context take on specific, quasi-sociological meanings: *externalist* in "He 'Digesteth Harde Yron,'" *literalists* (based, according to the Notes, on the phrase "literal realist") in "Poetry," *precisionists* in "Bowls," *rigorists* in the poem so titled.

Formal diction in poetry is always "traditional" in the very general sense that it perpetuates literary language in literary works. But the formal tradition is not one kingdom; it is a federation, and its member states are separated from one another by invisible barriers of restrictive usage as real as those that separate formal language in its totality from the language of everyday. These barriers Moore systematically disregards. Her raids on the vocabulary of science and technology and her excursions to the frontiers of Latinate polysyllabism are striking local signs of an innovative principle that crucially shapes her style: the wholesale importation into poetry of the idiom of prose at its most prosaic.

Formality in Moore, as in Stevens, manifests itself in the elaboration of syntax which is a corollary of high Romance-Latinate percentiles in literary language. There is naturally a good deal of variation among the poems. Like Stevens, Moore can be terse, giving us series of sentences that seem artificial in their very brevity, as witness these lines from "The Mind Is an Enchanting Thing:"

It

is like the dove-
neck animated by
sun; it is memory's eye;
it's conscientious inconsistency.

(For other examples, see "Nevertheless" and "Propriety.") And she can write in the simple, conversational syntax of "The Arctic Ox (or Goat)" and "Saint Nicholas," as well. But especially in major poems such as "Elephants," "The Pangolin," and "Virginia Britannia," sentence after sentence far outdoes the spoken language in the multiplicity of its parts and the ordered complexity of their interrelationships.

Formality of syntax in Moore and formality of syntax in Stevens have certain features in common—appositive constructions, for instance, and series of noun phrases. But the two poets differ crucially, in syntax as in diction, by virtue of their contrasting genre affiliations. The most significant difference is one that manifests itself within the compass of the individual phrase or clause: the proportionate frequencies of the four major or "open" grammatical classes—the nouns, the verbs, the adjectives, and the adverbs.[11]

These four kinds of words can be differentiated from one another in purely formal terms, membership in each class being marked by inflectional endings, prefixes and suffixes, and eligibility for use in certain positions in syntactic "frames." Such criteria enable us to construe Lewis Carroll's phrase "the slithy toves," whether or not we have seen the words *slithy* and *toves* before, as a noun phrase consisting of the definite article, a modifying adjective, and a noun in the plural. But the members of the four open classes also resemble each other in that they are primary signifiers of denotative meaning; for this reason, some grammarians call them "lexical" or "content" words.[12] Since denotation of necessity involves reference, their expressive values are, one might say, extramural, pointing beyond the closed system of language to a subject matter which, though manipulated by language, exists independently of it. In this respect, they differ collectively from the prepositions and conjunctions (which express relationships among terms), the pronouns (which are denotatively empty substitutes for nouns), the determiners, the numerals, the quantifiers, and all other sets of "closed-system" items. But though nouns, verbs, adjectives, and adverbs are alike in that they work together to express the terminological or descriptive content of language, they differ systematically in the nature of their contributions to that content. Each major part of speech, by virtue of its grammatical class, signifies a different aspect of experience as we conceptualize it in putting it into words.

We live in a conceptualized world, a world defined not only by the lexical meanings of words but by their grammatical meanings. The grammar of each language refracts the mind's apprehension of "reality" as through a prism and divides it arbitrarily into bands. One whose native language is English (or any other Indo-European language, for that matter) is foreordained to analyze the content of his experience into sets of stable *entities,* having more or less variable or changeable *attributes* of an innate or circumstantial sort, and participating in time-located *actions, processes,* and *relationships.*[13] The "parts of speech" constitute a model of the nature of things whose validity it does not occur to us to

90

doubt, and this model itself implies a kind of ontological hierarchy or order. The nouns correspond to our sense of a primary physical world made up of objects and substances that can be counted or measured. These entities are implicitly conceived of as prior to, and thus independent of, the characteristics attributed to them by adjectives, and the time-located actions, processes, and relationships predicated of them by verbs.[14] The meanings denoted by adjectives and verbs presuppose the meanings denoted by nouns; the meanings denoted by adverbs, at one further remove from the primary content of experience, presuppose the meanings denoted by verbs and adjectives.[15] In this naive or commonsensical account of the conceptual implications of our inherited parts-of-speech system, the finite verb element (the part of the verb having person, number, tense, and mood) is seen to be the only true verb, the infinitive and the gerund being verb-related nouns (designators of entities), and the present and past participles verb-related adjectives (designators of attributes).

Definitions of the parts of speech based solely on the referential aspect of meaning (e.g., "a noun is the name of a person, place, or thing") have been effectively discredited by C. C. Fries and others.[16] Their inadequacy is revealed by the fact that competence in the use of language includes the ability to choose among purely grammatical alternatives in making a given statement. Thus we can say (1) "They watched the sun as it set," or (2) "They watched the setting sun," or (3) "They watched the sunset." In (1), we analyze the subject of reference (the apparent motion of the sun in relation to the horizon) into two terms signifying, respectively, a concrete entity, the sun, and a time-located action, that of "set-ting", the former being construed as the agent of the latter. In (2), we analyze this same subject into a concrete entity and an attribute of that entity. In (3), we express the subject as a single abstract entity, an event. This event in turn can be treated as an attribute of something else (as in "sunset-watchers"), or as an attri-bute of another attribute (as in "sunset red"). Clearly such formulations differ in the meanings they express as well as in their structure, or, more precisely, in the *kinds* of meaning they express. The four main parts of speech supply us with four conceptual stamps or dies which impose their outlines on this or that aspect of our experience while simultaneously receiving denotative content from it. They thus contribute to the shaping of language at the subverbal level of "formulation," where the content of a given unit of discourse crystallizes into particular ideas. The terms denoting these ideas, in their grammatical roles as members of one or another major form-class, join to form syntactic structures. Language encourages flexibility in the imposition of the parts-of-speech model on content, partly by supplying us with sets of prefixes and suffixes which permit the "derivation" of one part of speech from another with retention of the terminological base, partly by permitting the "conversion" of one part of speech into another without change in form.

To the extent that they vary independently of what is said, the four open classes constitute a stylistic repertoire, their expressive values as grammatical elements working with their values as terms and as tags to give language its distinctive qualities and powers. The proportions in a given passage of nouns, finite verbs, adjectives, and adverbs will inevitably be affected somewhat by the subject matter of the passage. It would be strange if a play-by-play account of a baseball game did not contain a large number of finite verbs, or if an essay on the balance of trade did not contain a large number of nouns. But subject matter aside, the proportions of the parts of speech can be seen to vary in accordance with level of formality, in accordance with genre at the formal level, and, within this double constraint, in accordance with the imaginative bias of the individual speaker or writer.[17]

Of the four major parts of speech, it is the finite verb element (f.v.e.) which provides the single best index of syntactic elaboration, and which is therefore the single most significant statistical variable in comparative studies of style. Our earliest consecutive utterances, those characteristic of the first stages of language acquisition, are simple sentences in the grammatical sense, "largely made up," to quote Roger Brown's important study, "of nouns and verbs (with a few adjectives and adverbs)."[18] They are also short, consisting typically of three or four constituent structures such as noun phrases, finite verb phrases, and prepositional phrases; the constituents themselves exhibit little or no internal modification or compounding. Sentences fitting the above description, provided that their diction is also simple, remind us of a first-grade reader; thus William Empson said of "The cat sat on the mat" that it might have come from *Reading without Tears.* In the last stanza of Stevens's "Poetry Is a Destructive Force," the threat posed by the sleeping lion which symbolizes the creative imagination is conveyed not only in diction but in syntax of radical simplicity; the effect is one of disturbing understatement, of power held blandly in check:

> The lion sleeps in the sun.
> Its nose is on its paws.
> It can kill a man.

(It should be noted in passing that in three of the above four sentences, the proportion of finite verbs is one word in six; in Stevens's last sentence, it is one in five. While these figures obviously do not prove anything, it is interesting that they correspond to what seems to be the "high" average f.v.e. count in English text of about 16.5 percent.)

As we become more adept at using language, our sentences grow longer. We add words to phrases and phrases to clauses, and we turn clauses into infinitive and participial phrases. The effect of all these changes is to lower the proportionate frequency of the finite verb. When the adult speaker turns author, devising and revising language at leisure, he finds it both possible and desirable to develop the synthetic potentialities of the sentence as a means of expressing the complexity of thought, the continuity of narrative, the play of emotion, and the multiplicity of descriptive detail. As the speech of the adult contains proportionately fewer finite verbs than that of the young child, so *elaborate* formal language contains proportionately fewer finite verbs than colloquial language.[19] Statistically, this tendency manifests itself in an inverse correlation which seems to hold true for English text across the board: the higher the consecutive Romance-Latinate percentiles, the lower the consecutive percentiles of finite verbs. (Since "high formal" language of the sort marked by simple diction and biblical allusiveness is simple syntactically as well, it exhibits the correlation in its complementary form, with characteristically low Romance-Latinate percentiles and high f.v.e. counts.) Like all correlations, this one admits of exceptions in particular cases. Especially in the mimetic genres—fiction, drama, lyrical and narrative poetry—an author who uses elaborate diction may nonetheless simulate the grammatical structures of the spoken language (as Browning did), or may (as Stevens did) find the finite verb a peculiarly congenial implement for the formulation of experience.[20]

A cautionary statement should be added: though high and low finite verb counts may be of significance in the analysis of style, they differ from high and low Romance-Latinate counts in that they do not of themselves produce predictable effects. Everyday speech, to be sure, is rich in finite verbs, but the presence of numerous finite verbs will not make language sound like everyday speech, any more than the lack of finite verbs, per se, will make language sound elaborately formal.[21] This is partly because effects of colloquial and formal diction are produced by individual words having intrinsic value as "markers." Effects of colloquial and formal syntax are produced in the aggregate, by patterns perceived on the larger scale of the sentence or clause. Much depends on the particular words in which they are embodied.

The negative correlation between the proportion of finite verbs in a given passage and its level of (elaborative) formality can be demonstrated by devising "translations" of colloquial language into formal language and vice versa. In chapter 2, two well-known lines of Frost's, "Something there *is* that *does*n't love a wall," and "We *love* the things we *love* for what they *are*," were rewritten as "There *exists* an antipathy toward barriers" and "Our love of the object of love *is* based upon its nature in reality." We can now observe that the first revision uses one finite verb in place of two, the second, one in place of three. Working in the opposite direction, we can translate Marianne Moore's statement that the pangolin can roll himself into "a ball that *has* / power to defy all effort to unroll it" into "a ball that nobody *can* unroll, no matter how hard he *tries*." In all three cases, the two versions differ not only grammatically, in the proportions of the parts of speech, but conceptually, in degree of abstractness. Actions signified by finite verbs in the more colloquial versions (*does* [*not love*], *love* v., and *tries*) correspond to entities signified by nouns in the more formal versions (*antipathy, love* sb., and *effort*). These entities are of course abstract. And since the meanings of

A FORTNIGHT
IN THE 16ᵀᴴ CENTURY

It is only Two Days Away

Why, there's a girl who might have stepped out of the 16th century! Billowing skirt, gaily striped apron, tight black bodice, dainty striped wimple, bright silk kerchief —what a picture! There's another, with a baby slung to her back! And another! This must be weeks from England. But no —it's no further than Dalecarlia, the heart of Sweden, two days away!

They still dress like that in Dalecarlia. In their spotless wooden farmhouses you may still see the rare old Biblical wall paintings; you may still hear the whirr of the shuttle and watch the housewife deftly weaving her cloth. You can read by electric light and call up London by telephone, but the moment you lift your eyes or set down the receiver, you are back again in the days of folk songs and dances, of handcrafts and mediæval customs.

Why not go back a few centuries this summer to this land of lakes and sunshine, forest and mountain, where everything is so old that it has become refreshingly new ? Within easy reach is Stockholm, the fairest capital in Europe, with its great Exhibition of Swedish Industrial and Decorative Arts and Crafts from May to September; Visby, the city of ruins and roses ; primitive Lapland, lighted by the mysterious Midnight Sun ; and the marvellous scenic pageant of the 350 mile Göta Canal. They are all within the bounds of this one wonderful holiday.

*

For free, copiously illustrated booklets and full information write to the Swedish Travel Bureau, 21f, Coventry Street, London, W.1, The British and Northern Shipping Agency, 5, Lloyd's Avenue, E.C.3, or any of the leading tourist agencies.

nouns are not "time-located," by tense-inflection, like the meanings of verbs, an increase in the proportion of nouns to verbs works to "abstract" the content of a given statement by removing it from temporal process.

How high is "high" and how low is "low"? And how "low" is the proportion of finite verb elements in Moore? In trying to answer these questions, I thought it best to begin by looking for high and low counts elsewhere than in poetry and other literary genres, setting up a tentative range in terms of which the findings for Moore and my other two poets could then be evaluated. Accordingly, I sampled texts of three kinds: (1) tape-recorded conversations of a spontaneous and casual nature; (2) feature articles identified by Moore in her Notes as sources of her poems; and (3) scientific articles roughly contemporary with the feature articles and comparable in subject matter.[22] The results were predictable in that the counts of f.v.e.'s per 100 words in the tape-recorded conversations were consistently and considerably higher than those found in either kind of published article. There was also a small but possibly significant difference between the feature articles and the scientific articles, the counts for the latter running slightly lower than those for the former. Specifically, the range of percentiles of f.v.e.'s for the samples of conversational language was 12 to 21, the average was 16.4, and the median was 16.5. For the feature articles, the range was 4 to 13 and the average was 8.7; for the scientific articles, the range was 3 to 17 and the average was 7. The median for both was 8.

Of the three poets whose styles are the subject of this study, it is Moore, by a clear margin, whose language contains the fewest finite verbs.[23] The counts vary from poem to poem, as is to be expected, rising to 13 and 16 in the first 200 words of "The Arctic Ox (or Goat)" and to 16 in the first 100 words of "What Are Years?" But Moore's average for all 100-word sequences tabulated is 8.1, as compared to 11.4 for Stevens and 10.9 for Frost; her median is 8, as compared to 11 for Stevens and 11.5 for Frost,[24] and her range of 1 to 16 is lower, at both its low and high extremes, than either Stevens's of 4 to 18 or Frost's of 6 to 18. At its lowest, Moore's low count of one finite verb in a 100-word passage falls below the low extreme of three verbs in 100 words in my samples of scientific prose, and the total of 50 verbs in 900 consecutive words in "Virginia Britannia" is 8 lower than the lowest total I found for 900 consecutive words in those same samples.[25]

Where one grammatical element is lacking, others must be present in its place. One such, in Moore's syntax, is the present or past participial phrase, used where another author might have used a clause. There are a number of these in "Virginia Britannia," beginning with the second sentence of the poem:

> The air is soft, warm, hot
> above the cedar-dotted emerald shore
> *known* to the redbird, the red-coated musketeer,
> the trumpet flower, the cavalier,
> the parson, and the wild parishioner.

(Though here it is the noun series that most conspicuously occupies syntactic space, delaying the appearance on the scene of the next verb.) In the fourth stanza, an appositive construction with the noun *mockingbird* as head is followed by three present participial phrases:

> *alighting* noiseless, *musing* in the semi-sun,
> *standing* on tall thin legs as if he did not see.

The first sentence of "The Frigate Pelican" leads off with a compound present participial phrase and ends with a simple one:

> Rapidly *cruising* or *lying* on the air there is a bird
> that realizes Rasselas's friend's project
> of wings *uniting* levity with strength.

Participial phrases make up most of the third stanza of "He 'Digesteth Harde Yron'":

> How
> could he, *prized* for plumes and eggs and young,
> *used* even as a riding-beast, respect men
> *hiding* actor-like in ostrich skins, with the right hand
> *making* the neck move as if alive
> and from a bag the left hand
>
> *strewing* grain, that ostriches
> might be decoyed and killed!

(These lines contain only two finite verbs, *could* and *might,* in a total of fifty words.) It should be added that the participial phrase, present or past, is an important constituent of the extended complex noun phrase, a feature of Moore's syntax discussed at length below.

We can learn a good deal about Moore's syntax by counting finite verbs, spotting participial phrases, and in general observing the deployment of the parts of speech in her poems. What such investigations do not reveal is the *significance* of the proportions of the parts of speech in Moore's language, and notably of her sparing use of the finite verb, as symptomatic of the workings of her imagination. For that, we must turn from syntactic classification and statistics to an examination of the expressive values of particular words. In so doing, we can usefully invoke the important grammatical distinction between "stative" and "dynamic."[26]

Broadly speaking, words are called stative or dynamic depending on whether the concepts they signify are regarded as stable or changing, permanent or temporary, absolute or variable. The distinction is formal as well as conceptual. Stative verbs, for example, are regularly used in the simple present or past tense; when such a verb is recast in the progressive aspect, it changes from stative to dynamic, rendering the sentence in which it appears unidiomatic or changing its meaning. We cannot substitute "is going" for "goes" in "White wine goes with fish," where *goes* is clearly stative, but we can make the substitution in "All goes well," where *goes* is clearly dynamic. The first sentence is categorical, cast in a "timeless" present.[27] The second is factual; the condition it describes exists in a "historical" present, and is subject to change. But aside from "All goes well" and other set expressions, verbs of dynamic significance normally take the progressive aspect in the present tense. "He plays well," even though spoken at a concert, would be understood as describing a man's playing in general rather than at a particular moment. Verbs in the simple past tense may be either stative or dynamic. "He played well" may refer to a certain occasion or a number of occasions; it may also refer to the quality of a man's playing without specification of time.[28] Other tests reveal the comparatively stative or dynamic character of adjectives and nouns. We can say "He is being cooperative" but not "He is being wealthy." We can say either "He is cautious" or "He is being cautious," but in one statement we are describing a characteristic, in the other a kind of behavior. And we can say "He is being a pest" but we cannot say "He is being a reporter" without stretching the meaning of the latter term. Of the four open classes, it is the noun, as signifier of entities, that is most intrinsically stative. The finite verb, as signifier of time-located actions, processes, and relationships, is intrinsically dynamic; in fact, one might say that stative verbs are ipso facto less "verb-like" than dynamic ones.[29]

When language attempts to hold its subject matter constant, its grammar inevitably takes on stative characteristics. We can expect such language to contain few finite verbs; of the verbs it does contain, many, if not most, will be stative, and among these, the forms of *to be*, which can link any subject with any attribute in logical definition or factual statement, will tend to appear with obtrusive frequency. So will the passive voice, which in English usually takes the form of *to be* as "linking verb" followed by a past participle (i.e., a verbal adjective). Since *to be* is the most general, and hence the most empty, in meaning of the verbs, its use as predicating nexus in sentence after sentence makes for monotony and lifelessness—effects often singled out for dispraise in descriptive prose, whether scholarly or journalistic.

All the above statements hold true for the language of Marianne Moore. I have already spoken of her low finite verb counts. Stative verbs abound, notably in assertions of symbolic significance. The star on the steeple in "The Steeple-Jack" "stands for hope" (p. 7); we are told in "The Buffalo" that "Black in blazonry means / prudence; and niger, unpropitious" (p. 27); in "Light Is Speech," that "the word France means / enfranchisement; means one who can / 'animate whoever thinks of her'" (p. 98); in "Elephants," that the white elephant's "held-up foreleg for use // as a stair . . . expounds the brotherhood / of creatures to man the encroacher'' (pp. 129–30). There is of course much description of characteristic behavior, usually in the timeless present: the plumet basilisk ''feeds on leaves and berries'' (p. 22), the house-cat ''takes its prey to privacy'' (p. 91), the head of the ostrich ''revolves with compass-needle nervousness / when he stands guard'' (p. 99), and so on. Two modal auxiliaries, *can* (signifying an innate capacity) and *will* (signifying habitual and hence predictable action), appear frequently in such descriptions. Reindeer ''can run eleven / miles in fifty minutes'' (p. 96); the salamander ''can withstand // fire and won't drown'' (p. 144); ''the tuatera // will tolerate a / petrel in its den'' (p. 21); the ostrich ''will wade / in lake or sea till only the head shows'' (p. 100); the pangolin ''will drop [from a tree] and will / then walk away / unhurt'' (p. 118); the arctic ox (or goat) ''will open gates and invent games'' (p. 194). Such statements link Moore's language not only with the prose of feature articles on natural history, but with advertising, where the auxiliaries *can* and *will* are regularly used to signify the power and reliability of the product in question.[30]

The use of *have* as a stative verb meaning ''to be endowed with, to be characterized by having,'' is a mannerism in Moore.[31] The ancient Egyptians, she tells us, ''had a flax which they spun // into fine linen / cordage'' (p. 11); the state of Virginia ''has high-singing frogs'' and other attractions (p. 110); the mind ''has memory's ear'' (p. 134). In an especially curious turn of phrase, Moore's willingness to pardon the Spanish dancer Soledad for having once been a bullfighter is turned into an attribute of the person pardoned: ''Well; she has a forgiver'' (p. 169). This use of *have,* like the above-described uses of *can* and *will,* is characteristic of advertising language; products are regularly extolled as unique in ''having'' this or that ingredient or feature.

To be as linking verb appears in some passages to the point of obtrusiveness. It is used five times in the first four lines of ''What Are Years?''

> What is our innocence,
> what is our guilt? All are
>   naked, none is safe. And whence
> is courage. . . .?

''Propriety'' contains a total of thirteen finite verbs, of which nine are forms of *to be.* (Cf. also the passage from ''The Mind Is an Enchanting Thing'' quoted on p. 89 above.) Descriptions of habitual behavior are frequently cast in the passive voice and thus contain *to be* as ''linking verb.'' When the ''behavior'' in question takes the form of vigorous action, the choice of the passive may seem odd, as when Moore says of the Indian buffalo, menaced by a tiger, that its two horns ''are lowered fiercely'' (p. 28). Her account of how the paper nautilus protects its eggs is similarly deactivated, leading off with a past participial phrase:

Buried eightfold in her eight
   arms, for she is in
   a sense a devil-
fish, her glass ram's-horn-cradled freight
   is hid but is not crushed.

(p. 121)

The poem continues in similar syntactic vein:

   as Hercules, bitten

   by a crab loyal to the hydra,
was hindered to succeed,
   the intensively
   watched eggs coming from
the shell free it when they are freed—

Its final clause, characteristically, is a definition in which subject and subject complement are linked by the verb *to be:* "Love / is the only fortress / strong enough to trust to."

In view of the stative character of Moore's grammar, strikingly apparent in her treatment of the finite verb, we ought not to be surprised by the importance and dramatic saliency in her language of the most stative of the parts of speech, the noun. Squadrons of nouns in series, virtually devoid of modification, march through *The Complete Poems,* from the "trumpet vine, / foxglove, giant snapdragon . . . morning-glories, gourds" and other wild and domesticated plants growing in and near the village described in "The Steeple-Jack" to the "lindens, / maples and sycamores, oaks and the Paris / street-tree, the horse-chestnut" which had (no doubt) been seen by William Cullen Bryant and Timothy Cole before Asher Durand painted them conversing underneath an elm.

Particular nouns become conspicuous as a result of conversion to adjectival use, as in descriptions of the "quicksilver ferocity" of the plumet basilisk (p. 24), the "alligator-eyes" of the domestic cat (p. 43), and the "gnat // trustees" of the white elephant (p. 129). (For additional examples, see the discussion of nouns as premodifiers in the extended complex noun phrase below.) Moore had a propensity for joining two or more nouns together to form compound nouns and modifiers; as a result, eye-catching sequences of three or more nouns such as "ostrich-skin warts" (p. 108), "ram's-horn root" (p. 125), "grass-lamp glow" (p. 148), "backgammon-board wedges" (p. 151), "bowling-ball thunder" (p. 210), "fern-seed / footprints" (p. 15), "sawtooth leather lace" (p. 96), "birdclaw-ear-ringed" (p. 109) and "mouse-skin-bellows-breath" (p. 188), are a hallmark of her descriptive style. The business of description is sometimes carried on almost wholly by series, appositives, and subject complements in what Hugh Kenner has called a "rain of nouns"[32] (though *hail* might be a better word for the effect):

99

> This near artichoke with head and legs and grit-equipped gizzard,
> the night miniature artist engineer is,
> yes, Leonardo da Vinci's replica—
> impressive animal and toiler of whom we seldom hear.
>
> (p. 117)

> The split
> pine fair hair, steady gannet-clear
> eyes and the pine-needled-path deer-
> swift step; that is Sweden, land of the
> free and the soil for a spruce tree—
>
> vertical though a seedling—all
> needles: from a green trunk, green shelf
> on shelf fanning out by itself.
>
> (pp. 131–32)

> Style
>
> revives in Escudero's constant of the plumbline,
> axis of the hairfine moon—his counter-camber of the skater.
> No more fanatical adjuster
> of the tilted hat
> than Escudero; of tempos others can't combine.
>
> (p. 169)

A comparison with the syntactically similar passages in Stevens discussed in chapter 4 is interesting in that it points up a deep-seated contrast between the two poets. Whereas series and appositives in Stevens typically represent *alternative* modes of apprehension, equally valid but equally transient in validity, in Moore their elements are mutually supportive, serving as so many strokes to nail the subject ever more firmly in cognitive space.

Also noteworthy is an imaginative process characteristic of Moore whereby actions are treated as entities, named and cataloged like so many items on a shelf. "We do not like some things," says the speaker of "The Hero," "and the hero doesn't." The "things" in question are then enumerated; the first, "deviating headstones," is tangible, but the rest are not: "uncertainty; going where one does not wish / to go; suffering and not / saying so: standing and listening where something / is hiding." In "Tom Fool at Jamaica," the climax of a race, a subject that in the hands of another author might well have brought down a rain of verbs, is again formulated as a list of "things":

> You've the beat
> of a dancer to a measure or harmonious rush
> of a porpoise at the prow where the racers all win easily—
> like centaurs' legs in tune, as when kettledrums compete;
> nose rigid and suede nostrils spread, a light left hand on the rein, till
> well—this is a rhapsody.

100

The climactic finite verb one expects at the end (in a subordinate clause introduced by *till*) is omitted; the description breaks off, and the passage concludes
with a kind of definition of itself. So too the sinuous motions of the Spanish dancer
Soledad in "Style" are converted into patterns, "perhaps say literal alphabet-/S
soundholes in a 'cello / set contradictorily" (p. 169).

More examples could be supplied, but it is obvious by now that Moore's
grammatical preference for stative over dynamic bespeaks a deeper bias. Hers is
an imagination that sees more meaning in fixity than in flux, in the set of still
photographs than in the moving picture, in the wave "at the curl"[33] or "held up
for us to see / in its essential perpendicularity" than in the "wave, interminably
flowing" of Stevens's "Peter Quince at the Clavier." The appropriateness of syntax to conception is strikingly apparent in "Elephants." The 29-word sentence
which opens the poem contains only one finite verb, *fights,* and is replete with
past participles; it describes a tug-of-war between two elephants in which the
opposing forces have momentarily canceled each other out:

> Uplifted and waved till immobilized
> wistaria-like, the opposing opposed
> mouse-gray twined proboscises' trunk formed by two
> trunks, fights itself to a spiraled inter-nosed
>
> deadlock of dyke-enforced massiveness.

Though presented as a single event, this is in fact a kind of habitual activity, a
game. The fact that it is a game rather than a fight is important, for the captive
beasts are not venting pent-up hostility but enjoying themselves, demonstrating
the "equanimity" emphasized elsewhere in the poem.

> It's a
> knock-down drag-out fight that asks no quarter? Just
> a pastime, as when the trunk rains on itself
> the pool siphoned up.

The pose selected for detailed description in the opening of the poem is thus
emblematic; we can visualize the two elephants with their intertwined trunks as
forming a symmetrical design, as if on either side of an escutcheon. Other similar
pictures are held up for us to see in other poems: "the decorous frock-coated
Negro" who is a guide at Washington's tomb, "standing like the shadow / of the
willow" (p. 9), the Indian buffalo "standing in a mud lake with a / day's work to
do" (p. 28), "Hans von Marée's / St. Hubert, kneeling with head bent, / erect—in
velvet and tense with restraint—/ hand hanging down: the horse, free" (pp.
196–97) (this last of course based on an actual painting). Moore herself sometimes
speaks as a guide, drawing our attention to one or another of her "exhibits." She
prefaces her description of the mockingbird in "Virginia Britannia" with an invi-
tation to "observe the terse Virginian" (p. 108), and says of the human animal to

whom her attention turns at the end of "The Pangolin," "there he sits in his own habitat, / serge-clad, strong-shod" (p. 120). On the abstract plane, she shows us moral or spiritual entities: "This then you may know / as the hero" (p. 9); "This is mortality, / this is eternity" (p. 95). Unlike Stevens, who endlessly captures the flash of intimation in the nick of speech, only to discard the hard-won prize and begin again, Moore works toward an apprehension of her subject that, once achieved, need not change. It was Stevens who wrote that "There are many truths, But they are not parts of a truth" (p. 203). Marianne Moore's words on the same subject are, "Know that it will be there when it says, 'I shall be there when the wave has gone by'" (p. 42).[34]

Grammatical stativeness and "stability" of descriptive content in Moore are reinforced by a conspicuous feature of syntax shared by her language with that of the feature article and the advertisement: the "complex noun phrase" in its short and extended forms.[35] I follow Quirk et al.[36] in distinguishing the "basic" from the "complex" noun phrase. Aside from the noun or pronoun serving as head, the basic noun phrase contains only "closed-system items" such as determiners, quantifiers, possessive pronouns, and numerals. The complex noun phrase usually contains one or more of these, but it also contains at least one "open-class item." What I call the extended complex noun phrase contains two or more such items, one in premodifying and one in postmodifying position.

Open-class premodifiers in the complex noun phrase include adjectives, present and past participles, nouns converted to adjectival use, and nouns in the inflected genitive; postmodifiers, in addition to these, include prepositional phrases, present and past participial phrases, infinitive phrases, and relative clauses. The extended complex noun phrase assumes imposing proportions when a number of elements of a single grammatical type or a variety of types are directly dependent on the head, or when a noun serving as the head of a modifying element is itself heavily modified. The following sentences, taken from feature articles which we know were read by Marianne Moore and advertisements which she may have read, exemplify some of the many varieties of the construction:[37]

1. A good golf shoe because it has *turf gripping soles of ribbed rubber* and is made of *moisture resisting elk with a calf saddle* (*Times*, 6/8/34, p. 7)

2. On *the lightning-fast withdrawal of the tongue into its groove on the floor of the mouth*, the ants are swept off into the throat. . . . (Hatt, pp. 728–29)

3. "Daisy" is the name of *this dashing new off-the-face (yes, off-the-face!) sailor in shiny rough straw* (*Times*, 4/1/35, p. 20)

4. These are *those most extraordinary-looking lizards known as 'basilisks,' which are arboreal in habit, and live only on trees overhanging water* (Pycraft, col. 2)

5. It is *a really full-sized, four-door, four-seater family saloon that touches the sixty mark, and does 45–50 miles per gallon* (ILN, 1/16/32, p. 111)

6. The eggs are laid in *a shallow pit or depression of the soil scraped out by the feet of the old birds with the earth heaped around to form a wall or rampart* (Laufer, p. 262)

The complex noun phrase is clearly an information-compacting device. As is to be expected, it has been developed to extremes of elaboration in promotional prose and other genres in which language is characteristically loaded with descriptive detail. Each such phrase takes advantage, one might say, of an explicit reference to something in the descriptive content of a passage to add one or more facts about it to the sentence in which the reference is made. In styles of lower density, such facts would be stated in individual sentences, each with its own finite verb. Any of the examples quoted above can be "unpacked" to form a series of short statements. For the first complex noun phrase in (1), "turf gripping soles of ribbed rubber," we might substitute "Its soles grip the turf. They are made of rubber. The rubber is of ribbed design." In the resultant paraphrase, 16 words, including 3 finite verbs, correspond to 6 words lacking a finite verb in the original.

An extended complex noun phrase is often found in information-saturated language in apposition to another such phrase, and may contain a complex noun phrase in apposition to one of its own nominal elements. Of the two phrases joined by apposition in such structures, the second is regularly supplementary in descriptive content to the first, much like a postmodifying participial phrase or relative clause. (In the following examples and elsewhere, I use the plus sign to indicate apposition.)

7. Nearly three centuries ago merchant adventurers first noticed *mysterious bundles of gossamer tumbling across the tundra, + small fibrous clouds blown by the summer arctic winds, sometimes catching on the flat dwarf birches and stringing out in waving sheets* (Teal, p. 76)

(Note that "which looked like" or "resembling" could be inserted between the two phrases connected by apposition in this example.)

At its most elaborate, the extended complex noun phrase may be a hierarchical structure in which one phrase contains another which in turn contains another. When such nesting occurs, or when postmodifying phrases and clauses are linked in successively lower grades of subordination, the phrase may seem to drift away from its original topic:[38]

8. Such a group [i.e., of animals with so little hair that they can scarcely be called mammals] is the pangolins, + *bizarre anteaters which have largely sacrificed the typical coat for one of large, over-lapping, horny scales, worn practically everywhere except over the face and the underparts back to the tail* (Hatt, p. 725)

9. John J. Teal, Jr., is *an authority on the arctic, where his attention has been drawn to the musk ox, + that huge docile animal with its silken fleece which has been hunted almost to extinction* (Teal, headnote)

Similarly digressive effects, of the sort often singled out for criticism in discussions of journalistic prose, are produced by the inclusion in the extended complex noun phrase of material tenuously related to the gist of the sentence:[39]

10. Jack Ford, + *crack engineer of the Burlington on the "Zephyr's" amazing "dawn to dusk" dash,* says: [a testimonial to Camel cigarettes follows] (*Sun,* 10/3/34, p. 18)

11. In the course of *the excavations undertaken on the ancient site of Kish in Mesopotamia by the Field Museum–Oxford University Joint Expedition,* great quantities of fragments of ostrich egg-shell were brought to light . . . . (Laufer, p. 257)

12. Caelius Apicius, + *a renowned gormandizer at the time of Augustus and Tiberius, who committed suicide when he saw his fortune shrunk to two million and a half sestertii,* has handed down several culinary recipes as to how to prepare good ostrich meat (Laufer, p. 267)

The premodifying sequence in the complex noun phrase may itself attain to considerable size, and its elements appear in a variety of combinations and permutations. Each sequence, as noted earlier, contains at least one open-class or denotatively significant modifier. This modifier is frequently "designative" in the useful sense assigned that word by Geoffrey Leech, serving to classify or identify its referent.[40] Harking back to the grammatical distinction between stative and dynamic meanings, we can see that designative modifiers are highly stative. Not only are the attributes they signify regarded as inherent and stable; they themselves are "fixed," in that they cannot be qualified with respect to degree. In grammatical terms, they are "non-gradable."[41] Nouns used as modifiers—for example, *rubber* in "ribbed rubber soles" (1), *calf* in "calf saddle" (1), *merchant* in "merchant adventurers" (7), and *dwarf* in "dwarf birches" (7)—are of course designative. We cannot say that the soles of shoes are "more" or "less" rubber; we cannot say that the saddle of a shoe is "very calf," and so on. Modifiers other than nouns may be designative or nondesignative, depending on their meaning in a given phrase. *Ribbed,* in "ribbed rubber soles," and *overlapping,* in "overlapping horny scales" (8), are designative in that they signify a definite style and a definite configuration, respectively. Designative modifiers are often preceded by gradable modifiers denoting attributes regarded as variable in degree; these latter may have either objective or qualitative meanings. In "small fibrous clouds" (7), "flat dwarf birches" (7), and "large, overlapping, horny scales," the gradable modifier is objective; in "amazing 'dawn to dusk' dash" (10), it is qualitative.[42] In "dashing new off-the-face sailor" (3), where "off-the-face" signifies a style of hat, two gradable modifiers, the first qualitative, the second objective, precede the designative modifier. (*Sailor* itself is short for *sailor hat,* and is thus a designative modifier converted into a noun.) Designative, gradable-objective, and gradable-qualitative modifiers appear in various combinations in other phrases, for example, "sensitive fleshy pad" (Hatt, p. 726), "the powerful avian giant" (Laufer, p. 264), "a brilliant saffron yellow" (Pycraft, col. 1), "tiny multi-colored beads" (*Times,* 4/3/35, p. 7), "clear chalk-white prints" (*Times,* 6/6/34, p. 3), "a beautiful carved red lacquer bowl" (Davis, caption), "the lightest woven-wire pasture fence" (Teal, p. 80), "a loud, mournful kind of bellowing roar" (Laufer, p. 262). In all these, we see a progression from variable to stable attributes, and a corresponding grammatical progression from dynamic to stative.[43]

Three constituents of the premodifying sequence—the adjectival noun, the adjectival compound, and the noun in the inflected genitive case—are hallmarks of the descriptive style of promotional prose and journalistic prose generally.[44] Each, in comparison with other ways of expressing the same content, effects minor economies of space in the passage in which it appears.

Most of the nouns used as premodifiers in the examples quoted above are familiar to us in their attribute-signifying roles—for example, *golf* in "golf shoe" (1), *calf* in "calf saddle" (1), *family* in "family saloon" (5), and *dwarf* in "dwarf birches" (7). But in one phrase, "the Field Museum–Oxford University Joint Expedition" (11), two nouns have been taken from the descriptive content of the article and put into service as modifiers "for the nonce," at the same time being joined to form a compound. The result is a more compact equivalent of "the Expedition sponsored jointly by the Field Museum and Oxford University." The same sort of grammatical maneuver is responsible for such collocations in my source materials as "*dragon* designs" (Davis, col. 3), "*pangolin* tongues" (Hatt, p. 728), "*ostrich egg-shell* cups" (Laufer, title), "*musk* ox way of life" (Teal, p. 78), "*lace-stitch* design" (*ILN,* 6/15/35, p. 1093), and "*buyer* sales" (*Times,* 4/3/35, p. 4), each of which, like "Field Museum–Oxford University," can be paraphrased in expanded form.

Like the noun in the premodifying sequence, the adjectival compound may be familiar to us individually or in type, as is true of *turf-gripping* (1), *moisture resisting* (1), *off-the-face* (3), and *four-door, four-seater* (5). But the improvisational compounding of premodifiers is a regular practice among writers of promotional prose, and to it we owe such nonce formations as "*barren-ground* musk ox" (Teal, p. 77), "*multi-pellet* droppings" (Teal, p. 80), "*hundred-yards* sprinter" (Pycraft, col. 1), "*mile-high* golf" (*Sun,* 6/26/34, p. 23), "*shirts-skirts-and-shorts* suits" (*Times,* 6/8/34, p. 5), and "*May-through-September* sun" (*Geog.,* Jan. 39).

The inflected genitive of the noun, where spoken idiom would call for the phrasal genitive with *of,* seems more characteristic of the advertisement than of the feature article. (It often appears in the news article, a form not under consideration here.) Typical examples are "*Alaska's* island-dotted, mountain-sheltered seas" (*Geog.,* Jan. 1939), "*Yosemite's* four vivid seasons" (*Geog.,* Jan. 1935),

"*Luckies'* fine, smooth tobacco quality" (*Times,* 6/5/34, p. 46), "this little *wo-man's* washable silk crepe suit" (*Times,* 6/3/34, p. 15), and "*New York's* sultry summer days" (*Times,* 6/6/34, p. 11).

In addition to the three kinds of constituent I have been discussing, the pre-modifying sequence in the complex noun phrase abounds in modifiers which are in effect "condensed similes." This is not surprising; the simile lends itself to the purposes of promotional description in that it helps the reader to "see" the un-familiar in terms of resemblances to what he knows. The condensed simile at its simplest is formed by adding the suffix *-like* to a noun signifying the vehicle or second term of the comparison, as in "snake-like" (Hatt, p. 728), "porcelain-like" (Laufer, p. 257), "rod-like" (Pycraft, col. 2), "umbrella-like" (ibid.), and "beef-like" (*Times,* 6/8/44, p. 5). In other condensed similes, a noun signifying the vehicle is linked by compounding with a past participle or adjective which fo-cuses or explains the comparison, as in "ax-edged tails" (Hatt, p. 729), "yoke-shaped horns" (Teal, p. 76), "lightning-fast withdrawal" (Hatt, p. 728), "zephyr-light taffeta" (*Times,* 4/2/35, p. 2), and "bracelet-sleeved . . . dress" (*Times,* 6/9/44, p. 6). In still others, the vehicle alone is expressed, in the form of an adjectival noun, as in "gauntlet sleeves" (*Times,* 6/5/34, p. 6), "rich nut flavor" (*Times,* 6/3/34, p. 16), "mailbag beach bag" (*Times,* 6/8/34, p. 5), and "Bellows Pleat Back" (*Times,* 6/5/34, p. 11). This last type would seem to be especially favored in advertising copy, though the feature articles I surveyed do contain one striking formation, "ant-chute mouth [of the pangolin]" (Hatt, p. 728), that is, "mouth shaped like a chute for conveying ants."

Nowhere is the language of modification in advertising more creative than in the condensed simile specifying a shade of color, which soars to heights of originality in descriptions of men's and women's, especially women's, clothing.[45] Side by side with conventional comparisons like "geranium red" (*Times,* 5/10/34, p. 3) and "chalk-white" (*Times,* 6/6/34, p. 3), we find "claret red, butcher blue, or nigger brown" (*ILN,* 4/13/35, p. 622), "sherbet pink, lemon ice, sky blue or town black" (*Times,* 6/2/44, p. 5), "heaven pink, sport blue, sport green" (*Times,* 6/4/44, p. 12), and "suez blue, lilac water, patio green or lotus pink" (*Times,* 1/1/56, p. 2). A variety of summer hats is described in especially memorable terms: "golden toast lacy straw, pale coffee rough straw, café au lait lace straw, burnt toast coolie brim of rough sewn straw," and, last but not least, "cream-in-the-coffee butcher-weave spun rayon dashing buccaneer" (*Times,* 6/1/44, p. 6).

One characteristic of the premodifying sequence in promotional prose remains to be described: its length. In this respect, the advertisement outdoes the feature article, no doubt because ever-present considerations of space tend to make it the denser in style of the two forms. In the materials surveyed, I found one sequence of twelve premodifiers, two of eleven, and three of nine, in advertisements; the largest number of premodifiers in the feature articles was eight. The examples that

follow are given in descending order of length. (I have counted compound formations as two or more words, depending on the number of elements they contain.
Where the head of the phrase is a compound, as in *town coat, gearbox, milk-jug*, I
have counted the first element separately, whether or not it is joined typographi-
cally to the second.)

With twelve elements:

Hybrid everblooming, heavy 2 and 3 year old field grown dormant bushes
(*Times,* 4/2/35, p. 22)

(*Everblooming* has been counted as two elements.)

With eleven elements:

The classic Lady Chesterfield peak label, man-tailored, fly-front town coat
(*Times,* 4/3/35, p. 3)

(*Chesterfield,* a proper name, has been counted as one element.)

*Luxuriously-soft, long-wearing light-weight John David "Brompton" Fine
Gabardine* Suits (*Times,* 6/5/34, section L, p. 11)

With nine elements (see also no. 5, p. 103):

Our 3-piece plaid cotton shirts-skirts-and-shorts suits (*Times,* 6/8/34, p. 5)

Cream-in-the-coffee butcher-weave spun rayon dashing buccaneer (*Times,*
6/1/44, p. 6)

With eight elements:

The all-silent all-synchromesh fourspeed gearbox (*ILN,* 5/11/35, p. 864)

(*Syncromesh* has been counted as one element.)

A new blue-and-white Staffordshire pottery milk-jug (Davis, col. 1)

(*Staffordshire* has been counted as one element.)

With seven elements:

The two long, rod-like, backwardly directed supporting bones of the tongue
(Pycraft, col. 2)

(*Rod-like* has been counted as one element.)

The complex noun phrase in all the variety of its constituents was for Marianne
Moore an indispensable descriptive device, and she exploited it with inexhaustible ingenuity. The opening of "Elephants," discussed earlier in terms of its
emblematic significance, contains two striking examples:

Uplifted and waved till immobilized
wistaria-like, *the opposing opposed*
mouse-gray twined proboscises' trunk formed by two
trunks, fights itself to *a spiraled inter-nosed*

deadlock of dyke-enforced massiveness.

Several characteristic features will be recognized here: the inflected genitive, the adjectival compound, and the condensed simile specifying a color; the first phrase contains a sequence of seven premodifying elements. This aspect of Moore's language deserves fuller treatment; I shall return to it, as a part of my discussion of the similarities between her poetry and promotional prose, in the following chapter.

SIX

MARIANNE MOORE'S
PROMOTIONAL PROSE
A POEM'S GUISE
AT LAST

Marianne Moore is unique among poets in the nature and importance of her indebtedness to prose writings. The promotional prose of feature articles and advertisements, which is of special interest in this study, was for her a source not only of subject matter but at times of inspiration. Two of the five articles examined in chapter 5 for finite verb counts and examples of the complex noun phrase— "Pangolins" by Robert Hatt and "Golden Fleece of the Arctic" by John J. Teal, Jr.—are responsible for Moore's "Pangolins" and "The Arctic Ox (or Goat)," respectively (for full bibliographical information on the five articles see n. 24 to chap. 5). The other three figure in her Notes in much the same manner as items in the bibliography of a research theme. Mythological lore from Frank Davis's "The Chinese Dragon" and scientific description from W. P. Pycraft's "The Frilled Lizard" (Moore cites as "The Malay Dragon and the 'Basilisks'") appear side by side in the opening sections of "The Plumet Basilisk" (Notes, pp. 264, 265); Berthold Laufer's "Ostrich Egg-Shell Cups from Mesopotamia" is mentioned (p. 277) as a source of certain of the facts about the ostrich incorporated in "He 'Digesteth Harde Yron.'" Other feature articles that gave Moore ideas for poems are "Economies [actually "Economy"] in the Use of Steel," by Waldemar Kaempffert, for "The Icosasphere" (pp. 281–82), and "Festivals and Fairs for the Tourist in Italy," by Mitchell Goodman, for "The Web One Weaves of Italy" (p. 164). "Four Quartz Crystal Clocks" was largely derived from a Bell Telephone Company pamphlet (p. 280), a hybrid of feature article and advertisement of the sort described in chapter 5. Elsewhere the Notes acknowledge indebtedness to a variety of newspapers and magazines for information on a variety of subjects: on the diet of the fieldmouse, to the *National Geographic* (p. 264); on the legendary Persian nightingale, to the *New York Sun* (pp. 278–79); on the history of the herb rosemary, to *The Spectator* (p. 288); on the grasshopper-shaped weathervane atop Faneuil Hall in Boston, to the *Christian Science Monitor* (p. 293), to cite only a few instances. Advertisements and quasi-advertisements which provided Moore with poetic material include a catalog for "the Karl Freund collection sale" (p. 266), an advertisement for India paper in the *New York Times* (p. 269), an "advertisement entitled 'Change of Fashion'" in the *English Review* (p. 272), and an article in *What's New*, a pamphlet distributed by Abbott Laboratories (p. 287). In view of the prominence of fixed poses and scenes in Moore's descriptions, it is not surprising that some of her promotional sources are pictures. According to its headnote (p. 218), "Blue Bug" was written "upon seeing Dr. Raworth Williams' Blue Bug with seven other ponies, photographed by Thomas McAvoy: *Sports Illustrated.*" Photographs in the *National Geographic* and *Life* are cited in the Notes to "Camellia Sabina" (p. 264) and "Saint Nicholas" (pp. 293–94), respectively. Other visual credits are cinematic. The tuatera described in "The Plumet Basilisk" was "shown by Captain Stanley Osborne in motion pictures" (p. 265), and "Elephants" was written after Moore had attended "a lecture-film entitled *Ceylon, the Wondrous Isle*" (p. 281). There is one reference to a picture in an advertisement: the "bock beer buck" of "Armor's Undermining Modesty" with its "pale-ale-eyed impersonal look" (an animal the author of this study remembers well) was seen by Moore on a "poster unsigned, distributed by Eastern Beverage Corporation" (p. 283). (Cf. her allusion in "Style" to "the traditional unwavy / Sandeman sailor," i.e., the angular silhouette wearing a flat-brimmed hat on the label of Sandeman sherry.)

Moore gave us her notes because she honestly, though mistakenly, believed that the "chief interest" of much that she wrote was "borrowed" ("A Note on the Notes," p. 262). They gratify our curiosity in that they tell us the *sort* of reading she got her information from, but they are (fortunately) far from complete. The grasshopper-shaped weathervane in Boston is duly documented, but what of the four dragons with intertwined upright tails over the door of the bourse in Copenhagen (p. 21)? We are assured that Peter, in the poem of that title, is the real "cat owned by Miss Magdalen Hueber and Miss Maria Weniger," but in what zoo did Moore see the cat she celebrates, in "The Monkeys," as "that Gilgamesh / among the hairy carnivora"? We are not told, and it does not matter. Probity was never in question; accuracy can be taken on faith.[1]

The fact in itself is of no importance. What concerns us is the fact chosen for the poem, formulated and verbalized in the poem, imbued with the spirit of the poem. And it is here that we encounter at every turn the resemblances to the feature article and the advertisement which were posited at the outset of this study and which must now be spelled out in detail. But first, lest it should seem that these resemblances are intended to explain the *power* of the poetry, let me concede, nay assert, that Marianne Moore was always true to the conventions of promotional prose—in her fashion. We could not do without the admixture of eccentricity and originality that perfuses her language: the Latinate technical terms; the polysyllabic rarities and neologisms; the free-wheeling images that compare lions' heads to flowers, flowers to the feathers of Andalusian cocks, and the tails of cocks to scimitars; the ellipses and divagations; the sudden flashes of aphorism and satiric wit. Moore's poetry, rearranged by an operation the reverse of that performed at the beginning of this study, can deceive us into thinking we are reading promotional prose, but not for very long. Deprived of its lineation as verse, the statement in "The Steeple-Jack" that "You can see a twenty-five-pound lobster; and fish nets arranged to dry" may look for all the world like information in a guidebook, but it is immediately followed by a descriptive passage whose final comment, at least, is calculated to confuse the tourist: "The whirlwind fife-and-drum of the storm bends the salt marsh grass, disturbs stars in the sky and the star on the steeple; it is a privilege to see so much confusion." "He 'Digesteth Harde Yron'" leads off in the manner of a feature article about ostriches: "Although the aepyornis or roc that lived in Madagascar, and the moa are extinct . . ." Continued in conventional fashion, the sentence might run, "the ostrich, called 'a large sparrow' by the classical author Xenophon, who saw one walking by the Euphrates when travelling in northern Arabia, has survived in large numbers to the present day."[2] What Moore actually wrote was, "the camel-sparrow, linked with them in size—the large sparrow Xenophon saw walking by a stream—was and is a symbol of justice." Had I started my investigation on the assumption that Moore really *was* writing promotional prose, I should have had to conclude that she failed. This, of course, is the moral of the bathetic tale of her correspondence with the Ford company after it had engaged her to devise a name for a new car.[3] Much as we may deplore "Edsel," we can understand the rejection, inter alia, of "Mongoose civique," "Turcotingo," and "Utopian Turtletop."

I shall begin my examination of the promotional aspects of Moore's poetic language by discussing visual imagery, an aspect of her style treated in the preceding chapter under the heading of syntax. Like those we find in feature articles and advertisements, Moore's word pictures are literally "colorful." Colors themselves are definite and bright, their intrinsic qualities often heightened by contrast. The lizards of the Virgin Islands (described in "People's Surroundings") glitter "like splashes of fire and silver on the pierced turquoise of the / lattices" (p. 56); a sycamore tree is an "albino giraffe" against a "gun-metal sky" (p. 167); a brocade "blaze[s] green as though some lizard in the shade / became exact— // set off by replicas of violet" (p. 189). No poet has ever loved better than Moore to number the streaks of the tulip. Stripes, especially the distinctive markings of animals, are a signature of her imagery. The hairs of the jerboa's tail form a black and white tuft at the tip, "strange detail of the simplified creature" (p. 14); the plumet basilisk has eight green bands on its tail "as piano keys are barred / by five black stripes across the white" (p. 22); the fauna of Big Snow Mountain include "the nine-striped chipmunk" (p. 73); the skunk in "The Wood-Weasel" emerges in "sylvan black and white chipmunk / regalia" (p. 127); the roadrunner in "The Mind, Intractable Thing" is "stenciled in black / stripes all over" (p. 208). The poet's affection extends to spotted creatures as well: the calico horses of "New York" (p. 54), the "paddock full of leopards and giraffes" of "Marriage" (p. 64), the "conspicuously spotted little horses" of "An Octopus" (p. 74), the "snow-leopard wrap" worn by El Greco's possibly fictitious daughter, "the fur widely // dotted with black" (p. 233). Elsewhere, variegation creates a verbal technicolor. The translucent black water beneath the ocean cliff in "The Fish" is populated with blue mussels, pink jellyfish, and green crabs (p. 32); pink nectarines are painted beside "slender crescent leaves / of green or blue or / both" in "Nine Nectarines" (p. 29); in "Rosemary," the leaves of the herb are "green but silver underneath, / its flowers—white originally—turned blue" (p. 168); jet black and pale gray-blue pansies grow beside box hedges within a pink brick border in "Virginia Britannia" (p. 108). All this may remind us of *Natural History* and the *National Geographic,* but bright colors in clearly defined contrastive patterns and variegated arrays are equally characteristic of the descriptive content of advertisements for clothing, accessories, and jewelry. Accounts in Moore's poems of the "white pin-dots on black horizontal spaced- / out bands" on the back of the newt (p. 6), the "pink and black-striped, sashed or dotted silks" of racehorses (p. 162), and the decorations on the uniforms of the palace guards of the Sultan Tipu, "little woven stripes incurved like buttonholes" (p. 241), have their truest counterparts in "cool grey-and-white stripes, white piqué touches" (advertisement for women's suit-dresses, *Times,* 6/7/44, p. 13), "bare-midriff swim suit accented with bands of navy or red" (*Times* 6/4/44, p. 7), and "skinny streaks of beige, turquoise or licorice sharply drawn on the chalkiest white cotton knit" (advertisement for women's dresses, *Times* 1/1/56, p. 46). A significant pictorial analogue to both sets of passages is the vividly striped apron worn by the figure in the Swedish Travel Bureau advertisement reproduced on page 94.

In poems about places, the content of key passages seems chosen as a professional photographer assigned to illustrate a magazine article might choose scenes in a locale. Some "shots" are at close range, some at a distance. Particularly memorable is the sunset panorama that concludes "Virginia Britannia":

> The live oak's darkening filigree
> of undulating boughs, the etched
> solidity of a cypress indivisible
> from the now agèd English hackberry,
> become with lost identity,
> part of the ground, as sunset flames increasingly
> against the leaf-chiseled
> blackening ridge of green.
>
> (p. 111)

Vividness of color contrast is here enhanced by clarity of line, another recurrent feature of Moore's visual imagery. In some especially striking passages, contour and surface detail are meticulously rendered with the uniformly heavy lineation of a Dürer engraving. The rows of scales forming the armor of the pangolin overlap "with spruce-cone regularity until they / form the uninterrupted central / tail-row" (p. 117); the shell of the paper nautilus has "wasp-nest flaws / of white on white, and close- // laid Ionic chiton-folds / like the lines in the mane of / a Parthenon horse" (p. 122); the spines of the porcupine, in "Apparition of Splendor," are "thistlefine spears, among / prongs in lanes above lanes of a shorter prong" (p. 158).

Visual images of so high a degree of resolution, for all their authenticity, are far from realistic—they do not correspond to the selective and partially focused picture recorded by the seeing eye. The discrepancy between representation and experience is especially apparent when the subject is in motion or only momentarily at rest, as at the end of "The Jerboa" (p. 15). The creature pauses,

> pillar body erect
> on a three-cornered smooth-working Chippendale
>   claw—propped on hind legs, and tail as third toe,
>   between leaps to its burrow.

Since, as we have just been told, the jerboa moves with "kangaroo speed," neither its method of locomotion nor the shape of its claw could have been as precisely observed as the speaker's words imply, had it been seen running on a single occasion. Such details have their source in the repeated and careful observations of the naturalist or artist in the field, armed with pencil and paper, or in the freezing of motion made possible by the high-speed camera.[4] Other images suggest the "zoom shot" in which the camera eye can approach the subject far more closely than the human eye—for example, the description of the "minute legs" of the Malay dragon "trailing half akimbo" after it has dived from a tree top to a hanging spray (pp. 20–21). Moore's surreal word photographs bespeak an *intellectual* curiosity as readily satisfied by the printed page as by visible phenomena themselves. The minutiae of external appearance serve in the poems as data, pointing toward an apprehension of the object in terms of essential form or emblematic significance.

Facts as well as pictures are dramatized in the poems by such tried-and-true promotional techniques as the heightening of contrasts and incongruities latent in the subject matter.[5] In "Elephants," a "six-foot" mahout lying asleep on his mount is said to be "so feather light the elephant's stiff / ear's unconscious of the crossed feet's weight" (p. 128), while those officiating at the display of the Buddha's tooth are "gnat // trustees" in comparison with the bulk of the white elephant which leads the procession (p. 129). "Moon-vines [are] trained on fishing twine" in the village described in "The Steeple-Jack" (p. 6); early American history is summed up in "New York" as a progression from "the beau with the muff . . . to the conjunction of the Monongahela and the Allegheny" (p. 54); and "tobacco-crop / records" are inscribed "on church walls" in Virginia (p. 110). The poems are populated with creatures that excel: heroes, champions, sole survivors. The frigate bird, outmaneuvering all other birds in flight, is supreme in "the height and in the majestic / display of his art" (pp. 25–26); the ostrich, alone among large flightless birds, has resisted man's depredations (p. 99); the racehorse Tom Fool has "that mark of a champion, the extra / spurt when needed"; his performance reminds the speaker of "the time Ted Atkinson charged by on Tiger Skin— / no pursuers in sight" (p. 163); the Spanish dancer Escudero moves to "tempos others can't combine," while the skill and grace of the jai-alai champion Etchebaster "preclude envy" (p. 169). Moore's cast of heroic characters includes some notorious oddities: the pangolin, who "endures exhausting solitary trips" from dusk to dawn in search of food (p. 117); the ostrich, who guards the eggs at night, "his legs / their only weapon of defense" (p. 99), the paper nautilus, who "scarcely // eats until [her] eggs are hatched" (p. 121).

"Remarkable facts" are made the more impressive by statistics. The extinct wild aurochs, a beast well worth painting, had a "six- / foot horn spread" (p. 27); the elephant must break off enough branches daily to "provide his forty-pound bough dinner" (p. 128); a prickly pear leaf clinging to barbed wire once sent "a root . . . down to grow / in earth two feet below" (p. 125). The intensiveness of the persecution survived by the ostrich in ancient times is brought home by references to "six hundred ostrich brains served / at one banquet" and "eight pairs of ostriches / in harness" (p. 100). Such statements are at times amusingly reminiscent of advertising claims. Moore's description, in "People's Surroundings," of "paper so thin that 'one thousand four hundred and twenty / pages make one inch'" (p. 55) is in part quoted verbatim from an advertisement. The icosasphere is brought to our attention as a money-saving device, "since twenty triangles conjoined, can wrap one // ball or double-rounded shell / with almost no waste" (p. 143). We are informed in "Rigorists" that the reindeer "can run eleven / miles in fifty minutes," much as we might be told about the performance of an automobile, and the speaker's statement, in "The Buffalo," that the Indian buffalo "need not fear comparison" with "any / of ox ancestry" sounds for all the world like an advertisement for an expensive wristwatch. Moore's enthusiastic report on qiviut, "the underwool of the arctic ox," in "The Arctic Ox (or Goat)," concludes:

> Suppose you had a bag
> of it; you could spin a pound
>   into a twenty-four-or-five-
> mile thread—one, forty-ply—
> that will not shrink in any dye.

It is not surprising that she was impelled to add,

>   If you fear that you are
>   reading an advertisement,
>   you are.

As in promotional prose proper, the complex noun phrase does yeoman service, conveying much descriptive detail in little space. It tells us, inter alia, of "impassioned Handel— // meant for a lawyer and a masculine German domestic / career" (p. 25), of "the Indian buffalo, / albino- / footed, standing in a mud lake with a / day's work to do" (p. 28), of the reindeer, a "candelabrum-headed ornament / for a place where ornaments are scarce, sent // to Alaska" (p. 96), of elephants that are "ministrants all gray or / gray with white on legs or trunk" (p. 129), and of "Thanatopsis-invoking tree-loving Bryant / conversing with Timothy Cole / in Asher Durand's painting of them / under the filigree of an elm overhead" (p. 242). Some of Moore's more elaborate creations produce effects of drift or digressiveness such as were illustrated earlier from feature articles and advertisements:

> Pacific yet passionate—
>   for if not both, how
> could he be great?
>   Jerome—reduced by what he'd been through—
> with tapering waist no matter what he ate,
>   left us the Vulgate.
>
> (p. 201)

Lightness of tone and felicity of rhyme beguile us here; after all, this is a poem we are reading, not a biography. In the following example from "In Lieu of the Lyre," we are willingly led away from the gist of the sentence by the charms, both intrinsic and verbal, of the descriptive details themselves:

> To the *Advocate, gratia sum*
>   unavoidably lame as I am, *verbal pilgrim*
> *like Thomas Bewick, drinking from his hat-brim,*
> *drops spilled from a waterfall, denominated later by him*
>   *a crystalline Fons Bandusian miracle.*
>   (p. 206)

Yet at times we may feel that the cargo of the phrase has sunk the ship of the sentence, as in this example from "The Pangolin":

> The giant-pangolin-
>   tail . . .
> is not lost on *this ant- and stone-swallowing uninjurable*
> *artichoke which simpletons thought a living fable*
>   *whom the stones had nourished, whereas ants had done*
>   *so.*

Some especially striking examples of the extended complex noun phrase are found in one of Moore's longest and best poems, "Virginia Britannia." Early in the poem, we are introduced to Captain John Smith, in connection with a comparison between the fur crown of the Indian chief Powhatan, one of whose capitals was at "Werewocomoco," and Smith's coat of arms. A good deal of biographical information, some of it totally irrelevant to the relationship between the men, is given in two successive phrases of which the second is in apposition to the first:

We-re-wo-
co-mo-co's fur crown could be no
odder than we were, with ostrich, Latin motto,
and small gold horseshoe:
arms for *an able sting-ray-hampered pioneer—*
painted as a Turk, it seems[6]*— + continuously*
exciting Captain Smith
who, patient with
his inferiors, was a pugnacious equal, and to
Powhatan as unflattering
as grateful.

(p. 107)

The hedge sparrow whose singing at dawn ushers in the close of the poem is the referent of three phrases linked by apposition within the compass of a single sentence:

The mere brown hedge sparrow . . .
even in the dark
flutes his ecstatic burst of joy— + *the caraway seed-*
spotted sparrow perched in the dew-drenched juniper
beside the window ledge;
+ *this little hedge*
sparrow *that wakes up seven minutes sooner than the lark.*

At least one critic has complained in print of the irrelevance of the bit of bird lore contained in the final detail, credited in the Notes (p. 280), without indication of published source, to "the British Empire Naturalists' Association."[7] Other readers may enjoy it, as Moore no doubt did, for its own sake. But in view of the allusion to Wordsworth's Immortality Ode in the last lines of the poem, it seems possible that the comparison between the two species "works" by putting us in mind of Shelley's skylark. The American bird is equally a blithe spirit, equally a spokesman for the poet's imaginative vision, and a touch more ardent in his celebration of the dawn.

Other phrases in other poems bring us down to the terra firma of the documentary advertisement. The Irish grow

flax for damask
that when bleached by Irish weather
has the silvered chamois-leather
water-tightness of a
skin.

(p. 113)

In "Saint Nicholas," the speaker longs for

116

> *a chameleon with tail*
> *that curls like a watch spring; and vertical*
> *on the body—including the face—pale*
> *tiger-stripes, about seven;*
>
> (p. 196)

And her next two wishes are unmistakably inspired in content and idiom by Madison Avenue itself:

> If you can find no striped chameleon,
> might I have a dress or suit—
> I guess you have heard of it—of *qiviut?*
> and to wear with it, a taslon shirt, *the drip-dry fruit*
> *of research second to none;*
> *sewn, I hope, by Excello.*

Premodification in the complex noun phrase is rich and rife. All the distinctive features described in chapter 5 are present. As in promotional prose, the designative modifier is ubiquitous; it is frequently combined with one or more nondesignative (gradable) modifiers which may be either objective or qualitative terms. Each of the following sequences includes at least one designative modifier in its normal position immediately adjacent to the head (line division markers omitted): with two modifiers, "sweet sea air" (p. 5), "white plush dewlap" (p. 27), "'charming tadpole notes'" (p. 53), "comic duckling head" (p. 99), "fine pavement tomb" (p. 107); with three modifiers, "the true Chinese lizard face" (p. 20), "hollow whistled monkey notes" (p. 22), "innocent wide penguin eyes [of baby mockingbirds]" (p. 105), "exhilarating hoarse crow-note" (p. 160). An odd feature of some of the longer sequences is the placement of a designative modifier out of order, in front of a gradable one; the effect is to heighten our awareness of the individual components. In the phrase describing the ostrich as "an alert gargantuan little-winged, magnificently speedy running-bird" (p. 100), the designative modifier *little-winged* (signifying an ornithological characteristic) precedes the gradable modifier *speedy;* so too with *box-bordered* and *tidewater* in "box-bordered tide-water gigantic jet black pansies" (p. 108), *Indian* in "feminine odd Indian young lady" (p. 109), *left* in "Tom Fool's left white hind foot" (p. 162), and *equidistant* in "the equidistant three tiny arcs of seeds in a banana" (p. 170).

As in promotional prose, the premodifying sequence has three recurrent constituents: the noun used adjectivally, the adjectival compound, and the noun in the inflected genitive case. Nominal modifiers and compounds are regularly formed "for the nonce" from the descriptive content of the poems, as in "*grape* holiday" (p. 17), "*bird-reptile* social life" (p. 21), "*Old Dominion* flowers" (p. 109), "*Bell Laboratory* time vault" (p. 115), "*giant-pangolin*-tail" (p. 118), "*teatime* fame" (p. 121), "*Parthenon* horse" (p. 122), "*cork oak* acorn" (p. 151), "*hunt-mad* Hubert" (p. 197), and "*Christmas-fire* tale-spinner" (p. 228). Nonce compounds with present and past participles, whose content might alternatively have been expressed by clauses containing finite verbs, include "*gold-defending dragon*" (pp. 23–24), "*sting-ray-hampered* pioneer" (p. 107), "*ant- and stone-swallowing* uninjurable artichoke" (p. 118), "*ram's-horn-cradled* freight" (p. 121), and "*Thanatopsis-invoking tree-loving* Bryant" (p. 242), among others. And nouns in the inflected genitive increase the informational density of such sequences as "*philology's* determined, ardent eight-volume Hippocrates-charmed editor" (p. 97), which also contains two striking nonce compounds, "the house-high glistening green *magnolia's* velvet-textured flower" (p. 109), "the gently breathing *eminence's* prone mahout" (p. 128), "its terrorized *thieves'* whole camel-train" (p. 201), and "*China's* very most ingenious man" (p. 219).

The "condensed simile" appears in all the varieties described earlier. Formations with -*like* as suffix include "maple-leaflike" (p. 38), "froglike" (p. 43), "racoon-like" (p. 45), "parchment-like" (p. 48), "ladyfinger-like" (p. 72), "not unchain-like machine-like" (p. 118), "Iscariot-like" (p. 138), "catlike" (p. 169), and "Fate-like" (p. 209). Past participles and adjectives are preceded by nouns in adjectival compounds in "match-thin hind legs" (p. 14), "porcupine-quilled palm trees" (p. 23), "prune-shaped head" (p. 43), "house-high glistening green magnolia" (p. 109), "mandolin-shaped big and little fig" (p. 110), "hammer-handed bravado" (p. 160), and "pitchfork-pronged ears" (p. 218). The vehicle alone is expressed by a noun modifier in "water-whistle note [of an owl]" (p. 8), "kangaroo speed [of the jerboa]" (p. 15), "quicksilver ferocity" (p. 24), "swan's-down dress [of the young of the frigate bird]" (p. 25), "compass-needle nervousness [of the revolving head of the ostrich guarding his nest]" (p. 99), "bayonet beak" (p. 106), "ostrich-skin warts [on the stem of a climbing rose]" (p. 108), "mirror-of-steel uninsistence" (p. 152), and "puma paw [of a baseball catcher]" (p. 221).

Condensed similes specifying shades of color equal or outdo the language of advertising in dramatic interest, and are of course more recondite. The jerboa is "the sand-brown jumping-rat" (p. 13), camellias have "amanita-white petals" (p. 16), bison have "hematite-black, compactly incurved horns" (p. 27), the aurochs has diminished in modern times to "Siamese-cat brown Swiss size" (p. 27), a "brass-green bird" seen hopping from twig to twig has a "grass-green throat" (p. 103). As in advertising, such color comparisons often appear in groups. The ocean viewed from the fishing village in "The Steeple-Jack" changes from "the purple of the peacock's neck . . . to greenish azure,"

> as Dürer changed
> the pine green of the Tyrol to peacock blue and guinea
> gray.
>
> (p. 5)

Ancient Egyptian civilization presents to the eye of the student "an evident poetry of frog grays, duck-egg greens, and eggplant blues" (p. 12). The maiden who entraps the unicorn, in an echo of the language of advertising innocently reminiscent of medieval piety, wears a dress of "Virgin-Mary blue" (p. 79). The trunk of a sycamore, seen "against a gun-metal sky," is "chamois-white" (p. 167). The subjects of the Indian ruler Tipu, approaching his throne, kiss an "emerald carpet" with "velvet face of meadow-green" (p. 241). Moore is especially resourceful in describing shades of gray and brown; in addition to the above-quoted "guinea gray," "frog gray," "sand-brown" and "Siamese-cat brown," she has "beeswax gray" (p. 29), "lead-gray" (p. 108), "mouse-gray" (p. 128), "buff-brown" (p. 14), "fawn-brown" (p. 19), "snuff-brown" (p. 20), "soot-brown" (p. 27), and "cinnamon-brown" (p. 30).

It would seem that Moore's language outdoes the feature article in the length of the premodifying sequence, without, however, equaling the advertisement. The longest sequences I have observed in Moore contain nine elements; there are three of these, and four with eight, versus the high of eight, exemplified only once, in my sample feature articles. (Each sequence is quoted in italics in the context of the complex noun phrase in which it appears. For the method of counting, see p. 107, above.)

With nine elements:

The prompt-delayed loud- / low chromatic listened-for down- / scale which Swinburne called in prose, the / noiseless music that hangs about / the serpent when it stirs or springs (p. 23)

Business-like atom / in *the stiff-leafed tree's blue- / pink dregs-of-wine* pyramids / of mathematic / circularity (p. 103)

The fragile grace of *the Thomas- / of-Leighton Buzzard Westminster Abbey wrought-iron /* vine (p. 117)

With eight elements:

*An alert gargantuan / little-winged, magnificently speedy running-*bird (p. 100)

Rare / unscent- / ed, provident- / ly hot, too sweet, inconsistent flower bed! (p. 109)

The house-high glistening green magnolia's velvet- / textured flower (p. 109)

A vein // of resined straightness from *north-wind / hardened Sweden's once-opposed-to / compromise* archipelago / of rocks (p. 131)

With seven elements (a selection):

Émile Littré, / *+ philology's determined, / ardent eight-volume / Hippocrates-charmed /* editor (p. 97)

Their thickly filamented, pale / pussy-willow-surfaced / coats (p. 105)

A deliriously spun-out-level / frock-coat skirt (p. 199)

A thirteen / twisted silk-string three-finger solo (p. 218)

Sequences of six elements or fewer are present in abundance, but limits of space forbid the further multiplication of examples.

At this point, it would be possible to call a halt. There is a sense in which Marianne Moore's poetic language is an idiosyncratic and brilliant version of promotional prose, given an additional dimension of interest by the arbitrary patterns of line and stanza length, the "little intricate grids of visual symmetry," as Hugh Kenner calls them,[8] which interrupt the discursive flow of syntax and sense as traditional metrical patterns do in the language of other poets. And there is a sense in which the poems have the sort of effect on us that successful feature articles and advertisements have: if nothing else, they convince us of the existence of a world full of a number of remarkable things. So much for the real toads; what of the imaginary gardens? Can the factual details assembled in one of Moore's essays in promotional prose be seen as participating in the development of a *dramatic form*—a form that makes a vision of human experience imaginatively accessible to other human beings? If so, the most prosaic of them may indeed wear a poem's guise at last.

Consider "A Carriage from Sweden," a poem featuring, on the one hand, an artifact, the "country cart" of the title, and on the other hand, the country where it was made. We are given a good deal of information about both. Sweden is a rocky archipelago; it has spruce-tree forests through which run paths thickly covered with pine needles; Swedish folkdancers wear white stockings and thick-soled shoes; Swedish men wear Sunday jackets decorated with hanging buttons and frogs—and there is more. As for the carriage, it is described feature by feature with the enthusiasm of an automobile salesman:

> Seat, dashboard and sides of smooth gourd-
>   rind texture, a flowered step, swan-
>   dart brake, and swirling crustacean-
> tailed equine amphibious creatures
> that garnish the axletree!

(Compare "Hand-built coachwork, real leather upholstery, sliding roof, 4 wide (draught-proof) doors, 4-speed (silent 3rd) gearbox, rear safety petrol tank" [advertisement for the Singer Junior Saloon, *ILN*, 1/18/32, p. 111; typography and punctuation have been altered].) Documentation now gives way to lyricism: "What // a fine thing! What unannoying / romance!" (Compare "What a picture!" in the advertisement reproduced on p. 94.) The last stanza of the poem describes an ornamental flower bed that in context takes on the look and meaning of a trademark, and the concluding line contains a phrase stamped on imported merchandise:

it's a Sweden
of moated white castles—the bed
of white flowers densely grown in an S
meaning Sweden and stalwartness,
skill, and a surface that says
Made in Sweden: carts are my trade.

A notable feature of formulation in these lines is the reiteration of the name *Sweden;* we are made aware of it as of a brand name in advertising copy. (Compare "Regan meets your needs for coordinated furniture, floor coverings, draperies, and accessories. Your Reganized office is planned to take advantage of Regan's free decorating and its 29 years of experience" [*Times,* 1/11/56, p. 7].)

So far, so good. Yet it goes without saying that the poem as a whole is not a feature article about Sweden, or an advertisement for Sweden designed to attract tourists, or an advertisement for a carriage made in Sweden (which in any case "no one may see"). The sort of "unity, coherence and emphasis" we expect of the professionally written feature article are lacking; instead, we find lacunae and bewildering shifts of topic. The speaker describes the physical appearance of Swedish women but not of Swedish men; contrariwise, she describes the Sunday clothes of men but not those of women; she speaks (twice) about a champion Swedish runner, but ignores other national sports such as skiing. Her train of thought moves from an account of the configuration of the branches of the spruce tree, such as one might find in a tree handbook, to folk dancing, thence to "Denmark's sanctuaried Jews," and on to a list of miscellaneous Swedish items including "puzzle-jugs and hand-spun rugs," with never a connecting link. Toward the end of the poem, she asks rhetorically, as if setting the stage for a conventional promotional encomium,

Sweden,
what makes the people dress that way
and those who see you wish to stay?

The answer is convoluted and enigmatic. It begins by referring to a standard tourist attraction, Sweden's "moated white castles," but from these the eye of the camera zeroes in on the aforesaid single bed of white flowers "densely grown in an S." The concluding lines, like "What // a fine thing! What unannoying / romance!" are reminiscent of advertising language in its lyrical aspect. The name *Sweden,* of which the S-shaped flowerbed forms the initial letter, is linked with a series of attributes, two designated by qualitative terms of praise, all alliterating on the letter *s.* The first, "stalwartness," seems to hark back to the tireless strength of the runner named the Deer, but the second, "skill," points to the making of artifacts rather than to physical performance. The third, "surface," is clearly reminiscent of the cart and its "smooth gourd- / rind texture," while what the surface "says" in the last line of the poem is "Made in Sweden: carts are my trade."

If we now look in the poem for an imaginative order capable of superseding the prosaic order of exposition, a major clue offers itself—not surprisingly—in the image on which the speaker's thoughts finally dwell: the shape of the letter S, present not only in the descriptive content of the poem as the S-shaped bed of flowers we are made to "see" as we read, but literally, there before our eyes on the printed page in both capitals and lower case, repeated eight times in the two next-to-last lines. This shape is most definitely of the *surface,* but it is associated also with the words *stalwartness* and *skill,* which denote qualities invisible to the eye. Though the first of these, as I have said, seems calculated to remind us of the champion runner, it is also an attribute of the cart. And the curved shape of the S has been prefigured in the poem by the "swirling" seahorse decorations on the axletree. The axletree, a crucial structural component of the cart, forms a straight line, and the cart itself has been described as "a vein // of resined straightness" (presumably because it is built of pine boards). The complementary relationship between the curved line and the straight line can thus be understood to represent, on the visible plane, a more deep-seated relationship between appearance and structure, grace and strength, or, to use the language with which the poem concludes, "surface" and "stalwartness." The two qualities are conjoined in the carriage by the "skill" of its maker.

The nature of their conjunction is made clear by the speaker's description of the carriage in the opening stanzas. As "a vein // of resined straightness," it is a welcome reminder, in a "city of freckled / integrity," of the moral rectitude of centuries past, personified by great and pious leaders like King Gustavus Adolphus of Sweden and George Washington of the speaker's own United States of America. The trustworthy "stalwartness" of the carriage bespeaks the care with which it was made, but it is more than merely serviceable: it is a "country cart / that inner happiness made art." Its decorative elaboration is charming, an "unannoying / romance," because it is unpretentious, an authentic and unselfconscious expression of a tradition in which the craftsman takes pleasure. The key attribute of unpretentiousness is stressed by Moore's choice of the word *cart* (three times) in preference to the *carriage* of the title, and by the matter-of-fact tone of the statement that concludes the poem. The maker of the cart thinks of himself not as a "folk artist," still less as a "creative artist," but as a workman: "Carts are my trade."

The letter *s* stands for stalwartness, surface, and skill; it also stands, as the carriage itself does, for Sweden. Once we have grasped the speaker's imaginative definition of "the spirit of Sweden" as grace founded on strength, we can see it exemplified everywhere in the poem; indeed, it explains the selection and ordering of descriptive detail as principles of exposition do not. The lovely Swedish lady for whom the carriage comes to the door has "the natural stoop of the / snowy egret," but she also has a "deer- / swift step"; the branches of the spruce tree fan out gracefully from a trunk which is "vertical though a seedling"; the runner's stride has the "spring" conferred by pine-needle paths and is backed by inexhaustible energy. (He, like the maker of the cart, is motivated by "inner happiness," since "when he's won a race, [he] likes to run / more.") The curved line reappears in "the hanging buttons and the frogs / that edge the Sunday jackets," the straight line in "the sun-right gable- / ends due east and west." And if "the deft white-stockinged dance in thick-soled / shoes" and "Denmark's sanctuaried Jews" are read as exemplars of physical grace and moral strength, respectively, then their odd juxtaposition is not so odd after all.

Trying to formulate the theme in abstract terms, I am reminded of some well-known lines of nineteenth-century verse:

> Straight is the line of Duty;
> Curved is the line of Beauty;
> Follow the straight line, thou shalt see
> The curved line ever follow thee.[9]

Nothing is morally right, says the poet, that is not also beautiful. But the coin has another side: nothing is beautiful that is not also morally right. For human beings, "Duty," the moral imperative, has primacy—"Beauty" pursued for its own sake eludes the pursuer. Viewed retrospectively, *sub specie aeternitatis,* the two are one and the same. In the poetry of Marianne Moore, the expressiveness of outward form or action, whether perceived directly in the symbolic object or at second hand in the emblematic fact, elicits a response in which aesthetic pleasure merges with moral approval. Beauty for Moore is in the last analysis an ethical concept. Another name for it is "integrity"; still another is "genuineness."[10]

One of the exemplars of Swedish integrity mentioned along with the cart toward the end of "A Carriage from Sweden" is "a Dalen / lighthouse, self-lit." The lighthouse with its beam, at once visibly beautiful and helpful to the traveler, is an especially apt embodiment of Moore's conception; it appears not only here but in "Light Is Speech," where it stands for the moral qualities that are "the spirit of France." Two similar emblems contribute to the definitional passage that concludes "The Hero":

> He's not out
> seeing a sight but the rock
> crystal thing to see—the startling El Greco
> brimming with inner light—that
> covets nothing that it has let go. This then you may know
> as the hero.

The poet has just spoken of Moses, who "would not be grandson to Pharaoh." This historical figure is the last of a group of textbook heroes paraded before us in the poem, including Jacob, Joseph, Cincinnatus, Regulus, Christian in *Pilgrim's*

Progress, and George Washington. Though the speaker does not deny heroic status to any of them, she looks longest and most appreciatively at one who is not a biblical patriarch, general, or father of his country, but merely a "decorous frock-coated Negro" guide at Washington's tomb. Ignored by the significantly "fearless" lady tourist who "asks the man she's with, what's this, / what's that, where's Martha / buried," he nevertheless carries out his official task with composure, voluntarily answering her questions, "speaking / as if in a play—not seeing her . . . standing like the shadow / of the willow." His behavior fulfills the definition of courage quoted in "In Distrust of Merits":

> "When a man is prey to anger,
> he is moved by outside things; when he holds
> his ground in patience patience
> patience, that is action or
> beauty."

The Negro guide in "The Hero" is one of a number of unprepossessing, humble, little-known, or lightly regarded figures singled out for special commendation in Moore's poems, including the jerboa, "a small desert rat, / and not famous," whose "shining silver house // of sand" surpasses the treasures of the pharaohs (p. 13), the mule, whose "neat exterior / [expresses] the principle of accommodation reduced to a / minimum" (p. 53), the ostrich with its "comic duckling head" and "leaden-skinned back" (p. 99), the freakish pangolin, and that perennial figure of fun, the skunk.

Perhaps the unlikeliest of Moore's unlikely heroes are the plants whose feats are recorded in "Nevertheless" in a kind of "Wonders of Nature" catalog. Among them is a prickly pear leaf clinging to barbed wire which has sent down a root "to grow / in earth two feet below." Another is a carrot; meeting an obstacle in the earth, it has turned back on itself in a coil to form a "ram's-horn root." From these and other examples the speaker draws a general conclusion: "Victory won't come // to me unless I go / to it." Hearing this aphorism out of context, one might think it endorsed an aggressive courage, urging us to go forth and crush the enemy. Actually, it does almost the opposite. "Victory," as we see it dramatized in the poem, comes from acquiescence; it is achieved by yielding to obstacles rather than by shouldering them aside. Even the prickly pear, in sending down its root, has shown a kind of Mohammed-goes-to-the-mountain compliance with circumstance.

In the plant protagonists of "Nevertheless," as in the cart of "A Carriage from Sweden," integrity manifests itself visibly as "expressive form." The tenacity of the carrot in continuing to grow while conforming to the obstacles in its way has not only brought about its survival but has given it a graceful shape, as the sap of the cherry tree in passing through the narrow stem has made the cherry red. So too in other poems. The pangolin flattens his scales as a defense against

124

stinging ants and "rolls himself into a ball" when attacked; he is "a thing / made graceful by adversities, con- // versities." The contours of the jerboa have been "simplified" and thus made aesthetically pleasing by the exigencies of life in the desert. And such triumphs bring joy as well. The jerboa "has / happiness," and the caged bird of "What Are Years,"

> grown taller as he sings, steels
> his form straight up. Though he is captive,
> his mighty singing
> says, satisfaction is a lowly
> thing, how pure a thing is joy.

In this passage, the biblical archaism *lowly* is a verbal sign of the Christian affinities of Moore's moral vision, evident especially in poems that celebrate the voluntary meekness of a powerful being. The white elephant, capable of crushing his keepers with one foot, nonetheless quietly holds up his foreleg "for use // as a stair"; he is "a life prisoner but reconciled." The gray elephants who follow him in the procession are "elephant-ear-witnesses-to-be of hymns / and glorias." But the procession itself is a Buddhist ceremony, and the movement of the speaker's thoughts in the latter half of the poem is ecumenical, assimilating the humility of Socrates and the wisdom of the Buddha to Christian meekness and love. The white elephant's "held-up foreleg . . . expounds the brotherhood / of creatures to man the encroacher, by the / small word with the dot, meaning know—the verb bŭd." The Indian buffalo is eulogized in similar terms. Though capable of killing a tiger on the spot, it allows itself to be "led by bare-leggèd herd-boys to a hay / hut where they / stable it." It willingly carries the Buddha and helps him dismount at the shrine, serving him better than any "white / Christian heathen." The same tranquility in servitude is shown by the Negro guide whose ancestors were slaves; he, like the white elephant, "covets nothing that [he] has let go." A moving passage of "What Are Years?" states the theme with unusual explicitness:

> He
> sees deep and is glad, who
> accedes to mortality
> and in his imprisonment rises
> upon himself as
> the sea in a chasm, struggling to be
> free and unable to be,
> in its surrendering
> finds its continuing.

Imprisonment ultimately becomes a metaphor for the human condition, for mortality itself.

Moore said of art that "it must acknowledge the spiritual forces which have made it" (p. 48). We have seen such forces in action in "The Hero," "Nevertheless," and other poems. In "A Carriage from Sweden," the conjunction of under-lying strength and outward grace, both physical and spiritual, reveals itself in a diverse and colorful assortment of "things," from "the split / pine fair hair, steady gannet-clear / eyes and the pine-needled-path deer- / swift step" through "the deft white-stockinged dance" and "Denmark's sanctuaried Jews" to "the table / spread as for a banquet" and "a Dalen / lighthouse, self-lit." Diversity itself is the theme of another travel poem, "The Web One Weaves of Italy," which, as we observed earlier, was inspired by a feature article in the *New York Times*, "Festivals and Fairs for the Tourist in Italy" by Mitchell Goodman. The poem is short. Of the sixty-odd events listed by Goodman in his five-column spread, Moore mentions only six, but these stand for an array of possibilities that becomes overwhelming, "blurred by too much." Overwhelming, yet delightful too:

> Are we not charmed by the result?—
>
> quite different from what goes on
> at the Sorbonne; but not entirely, since flowering
>   in more than mere talent for spectacle.
> Because the heart is in it all is well.

The entertainments offered the tourist at Italian festivals and fairs may not be edifying in the high cultural sense, yet they are not unworthy after all of compari-son with "what goes on / at the Sorbonne." Such popular art forms, like those we take more seriously, deserve our admiration if "the heart" is in them—if they manifest what Moore in "Tom Fool at Jamaica" calls *ardeur,* ardor, the mark of the champion. In a significant image borrowed from one of her own translations of La Fontaine, Moore calls Italy a "fount by which enchanting gems are spilt." For *fount,* we must read *source* in the root sense of that word. The spiritual forces reflected in all valid expression, humble or exalted, are for Moore a kind of Platonic unity underlying diversity, a One manifest in the Many, jets of a single "fount" beside which lie varicolored gems, all alike enchanting. So, in "Tom Fool at Jamaica," championship is exemplified not only by the horse that wins the race, but by a Spanish schoolboy's drawing, the play of porpoises about the prow of a ship, the jazz performances of Fats Waller, Ozzie Smith, and Eubie Blake, the acrobatics of Lippizan horses, and a monkey riding a greyhound (perhaps in a circus).

In the poem called "Style," the virtuosity shared by the flamenco dancer with the figure skater and the court tennis champion is likened to the spirit (expressed in "a letter") of Pablo Casals, the darting movements of the lizard, the hovering flight of fireflies, and the whorls in water brought about by the skillful manipulation of a canoe paddle. The speaker hesitates among alternative similes. The dancing of Soledad is

> like a letter from
> Casals; or perhaps say literal alphabet-
> S soundholes in a 'cello
> set contradictorily; or should we call her
>   *la lagarta?*

More images follow: Etchebaster's grace in the court tennis game is "catlike"; Escudero's silhouette resembles that of the Sandeman sherry sailor, and Rosario Escudero's guitar is a "wrist-rest for a dangling hand / that's suddenly set humming fast fast fast and faster." With this last line, the grammatical mode of the passage changes, hovering momentarily between stative and dynamic. The abrupt shift of tempo is characteristic of flamenco dancing, but it also occurs "suddenly," now, at this moment in the train of thought. Overwhelmed as if by an actual display of virtuosity on stage, the speaker throws up her hands and abandons her attempts to find "a suitable simile." There is none, because the only adequate vehicle would be an impossible conjunction, "as though" music could render visual pattern, or an artist could interpret a composer's music by painting the expression of his eyes or face. At the end of the poem, descriptive terminology is abandoned in favor of a series of proper names, each of which "means" only the individual it refers to. Multiplicity has triumphed. And yet the "unsuitable" similes have been expressed, the impossible conjunctions have occurred on the imaginative level, just as the individuals belonging to different realms—dancing, music, sport—have been joined in the intensity of a single invocation.[11]

Unity in diversity, or rather, unity arising from diversity, is the presiding theme of Moore's great poem "Virginia Britannia."[12] The Virginia of the present is conceived of as a cultural amalgam to which each phase of American history has made its contribution: the native Indians, the British colonials, the founders of the Republic, the frontiersmen, the enslaved blacks (Moore incorporates in the poem an idiom they have contributed to the language), and the well-to-do modern Virginians with their fine country homes and their fine horses, their "buckeye-burnished jumpers / and five-gaited mounts." Underlying all the accretions brought about by human settlement, both Indian and white, is the land itself with its indigenous flora and fauna. The poem begins with the "pale sand," the "soft, warm, hot" air, and the "cedar-dotted emerald shore" of the Virginia coastline

> known to the redbird, the red-coated musketeer,
> the trumpet flower, the cavalier,
> the parson, and the wild parishioner.

The musketeer was preceded in Virginia by the redbird, and the cavalier by the trumpet flower; the "wild parishioner" at the end of the series is presumably a deer, since the next detail mentioned is "a deer- / track in a church-floor / brick." The trumpet flower initiates a catalog of flowers, shrubs, and trees that runs through the poem. The theme of amalgamation—the coalescence of indigenous and alien which has given the state its present form—is epitomized by complementary groups of plants: the native live oak, cotton, and tobacco, on the one hand; the imported white wall-rose, fig, and silkworm mulberry on the other. The subject matter encourages "incongruities" of the sort that characterize the descriptive style of the feature article, leading off with the "deer- / track in a church-floor / brick." The mockingbird, a wild creature native to the state, stands on a "stone- / topped table with lead cupids grouped to form the pedestal"; the Virginian "cavalcade" of horses and mules includes the "witch-cross door" harking back to a superstitious past; the modern lady, played off against a "birdclaw-ear-ringed" Indian princess and a "gauze-and-taffeta-dressed" English lady of colonial times, eats the meat of the native sea turtle from a "crested spoon." She is

> mistress of French plum-and-turquoise-piped chaise-longue;
> of brass-knobbed slat front door, and everywhere open
> shaded house on Indian-
> named Virginian
> streams in counties named for English lords.

The poem is strewn with personal and place names that bespeak the history of the state: *Virginia Britannia, England, Old Dominion, We-re-wo- / co-mo-co, Captain Smith, Powhatan, Christopher Newport, Daniel Boone, Fort Old Field, Jamestown, Potomac, Chickahominy, Pamunkey, Mattaponi, Jefferson.*

Other themes we have noted in Moore appear in passing. Virginia itself is presented throughout the poem as an example of "expressive form," a veritable rebus spelling out its own history. Among the living cast of characters, important parts are played by two outwardly unprepossessing figures. The "meditative" mockingbird who stands for the speaker's train of thought is "lead- / gray" and "lead-legged"; his eye is "as dead / as sculptured marble / eye." He alights noiselessly and holds his head to one side, "standing on tall thin legs as if he did not see" as the Negro guide stands by the lady tourist, "not seeing her," in "The Hero." And the bird who becomes the speaker's emotional surrogate as the poem moves toward its conclusion is a "mere . . . hedge sparrow," a little brown bird with spots like caraway seeds. The theme of acquiescence as moral victory is touched on in the reference to the enslaved Negro, dubbed "inadvertent ally and best enemy of tyranny."

In the last two stanzas, the speaker's thoughts move from the joyous singing of the hedge sparrow in the darkness before the dawn to the coming of darkness at the close of day. Visible disparities are obliterated as live oak, cypress, and English hackberry "become with lost identity, / part of the ground," one silhouette against a flaming sky.[13] I have already quoted the passage in another connection, but it will bear repetition:

> The live oak's darkening filigree
> of undulating boughs, the etched
> solidity of a cypress indivisible
>   from the now agèd English hackberry,
>   become with lost identity,
>   part of the ground, as sunset flames increasingly
> against the leaf-chiseled
>   blackening ridge of green; while clouds, expanding above
>   the town's assertiveness, dwarf it, dwarf arrogance
>   that can misunderstand
>   importance; and
> are to the child an intimation of what glory is.

If we are to understand this passage fully, we must understand *arrogance* not only in its usual meaning, but in the Latinate meaning preserved in the modern English word *arrogation:* the preempting of what is not rightfully one's own. The charge of "arrogance" in this sense has already been leveled by the speaker against us and our ancestors:

> not an explorer, no imperialist,
> not one of us, in taking what we
> pleased—in colonizing as the
> saying is—has been a synonym for mercy.

And we have "misunderstood importance" in acting with the arrogance of prejudice, in failing to see that "the redskin with the deer / fur crown, famous for his cruelty, is not all brawn / and animality," or, to quote the quoted conclusion of another poem,

> "that the Negro is not brutal,
> that the Jew is not greedy,
> that the Oriental is not immoral,
> that the German is not a Hun."

The sort of behavior Moore calls "arrogance" at the end of "Virginia Britannia" is singled out for reproof also at the end of "Apparition of Splendor," a poem whose literal subject is the porcupine. The speaker defends the animal against the superstitious charge that, when embattled, it shoots its quills, and goes on to commend it for its lack of aggressiveness: "Maine should be pleased that its animal / is not a waverer, and rather / than fight, lets the primed quill fall." In that it is "not a waverer," the porcupine reminds us of the soldier or hero who "stands his ground." In that it "lets the primed quill fall" rather than fight, it reminds us of those powerful but docile creatures, the Indian elephant and the Indian buffalo, and of the pangolin, who "draws / away from danger unpugnaciously, / with no sound but a harmless hiss" (p. 117). The poem ends with a summarizing accolade: "Shallow oppressor, intruder, / insister, you have found a resister." "Intrusion" and "insistence" in personal relationships correspond to "oppression" on the larger scale of relationships within and among societies. All three are expressions of the spiritual "shallowness" or pettiness stigmatized in "In Distrust of Merits":

> O alive who are dead, who are
> proud not to see, O small dust of the earth
> that walks so arrogantly,
> trust begets power and faith is
> an affectionate thing.
>
> (p. 137)

Just as "arrogance" in Moore manifests itself in a number of forms, so too does the opposite kind of behavior that "makes us who look, know // depth" (p. 136). It appears as self-effacement, tolerance, the encouragement of others, self-sacrifice, charity in the New Testament sense. In "Armor's Undermining Modesty," the speaker muses on the knights of old who sought the Grail: "They did not let self bar / their usefulness to others who were / different" (p. 152). The armor they wore in battle conferred on them "a mirror-of-steel uninsistence" which is the appropriate outer form or "countenance" of inner moral strength or "continence." Paradoxically, the mirror of steel is at once an expressive emblem and an invulnerable disguise, giving back to the aggressor only his own reflected face. Hence the title: the "modesty" of armor "undermines" the antagonistic forces that would penetrate it.[14]

Elaborate diction and syntax combine in the final stanza of "Virginia Britannia"—a peroration made up of a single sentence—to produce an effect of high formality such as we rarely find in Moore. Here are no eccentric Latinate polysyllables, no scientific or quasi-scientific terms, no informative nonce compounds or condensed similes to inhibit the gathering solemnity of the panoramic description. Romance and Latinate words like *filigree, undulating, flames,* and *chiseled,* become, in context, idealizing qualitative terms. Important meanings are expressed by finite verbs—*become, flames, dwarf* (twice)—and these verbs are dynamic in the grammatical sense, signifying action in process. The poem ends with an allusion to another poem, Wordsworth's "Ode: Intimations of Immortality," again unusual in a poet who more characteristically alludes to prose. But the rhetorical intensity of the passage diminishes noticeably in the last few lines. The full meaning of the word *arrogance* is operative only if we can penetrate its etymological disguise, and the description of arrogant behavior as capable of "misunderstanding importance" is surely a charitable understatement for centuries of exploitation and prejudice. Even the allusion to Wordsworth comes wrapped in a prosy syntax, including two instances of *to be* as link verb and an awkwardly periphrastic indirect question. (Imagine Wordsworth's poem entitled "Intimations of What Immortality Is.") The sunset continues to flame as the last words of the poem are spoken, but the colors of the language have faded.

We note a similar damping down or withholding of eloquence in the concluding passages of other poems. In "He 'Digesteth Harde Yron'," the speaker's contemplation of the ostrich's survival of persecution leads to the resonant manifesto beginning, "The power of the visible / is the invisible." But the last two lines, with their final reminder of the ludicrous appearance of the bird, are as flat as they are pat:

> This one remaining rebel
> is the sparrow-camel.

The concluding passage of "The Hero" moves from the vivid evocation of emblems to a Q.E.D. which comes perilously close in form to the "Thus we see" of the undergraduate theme: "This then you may know / as the hero." And the celebration of French ardor and courage in "Light Is Speech" winds up with a definition whose last phrase is quoted from a prose essay:

> "The word France means
> enfranchisement; means one who can
> 'animate whoever thinks of her.'"

Here, as in the final allusion of "Virginia Britannia," Moore leaves the last word to someone else. A similar retreat from center stage takes place in other poems in which she allows her subjects to speak for themselves rather than undertaking to speak for them.[15] "The Monkeys" ends with the astringent remarks of the Gilgamesh-cat; "In the Days of Prismatic Color" ends with the words uttered by "truth"; what the captive songbird "says" forms the conclusion of "What Are Years?" The final stanza of "The Pangolin" is similarly stage-managed, with man himself as the designated spokesman:

> The prey of fear, he, always
> curtailed, extinguished, thwarted by the dusk, work partly done,
> says to the alternating blaze,
> "Again the sun!
> anew each day; and new and new and new,
> that comes into and steadies my soul."

In all these poems, and in others, we see the self-effacement which is a central value in Moore's moral pantheon dramatized as an "uninsistence" enacted on the level of language. In pushing in the stops, in descending from flights of eloquence to the ground of prose, Moore is practicing her own precept, an odd one for a poet: "The deepest feeling always shows itself in silence; / not in silence, but restraint" (p. 91). And the self-effacement of the poet in the poem is also the self-effacement of the real Marianne Moore. In her work, if anywhere, person and persona are one; to distinguish them would be to multiply entities unnecessarily. "One should be as clear," she wrote in a prose essay, "as one's natural reticence allows one to be";[16] asked in an interview why she had delayed publishing her early poems, she replied "To issue my slight product—conspicuously tentative— seemed to me premature. I disliked the term 'poetry' for any but Chaucer's or Shakespeare's or Dante's. . . . What I write, as I have said before, could only be called poetry because there is no other category in which to put it."[17]

But self-effacement in Moore also has a particular significance in relation to the style in which she chose to write much of her poetry: it is in accord with the conventional self-presentation of the "expounding I" in promotional prose. The author of the feature article is "there" to draw our attention to the subject, as the copywriter is there to draw our attention to the product. (Testimonials in advertisements are of course an entirely different thing.) In adopting the descriptive and verbal techniques of promotional prose, Moore plays the part of a high-minded publicity agent or honest advertiser, one who is giving us information for what he sincerely believes to be our own good. Tirelessly she describes the important accomplishments of others, turns the spotlight on beauties or excellences that might otherwise have remained obscure, vindicates the unjustly maligned by dispelling popular misconceptions. And her habit of quoting serves in similar fashion to publicize the words of other authors. "If I wanted to say something," she explained, "and somebody had said it ideally, then I'd take it but give the person credit for it."[18]

In an essay called "Subject, Predicate, Object," Moore wrote, "One thinks of poetry as divine fire, a perquisite of the gods. When under the spell of admiration or gratitude, I have hazarded a line, it never occurred to me that anyone might think I imagined myself a poet."[19] Yet in acknowledging the spiritual forces that have made them, in expressing a moral vision in which her readers can imaginatively join, Moore's poems too are carriers of the divine fire, whether or not their author thought they were. Moore's promotional prose is at once a "guise" and a "disguise," an outer aspect which, as with armor's mirror-of-steel uninsistence, may all but conceal the soul within. Her poems have the unprepossessing aspect of a number of her chosen subjects: the jerboa, the pangolin, the coiled-up carrot, the mule. And we can see in both the visible effect of constraining circumstances—the poet's acquiescence in what she considered to be her own imaginative limitations. Speaking, as she rarely did in her poems, of her own art, Moore hinted at this in a memorable aphorism: "Ecstasy affords / the occasion and expediency determines the form" (p. 88).[20]

Though she felt duty-bound to leave the quotation marks in, Moore regretted their presence, fearing that they were "disruptive of pleasant progress."[21] For us, her readers, they are a mild distraction, an eccentricity we can find forgiveable, even touching, in view of the self-deprecation that underlies it. On occasion, however, the quoting of a phrase or line has a positive value, adding an expressive nuance to the passage in which it occurs. Here again, we must look to the advertisement for an analogue: the descriptive statement put in quotation marks to simulate a chorus of public enthusiasm for a particular brand of this commodity or that:

> Any place you may elect, you can always get Sealect . . . "the milk that tastes like cream!" (*Sun*, 6/25/34, p. 13)

> When the children join the grown-ups to enjoy a refreshing glass of ginger ale, then, more than ever, "it must be Canada Dry!" (*Sun*, 6/28/34, p. 16)

And, without a dramatic matrix,

> "Just that much better." (*Sun*, 6/27/34, p. 32 [advertisement for Seagram's Gin])

Certain of the quoted phrases in Moore's poems have an oddly similar effect: the word *France* "means one who can / 'animate whoever thinks of her'" (p. 98); what matters about New York City "is not the plunder, / but 'accessibility to experience'" (p. 54); the racehorse Tom Fool "'makes an effort and makes it oftener / than the rest'" (p. 162).

The quotation in advertising expresses as dramatic "fiction" what the device of the slogan, if successful, achieves in reality: a link in the mind of the consumer between a certain product and a certain descriptive statement or phrase. All the quoted statements in the above examples were in fact slogans in their day, as was another that every American of a certain age, at least, will remember: "Woodbury's Facial Soap for 'The skin you love to touch'" (*Sun*, 6/28/34, p. 14). But the slogan does more than describe what has been; it is also a pledge that the quality of the past will be maintained in the future. We can count on Sealect milk to continue to taste like cream, on Seagram's Gin to be just that much better, on Woodbury's soap to give us the skin we love to touch. In its promissory aspect, the slogan is a humbler analogue of the personal or family motto, especially the visible motto which forms part of the crest of a coat of arms (it is not wholly surprising that the word *slogan* originally meant battle cry, or that the promotion of a product frequently includes the fabrication of a coat of arms complete with crest and motto).

Moore's poems contain a number of phrases and statements, with or without quotation marks, that sound, depending on the subject matter, like slogans or mottoes, from "Carts are my trade" (p. 133) and "Will not shrink in any dye" (p. 195) to "Dignity with intimacy" (p. 160) and "'Diversity; controversy; tolerance'" (p. 173; credited in the Notes to James B. Conant). And a number of her moral aphorisms take on the force of mottoes in that we recognize the speaker's aspiration or determination to behave accordingly: "'If I do well I am blessed / whether any bless me or not, and if I do / ill I am cursed'" (p. 26; identified in the Notes as a Hindu saying). "Don't be envied or / armed with a measuring-rod" (p. 144); "One need not shoulder, need not shove" (p. 172). There is a scattering of actual mottoes, personal and national, as well: "'Liberty and union / now and forever'" in "Marriage"; "*Lux et veritas, / Christo et ecclesiae, Sapient / felici*" in "The Student"; "'By Peace / Plenty; as / by Wisdom Peace'" in "Smooth Gnarled Crape Myrtle"; "'rather dead than spotted'" and "*Mutare sperno // vel timere*" in "Then the Ermine." And the poet herself sets her habitual reticence aside on occasion and steps to center stage to make a pledge of her own: "Renouncing a policy of boorish indifference / to everything that has been said since the days of Matilda, / I shall purchase an etymological dictionary of modern English" (p. 59); "Only / wood-weasels shall associate with me" (p. 127); "I vow ... I am going // to flee ... the viper's traffic-knot—flee / to metaphysical newmown hay" (p. 231). In "In Distrust of Merits," the speaker joins with "us" to make her commitment, as in a spiritual congregation:

> We
> vow, we make this promise
>
> to the fighting—it's a promise—"We'll
> never hate black, white, red, yellow, Jew,
> Gentile, Untouchable."

A retrospective look at "Virginia Britannia" with this recurrent feature of Moore's poems in mind immediately yields an insight: underlying the portrayal of the state is the unspoken motto "E pluribus unum." And as we reread the conclusion of the poem, we can catch an additional nuance in the reference to

> the etched
> solidity of a cypress indivisible
> from the now agèd English hackberry.

On first inspection, *indivisible* may strike us as another instance of Moore's idiosyncratic Latinity; a more idiomatic (though equally Latinate) word for the meaning would have been *indistinguishable*. But it is now possible to see in *indivisible* an allusive value as important (for Moore) as that of *intimation*. The word appears in a text of the utmost solemnity that every American child once knew by heart and recited in school daily, expressing a patriotism now fallen into disrepair. I mean, of course, the Pledge of Allegiance, with its reference to "one nation, indivisible, with liberty and justice for all." Moore, who could without embarrassment use "flying Old Glory full mast" as a symbol of spiritual self-affirmation (p. 157), manages the allusion here with the utmost delicacy, not thrusting it upon us, but allowing us to find and feel it for ourselves.

"Out of many, one." Marianne Moore made her country's aspiring motto come true imaginatively, in her vision of genuineness: the perceived authenticity of aspect or action that can "unite" the deer-fur crown of the Indian chief with the coat of arms of the English colonist, and the singing of the hedge sparrow with the affirmation of human rights in the Preamble to the Declaration of Independence. Her career as a poet was a promotional campaign waged on behalf of that ideal, and we can say of her achievement what she herself said, in her curiously prosaic accents, of that greatest of spiritual forces, a self-effacing love.

> Thus wholeness—
>
> wholesomeness? best say efforts of affection—
> attain integration too tough for infraction.

ROMANCE-LATINATE TABULATIONS AND FINITE VERB COUNTS

NOTE ON METHOD

The tabulations that follow give the percentiles of words of "Romance" and "Latinate" origin, including lists of words, and the percentiles of finite verbs, in successive 100-word passages of representative poems by Frost, Stevens, and Moore, amounting to a total of 30 passages, or 3,000 words, apiece. The poems are in alphabetical order by title. It is of course possible to determine Romance-Latinate and finite verb percentiles for entire poems, but I have preferred the unit of 100 words here and in teaching. Counts derived from it are automatically percentiles, and the size of the unit is such that successive counts correspond to successive stages in the reader's serial perception of the text. I have not determined percentiles for final groups of words in the poems smaller than 100 (they can easily be estimated), though in several cases I have treated passages of 97 or 98 words as 100s.

ETYMOLOGIES

The Latinate element in English diction cannot be correctly assessed unless Latinate words whose immediate source is French are counted together with direct Latin borrowings. The distinction, within the body of French loan words, between "Latinate French" and "Romance" words is explained in chapter 2, n.2, and instructions are given for determining the category to which a given French loan word belongs on the basis of the etymologies in *SOED* and *ODEE*. Latinate words in the lists are italicized.

The correlation in English between statistically high Romance-Latinate percentiles and perceptible ornateness of diction depends on the social and cultural status of the French and Latin loan words incorporated in the language from the beginning of the Middle English period. For the purposes of an etymological-stylistic correlation, all words that were in Old English at the time of the Conquest are "native." This includes words borrowed from Latin during or preceding the Old English period (e.g., *candle, cup, priest*).

NOTE: A few words in modern English represent the coalescence of an Old English with an Old French ancestral form (e.g., *rich, line, turn* v.). I have included such words in the lists, marking them with an interrogation point. Words for which French origin is possible but not certain (e.g., *boy, lumber, mooch*) have been similarly treated. When the etymology of a word indicates that it is either Romance or Latinate, I have classified it as Romance. I have not etymologized proper names (*Phoebus,*

Procrustes, Old Dominion, Panther Mountain, Vermont, Virginia, Westminster Abbey, April, March), except when used generically (*Jew, Turk*) or in adjectival bases (*Virginian, Indian*). Titles preceding names have been etymologized (*Captain, General, Saint*). Italicized French words have not been etymologized on the ground that they are not elements of English diction.

METHOD OF COUNTING WORDS

Especially in tabulating the language of Marianne Moore, it is important to anatomize compound words into their component elements or "bases." *Leafpoint* and *soundholes,* for example, contain one native and one Romance element; syntactically, they consist of two nouns, of which the first modifies the second. I have therefore anatomized all compounds of which both elements belong to the four major form-classes (nouns, verbs, adjectives, and adverbs). In addition to these, the language contains many compounds which belong to the minor form-classes and are members of "closed systems": the indefinite pronouns, the reflexive pronouns, and certain conjunctive adverbs, to name only three categories. These have been treated as single words. (See Appendix I, "Word Formation," in Quirk et al., for the distinction between compounding and affixation [I.4], and for a classified list of "open class" compounds of the "productive" sort [I.44–57]). In addition to compounds in which both elements belong to the major form-classes, I have anatomized those in which one element is a "closed-system" adverb (as distinguished from adverbs in *-ly* related to open-class adjectives), e.g. *upspringing, put-in, everlasting, underwool.*

NOTE: I have not anatomized Romance and Latinate compounds (e.g., *rendezvous, atmosphere*). *Over-* and *under-* as prefixes (e.g., in *over-serious*) are to be distinguished from *over* and *under* as adverbs (e.g., in *over-gone, under-gone*); see the lists of prefixes and suffixes in Quirk et al., App. I, 10–20, 21–30. I have treated as compounds certain words which are not understood by present-day speakers as formed of two separate lexical elements, e.g., *butterfly, cockroach, hackberry,* and *mulberry* (significantly, almost all of these occur in Moore). I have not anatomized proper names (*Jamestown, Newport, Sunday, Westminster*), with the exception of *Woodyard* in "Devil's Woodyard," which seems to be used as a common noun.

ROBERT FROST

1. "Directive"	*direct*	*ruled*
1–100 (11%):	*quarry*	chisel
simple	monolithic	*enormous*
detail	F.v.e.: 8%	Glacier
dissolved		braced
marble	101–200 (18%):	*Arctic*
sculpture	*pretense*	*Pole*
farm	covered	certain
farm	*story*	haunt
guide	lines (?)	*serial*

cellar
pairs
excitement
rushes
F.v.e.: 7%

201–300 (10%):
charge
inexperience
cheering
just
grain
adventure
country
village
cultures
faded
F.v.e.: 11%

301–400 (7%):
sign
CLOSED
harness
belilaced
cellar
closing
dent(?)
F.v.e.: 8%

401–500 (14%):
destination
destiny
source
original
rage
valley
barb
arch
cedar
goblet
Grail
saved
Saint
goblet
F.v.e.: 9%

501–20:
place
confusion

2. "Hyla Brook"
1–100 (7%):
Hyla
flourished
jewel
foliage
faded
paper
remember
F.v.e.: 7%

101–26:
. . . .

3. "The Investment"
1–100 (10%):
staying
paint
counting
dinners
vigor
paint
money
suddenly
extravagance
impulse
F.v.e.: 7%

101–14:
color
music

4. "Mending Wall"
1–100 (5%):
pass
repair
rabbit
please
mending
F.v.e.: 14%

101–200 (6%):
line (?)
use
balance
stay
turned (?)
just
F.v.e.: 13%

201–300 (5%):
cones
fences
mischief
notion
offense
F.v.e.: 17%

301–398 (6%):
exactly
firmly
savage
armed
moves
fences
F.v.e.: 14%

5. "Mowing"
1–100 (6%):
sound
sound
hours
easy
fay
feeble
F.v.e.: 12%

101–31:
pointed
spikes
flowers
pale
orchises
fact
labor

6. "Out, Out—"
1–100 (8%):
scented
stuff
count
mountain
ranges
please
boy (?)
hour
F.v.e.: 18%

101–200 (13%):
boy (?)
counts
saved
apron
supper
prove
supper
boy's (?)
refused
boy's (?)
cry
appeal
boy (?)
F.v.e.: 13%

201–300 (6%):
boy (?)
spoiled
doctor
doctor
ether
pulse
F.v.e.: 13%

301–5:
turned (?)
affairs

7. "The Oven Bird"
1–100 (9%):
solid

trunks
sound
flowers
petal
past
cherry
moment
cease
F.v.e.: 15%

101–19:
question
diminished

8. "Putting in the Seed"
1–100 (11%):
supper
table
petals
petals
barren
quite
slave
passion
just
soil
tarnishes
F.v.e.: 9%

101–17:
sturdy
arched

9. "Stopping by Woods
on a Snowy Evening"
1–100 (7%):
village
farm
lake
harness
sound
easy
promises
F.v.e.: 11%

101–10:
. . . .

10. "The Strong Are
Saying Nothing"
1–100 (14%):
soil
regard
future
final
approval
stamp
reserved
selected
piece
apart
chain
crease (?)
squares
doubt
F.v.e.: 6%

101–55:
serve
beauty
farm
farm
carries
cry

11. "The Tuft of Flowers"*
1–100 (8%):
turn (?)
view
levelled
scene
isle
apart
passed
noiseless
F.v.e.: 15%

*I have counted *resting* in line 14 as native, despite the possibility of a pun on *rest* "repose" (OE) and *rest* "remainder" (R).

101–200 (13%):
memories
flower
delight
round
round
flower
tremulous
questions
reply
turned (?)
turned (?)
tuft
flowers
F.v.e.: 10%

201–300 (4%):
flourish
message
around
spirit
F.v.e.: 7%

301–45:
aid
apart

12. "Two Tramps in Mud Time"
1–100 (13%):
strangers
caught
aim
cheerily
pay
blocks
large
around
block
piece
squarely
rock
control
F.v.e.: 15%

101–200 (5%):
common
spent

unimportant
arch
tenderly
F.v.e.: 13%

201–300 (10%):
turns (?)
plume
excite
single
flower
except
color
advise
rut (?)
print
F.v.e.: 10%

301–400 (7%):
crystal
task
poised
muscles
moist
vernal
lumber (?)
F.v.e.: 8%

401–500 (13%):
camps
lumber (?)
jacks
judged
appropriate
except
fool
stay
stay
logic
gain
exist
agreed
F.v.e.: 15%

501–53:
separation
object

unite
avocation
vocation
mortal
future's

13. "The Wood-Pile"
1–100 (8%):
paused
turn (?)
save
view
lines (?)
place
certain
just
F.v.e.: 12%

101–200 (5%):
foolish
personal
undeceived
pile
carry
F.v.e.: 13%

201–300 (10%):
cord
piled
measured
tracks
looped (?)
sure
pile
clematis
round
round
F.v.e.: 8%

301–58:
turning (?)
fresh
tasks
spent
labor
useful
place
decay

141

WALLACE STEVENS

1. "Anatomy of
Monotony"
1–100 (10%):
part
nature
nature
nature
parallel
autumn
ampler
cries
spirits
space
F.v.e.: 17%

101–78:
tenderness
grief
comfort
phantasy
device
apt
versatile
motion
touch
sound
covetous
desire
finer
implacable
chords
spaciousness
deceived
fatal
spirit
aggrieved

2. "The Auroras of Au-
tumn," V
1–100 (26%):*
invites
humanity
table

musicians
mute
muse
negresses
dance
curious
pattern
dance's
musicians
insidious
tones
instruments
jangle
air
scenes
theatre
blocks
curtains
naive
pretence
musicians
instinctive
poem
F.v.e.: 11%

101–78:
barbarous
panting
obedient
trumpet's
touch
please
tumult
festival
festival
disordered
mooch (?)
hospitaliers
brute
musicians
tragedy
persons

act
merely

3. "The Auroras of Au-
tumn," IX
1–100 (7%):
idiom
idiom
innocent
enigma
decorous
drama
sense
F.v.e.: 11%

101–98 (13%):
activity
fate
rendezvous
isolation
disaster
imminence
around
cloaks
embellishment
simplest
part
tenderest
part
F.v.e.: 9%

4. "The Candle a
Saint"
1–100 (18%):
apparelled
astronomers
rabbit
noble
figure
moving
chanting
astronomers
astronomers

*The word *vistas,* in line 11, is from Italian.

142

topaz
rabbit
emerald
noble
figure
essential
moving
image
source
F.v.e.: 10%

101–9:
abstract
archaic
  (French-Greek)

5. "Credences of
Summer"
 1–100 (14%):
fools
infuriations
autumnal
inhalations
roses
fragrance
trouble
trouble
considers
remembrance
certain
imagination's
inscribed
comfort
F.v.e.: 11%

101–200 (20%):
false
disasters
round
touching
waiting
postpone
anatomy
physical
metaphysical
very

part
trace
evasion
metaphor
essential
barrenness
centre
fix
eternal
foliage
F.v.e.: 10%

201–300 (34%):
foliage
arrested
peace
joy
permanence
ignorance
change
possible
exile
desire
barrenness
fertile
attain
natural
tower
point
survey
apogee
tower
precious
view
point
survey
squatting
throne
axis
apogee
marriage
hymns
mountain
tower
final
mountain

inhales
F.v.e.: 10%

301–400 (23%):
proper
air
refuge
creates
tower
ancientness
absorbs
appeased
age
capable
limits
reality
presents
piled
enigmas
serene
distant
fails
clairvoyant
secondary
senses
secondary
sounds
F.v.e.: 13%

401–500 (19%):
choirs
evocations
choirs
sounds
compounded
carried
rhetoric
language
direction
direction
accept
fortune
colors
festival
enriches
rest

race
perpetual
enrich
F.v.e.: 13%

501–600 (22%):
humble
charitable
majesty
soldier
filial
form
easily
fustian
casual
blue
contains
hymns
people
souvenir
enriches
embellishment
remembrance
displays
vital
heroic
power
covers
F.v.e.: 10%

601–700 (29%):
mountain
immeasurable
rock
placid
air
hermit's
symbol
hermitage
visible
rock
audible
brilliant
mercy
sure
repose

present
vividest
repose
certain
sustaining
certainty
rock
extreme
mountain
luminous
extremest
sapphires
central
princes
F.v.e.: 7%

701–800 (24%):
unreal
secure
difficult
face
object
avert
avert
object
common
desiring
object
face
desire
moved
concentred
concentred
possessed
object
savage
scrutiny
captive
subjugate
subjugation
proclaim
F.v.e.: 10%

801–900 (25%):
capture
prize

apparent
trumpet
visible
announced
visible
illustrious
scene
trumpet
cries
successor
invisible
substitute
stratagems
spirit
memory
place
possible
replaces
resounding
cry
trumpet
supposes
exists
F.v.e.: 13%

901–1000 (25%):
division
cry
clarion
diction's
personage
multitude
venerable
unreal
wait
motionless
gardener's
gardener
garden
salacious
complex
emotions
apart
abandoned
civil
decay

regard
arranged
spirit
arranged
fund
F.v.e.: 9%

1001–1100 (23%):
suave
polished
beast
complex
apart
detect
complex
emotions
civil
sound
part
sense
personae
characters
inhuman
author
meditates
blue
characters
mottled
costumes
blue
pales
F.v.e.: 9%

1101–62:
pales
appropriate
habit
huge
decorum
manner
mottled
characters
roseate
characters
moment

malice
sudden
cry
complete
completed
scene
parts

6. "Debris of Life and Mind"
1–100 (6%):
close
violent
brush
line
quite
able
F.v.e.: 16%

101–30:
color
meditation
gay
gay
stay
familiar

7. "Final Soliloquy of the Interior Paramour"
1–100 (19%):
reason
imagined
ultimate
intensest
rendezvous
collect
indifferences
single
single
round
poor
power
miraculous
influence

obscurity
order
arranged
rendezvous
vital
F.v.e.: 11%

101–45:
boundary
imagination
central
air

8. "The House Was Quiet and the World Was Calm"
1–100 (14%):
quiet
calm
conscious
quiet
calm
except
page
scholar
perfection
quiet
because
quiet
part
part
F.v.e.: 16%

101–41:
access
perfection
page
calm
calm
calm

9. "The Idea of Order at Key West"*
1–100 (17%):
genius

*Demarcations, in the last line of the poem, is from Spanish.

formed
voice
mimic
motion
constant
cry
caused
constantly
cry
inhuman
veritable
ocean
mask
medleyed
sound
phrases
F.v.e.: 16%

101–200 (11%):
tragic
gestured
merely
place
spirit
because
spirit
voice
colored
voice
coral
F.v.e.: 17%

201–300 (22%):
clear
air
air
sound
repeat
sound
voice
plungings
theatrical
distances
bronze
horizons

mountainous
atmospheres
voice
acutest
vanishing
measured
hour
solitude
single
artificer
F.v.e.: 8%

301–400 (13%):
except
turned
descended
air
mastered
portioned
fixing
emblazoned
zones
poles
arranging
enchanting
rage
F.v.e.: 17%

401–32:
order
rage
order
fragrant
portals
origins

10. "Notes toward a Supreme Fiction": "It must be Abstract," I–II
1–100 (21%):
ephebe
perceiving
idea
invention
invented
inconceivable

idea
ignorant
ignorant
clearly
idea
suppose
inventing
source
idea
compose
voluminous
idea
remotest
expelled
images
F.v.e.: 7%

101–200 (16%):
umber
autumn
umber
ephebe
project
project
flourisher
difficulty
celestial
ennui
apartments
idea
invention
poisonous
ravishments
fatal
F.v.e.: 12%

201–300 (25%):
idea
hermit
poet's
metaphors
ennui
idea
prodigious
scholar
monastic

146

artist
philosopher
appoints
place
music
desires
philosopher
desires
desire
ancient
cycle
desire
observes
effortless
blue
myosotis
F.v.e.: 18%

301–36:
virile
calendar
hymn
stale

11. "On the Manner of Addressing Clouds"
1–97 (33%):
grammarians
gowns
mortal
rendezvous
eliciting
sustaining
pomps
music
profound
exaltation
sound
funest
philosophers
ponderers
evocations
processionals
returns
casual
evocations
across

stale
mysterious
seasons
music
resignation
responsive
sustaining
pomps
magnify
waste
accompanied
mute
splendors
F.v.e.: 7%

12. "An Ordinary Evening in New Haven," I–II
1–100 (25%):
plain
version
apart
vulgate
experience
part
meditation
part
question
giant
composed
difficult
objects
dilapidate
appearances
appearances
communications
double
second
giant
recent
imagining
reality
resemblance
inevitable
F.v.e.: 4%

101–200 (27%):
larger

poem
larger
audience
crude
mythological
form
festival
sphere
age
suppose
composed
impalpable
impalpable
transparencies
sound
sounding
transparent
impalpable
habitations
move
movement
colors
coned
sense
poised
regard
F.v.e.: 6%

201–56:
perpetual
reference
object
perpetual
meditation
point
enduring
visionary
obscure
colors
uncertain
clearest
spirit's
indefinite
confused
illuminations
sonorities

apart
idea
idea

13. "A Postcard from the Volcano"
1–100 (9%):
picking (?)

autumn
grapes
air
mansion
cries
literate
despair
mansion's
F.v.e.: 15%

101–64:
part
aureoles
mansion
spirit
blank
opulent

MARIANNE MOORE

1. "The Arctic Ox (or Goat)"
1–100 (10%):
arctic
arctic
coat
conscience
suit
course
musk
musk
illiterate
epithet
F.v.e.: 13%

101–200 (12%):
browses
distinction
egocentric
scent
intelligent
musk
ounces
exposed
dominate
rare
choicer
join
F.v.e.: 16%

201–300 (21%):
invent

incapable
courtship
servitude
decide
stay
camels (?)
unintelligent
neurasthenic
serious
scarce
fur
quiet
demand
dandelions
carrots
encouraged
roll
revel
insatiable
qivi-curvi-capricornus *
F.v.e.: 6%

301–67:
ideal
suppose
ply
advertisement
cordial
creatures'
deserve

2. "A Carriage from Sweden"
1–100 (21%):
air
castle
atmosphere
events
museum
piece
country
art
city
integrity
vein
resined
opposed
compromise
archipelago
rocks
decay
gourd
texture
flowered
dart
F.v.e.: 10%

101–200 (16%):
crustacean
equine
amphibious
creatures
garnish

curvi- and -*capricornus* have not been etymologized separately; see Note on Method, above, for treatment of Latinate compounds as single words.

fine
unannoying
romance
beautiful
natural
egret
clear
soil
spruce
vertical
trunk
F.v.e.: 4%

201–300 (13%):
dance
sanctuaried
Jews
buttons
jackets
gable (?)
due
table
banquet
vest
pleats
effect
dress
F.v.e.: 8%

301–84:
stay
dolphin
graceful
responsive
responsible
moated
castles
flowers
densely
surface

3. "The Hero"
1–100 (13%):
personal

hypodermic
voice
neglected
semiprecious
extended
fine
points
hero
deviating
uncertainty
suffering
hero
F.v.e.: 11%

101–200 (10%):
muffled (?)
note
vexing
vexing
devout
roll
vanished
lenient
creature's
error
F.v.e.: 10%

201–300 (11%):
decorous
frock
coated
Gen'ral
sense
human
dignity
reverence
mystery
natural
hero
F.v.e.: 12%

301–31:
rock

crystal
covets
hero

4. "The Icosasphere"
1–100 (25%):
merged
density
parabolic
concentric
curves
concavity
spherical
feats
rare
efficiency
integration
avid
fortune
committed
perjury
paid
fines
risks
icosasphere
summit
economy
triangles
conjoined
double
rounded
F.v.e.: 11%

101–44:*
waste
geometrically
neat
engineers
solid
vertically

5. "Nevertheless"
1–100 (9%):
fragments

Icosahedron and *granite* in this section of the poem are loan words from Greek and Italian, respectively.

multitude

fruit

fruit

counter-curved

plant

barbed

carrots

form

F.v.e.: 10%

101–67:

victory

grape

tendril

menace

fortitude

cherry

6. "The Pangolin"

1–100 (33%):*

armoured

animal

scale

scale

spruce

cone

regularity

form

uninterrupted

central

equipped

gizzard

artist

engineer

impressive

animal

toiler

armour

extra

closing

eminence

similarly

safe

contracting

apertures

impenetrably

closable

endures

exhausting

solitary

trips

unfamiliar

returning

F.v.e.: 6%

101–200 (18%):

peculiarly

save

serpentined

danger

unpugnaciously

sound

fragile

grace

Buzzard

vine

rolls

power

defy

effort

unroll   *O*

neat

proof

scales

F.v.e.: 5%

201–300 (16%):

rocks

closed

beast

splendour

vileness

excellence

armoured

turn (?)

engulfs

points

plates

violently

retaliates

compact

furled

fringed

F.v.e.: 7%

301–400 (18%):

unhurt

unintruded

cautiously

giant

graceful

elephant's

trunk

special

uninjurable

simpletons

fable

nourished

aggressive

animals

unchain-like

machine-like

form

frictionless

F.v.e.: 9%

401–500 (28%):

graceful

adversities

conversities

explain

grace

requires

curious

graced

animals

luxurious

ingenious

supports

slaved

confuse

grace

Artichoke, miniature, and replica in this section of the poem are loan words from Italian.

manner
pay
debt
cure
graceful
use
approved
mullions
branching
perpendiculars
machine
moving
quietly
F.v.e.: 9%

501–600 (15%):
models
exactness
plantigrade
certain
postures
slaving
flowers
use
paper
tractor
stuffs
mechanicked
human
master (?)
griffons
F.v.e.: 5%

601–700 (23%):
obnoxious
error
animals
sense
humor
humor
saves
saves
unignorant
modest

unemotional
emotion
vigor
power
creatures
erecter
afraid
paced
obstacle
consistent
formula
pairs
mammal
F.v.e.: 11%

701–48:
habitat
serge
prey
curtailed
extinguished
partly
alternating

7. "Style"*
1–100 (25%):
style
revives
constant
plumb
line (?)
axis
fine
counter
camber
fanatical
adjuster
combine
evolving
classic
silhouette
Iberian
American
champion

entranced
solitude
letter
literal
alphabet
sound
contradictorily
F.v.e.: 7%

101–200 (21%):
lake
vertical
turned (?)
bisecting
viper
dart
recover
disaster
art
ease
pose
genius
anticipatory
tactics
preclude
envy
traditional
suddenly
suitable
simile
equidistant
F.v.e.: 8%

201–32:
arcs
conjoined
face

8. "Virginia Britannia"
1–100 (28%):
pale
air
cedar
emerald

*I have counted the title in the tabulation, as it is part of the first sentence of the poem.

coated
musketeer
trumpet
flower
cavalier
parson
parishioner
fine
pavement
tomb
engraved
remain
tremendous
vine
encompassed
flower
tower
sycamore
fritillary
chancel
place
unusual
waits
joyful
F.v.e.: 7%

101–200 (30%):
resurrection
fur
crown
ostrich
Latin
arms
able
ray
pioneer
painted
Turk
continuously
exciting
Captain
patient
inferiors
pugnacious
equal
grateful

rare
Indian
crowned
sculptured
surrounds
formed
insect
sounds
grape
vine
spaced
F.v.e.: 8%

201–300 (16%):
alternating
ostrich
formed
Indians
observe
terse
Virginian
mettlesome
imitates
mocking
meditative
sculptured
marble
noiseless
musing
conspicuous
F.v.e.: 8%

301–400 (26%):
table
cupids
grouped
form
pedestal
bordered
pansies
arbor
cemetery
lace
bordered
gigantic
jet
pansies

splendour
decade
dressed
overpowering
velvet
pale
ink
fur
ochre
cavalcade
furnished
mounts
F.v.e.: 1%

401–500 (27%):
mule
mule
prison
idiom
advancin'
circle
establishing
inadvertent
ally
enemy
tyranny
rare
unscented
providently
inconsistent
flower
flowers
curious
close
perfume
scarlet
fruiting
pomegranate
African
violet
fuchsia
camellia
F.v.e.: 7%

501–600 (28%):
magnolia's

velvet
textured
flower
anesthetic
scent
inconsiderate
gardenia's
gardenia
vein
substanceless
faint
flower
crape
myrtle
princess
feminine
Indian
gauze
taffeta
dressed
crested
mistress
turquoise
chaise
longue
slat
front
F.v.e.: 4%

601–700 (20%):
Indian
Virginian
counties
undiffident
tactless
symbol
republic
priorities
region
noted
humility
cotton
cotton
unique
pottery
design

unvenomous
tepid
record
serpentine
F.v.e.: 4%

701–800 (24%):
strangler
figs
explorer
imperialist
pleased
colonizing
synonym
mercy
fur
crown
famous
cruelty
brawn
animality
table
mandolin
fig
dress
vine
accompanied
compared
colonists
luxuries
mere
F.v.e.: 6%

801–900 (22%):
ardor
unable
suppress
satisfaction
flutes
ecstatic
joy
perched
juniper
minutes
filigree
undulating
solidity

cypress
indivisible
aged
identity
flames
increasingly
chiseled
expanding
assertiveness
F.v.e.: 5%

901–18:
arrogance
importance
intimation
glory

9. "What Are Years?"
1–100 (18%):
innocence
safe
courage
question
resolute
doubt
misfortune
encourages
defeat
accedes
mortality
imprisonment
chasm
unable
surrendering
continuing
very
form
F.v.e.: 16%

101–26:
captive
satisfaction
pure
joy
mortality
eternity

SUMMARY FOR
ALL PASSAGES TABULATED

	Frost	Stevens	Moore
Romance-Latinate Percentiles			
Range:	18-4	34-6	33-9
Median:	8	20	20
Average:	9	19.7	19.9
Finite Verb Counts			
Range:	18-6	18-4	16-1
Median:	11.5	11	8
Average:	10.9	11.4	8.1

Averages are rounded off to one decimal point.

APPENDIX B
WORD FREQUENCY COUNTS

A great deal of new statistical information on word frequencies has become available during the past ten years, the advent of the computer having made it possible to process vast quantities of printed text with speed and accuracy. In addition to *The Teacher's Word Book of 30,000 Words,* ed. Edward L. Thorndike and Irving Lorge (New York, 1944), long a standard reference source, we now have the *Computational Analysis of Present-Day American English,* by Henry Kučera and W. Nelson Francis (Providence, R.I., 1967), with figures for the occurrence of 50,406 different words in over a million words of text; *The American Heritage Word Frequency Book,* ed. John B. Carroll, Peter Davies, and Barry Richman (Boston and New York, 1971), with figures for the occurrence of 86,741 different words in over 5 million words of text; and "A Word Count of Spoken English," by Davis Howes (*Journal of Verbal Learning and Verbal Behavior* 5 [1966]: 572–606), with figures for the occurrence of 9,699 different words in 250,000 words of spoken discourse. For a number of reasons, the published counts are not of much help in determining comparative frequencies of occurrence at formal and colloquial levels. For one thing, the materials surveyed to produce them are limited in range. Thorndike and Lorge, Kučera and Francis, and Carroll et al. used only published writings, though these included fiction and magazine articles as well as materials of a less popular nature. The "American Heritage Intermediate Corpus," analyzed by Carroll et al., was assembled from texts chosen "to represent, as nearly as possible, the range of required and recommended reading to which students are exposed in school grades 3 through 9 in the United States" (p. xiii). The speakers whose language was tabulated in the Davis Howes count talked in the presence of "interviewers," who told them that samples of their speech were to be obtained for a statistical study of language; they were asked general questions, "such as 'tell me what brought you to the hospital' or 'tell me about the field you're majoring in,' depending on whether the [respondent] was a hospital patient or a student" (p. 573). Other difficulties arise as a result of the limitations of the computer, which does not distinguish between homographs, that is, identically spelled forms. The frequency statistics in a computerized list for the entry-form *tear,* for example, would include both the noun that means "teardrop" and the verb that means "rend." More important for the investigator concerned with style is the fact that distinctions are not made among the different senses and uses of a single word on which stylistic value so often depends—between *howl* "ululate" and *howl* "laugh," or *laugh* in "a hearty laugh" and *laugh* in "that's a laugh." The use of colloquial alternatives in a given area of meaning is particularly hard to tabulate, since, as we have already observed, the colloquial level of language has very few words it can call its own—that is, distinctively colloquial words are few in proportion to distinctively colloquial meanings and uses. Such spot checking as I have done provides some corroboration for the general notion that "commonness" as diction and "commonness" in the sense of frequent use tend to go hand in hand. The picture is clearest when, as is all too seldom the case, a set of formal, common, and colloquial synonyms is available in the language. One would imagine, for example, that *converse* "conversation" occurs less frequently than the common words *conversation* and *talk,* and that the same is true of the colloquial word *chat.* The figures in the counts bear this out; in Kučera and Francis, the numbers of occurrences are listed as 5, 50, 154, and 5, respectively; in Carroll et al., they are 24, 209, 1,133, and 9; in Davis Howes, they are 0, 3, 124, and 2. In contemplating these statistics, we must take into consideration the fact that *converse, talk,* and *chat* function as both nouns and verbs, whereas *conversation* is only a noun; in addition, some of the instances of *converse* must belong to the adjective meaning "contrary," and some of the instances of *talk* must mean "lecture" or "rumor." Looking at three words related to the action of laughing, we find that *ludicrous* occurs three times, *ridiculous* 19, and *funny* 41, according to the tabulations in Kučera and Francis. Here, the occurrences of a distinctively colloquial word outnumber those of a common word in printed texts (the figures 0, 11, and 45 for the three words in Davis Howes are less surprising), but *funny* may well mean "odd" more often than it means "ridiculous," in which case the results of the comparison would again be as expected. At the elementary and junior high school reading levels represented by Carroll et al., a total of 314 occurrences is recorded for *funny* versus 34 for *ridiculous* and two for *ludicrous; ridiculous,* as well as *ludicrous,* would seem to be avoided at these levels as a "hard word," but again, one would like a breakdown of meanings and uses in particular contexts. To give one final example, it seems reasonable that the word *merry* should occur only 8 times in Kučera and Francis and not at all in Davis Howes, but the total of 97 times in Carroll et al. seems surprisingly high, until one remembers the expression "Merry Christmas." (Davis Howes lists one occurrence of *merrier,* which does not occur at all in the other two counts; someone must have used the phrase "the more the merrier.")

NOTES

INTRODUCTION

1. For a recent statement to this effect about words of Latin origin, see G. W. Turner, *Stylistics* (Harmondsworth, England, 1973): "Even popular stylistics recognizes a category of 'big words' which corresponds generally to the part of our vocabulary which is derived from the classical languages" (p. 117; cf. pp. 121 ff.).

CHAPTER ONE

1. Unless otherwise stated, the poetry of Wallace Stevens is quoted from *The Collected Poems* (New York, 1954), that of Marianne Moore from *The Complete Poems* (New York, 1967), and that of Robert Frost from *The Poetry of Robert Frost,* ed. Edward Connery Lathem (New York, 1969).

2. The terms used in my discussion of the three passages reappear in later chapters, where they are defined and exemplified more fully. References may be found in the Index.

3. See Randolph Quirk et al., *A Grammar of Contemporary English* (New York, 1972), §11.27 note b: "A complete reversal of the normal relation between subordinate and superordinate clauses takes place with a type of *when*-clause which occurs finally in sentences in formal narrative style . . . . This type of *when*-clause introduces a new piece of information . . . . It gives dramatic emphasis and climax to the event so described." I take "formal narrative style" here to mean "narrative form," whether or not used in literary works. *When*-clauses of this type occur in the informal narration of anecdotes, usually elaborated by some such expression as "the next thing I knew" or "all of a sudden." They also occur in popular narratives such as stories for children; cf., in Clement Clarke Moore's "A Visit from St. Nicholas,"

> And mamma in her 'kerchief, and I in my cap,
> Had just settled our brains for a long winter's nap—
> When out on the lawn there arose such a clatter,
> I sprang from my bed to see what was the matter.

4. A classic of stylistic criticism carried out in terms of features of language in the literal sense is W. K. Wimsatt, Jr.'s, *The Prose Style of Samuel Johnson,* first published in 1941, successive chapters of which are entitled "Parallelism," "Antithesis," and "Diction"; a chapter on "Other Qualities" includes discussions of sentence-length, imagery, inversion, and chiasmus. Alan Sinfield's *The Language of Tennyson's "In Memoriam"* (Oxford, 1971) includes two chapters on diction, two on syntax, two on imagery and one each on sound and rhythm. Space forbids more than a minimum of additional citations, but cf. Stanley Greenfield, "Grammar and Meaning in Poetry," *PMLA* 82 (1967): 377–87; Seymour Chatman, "Milton's Participial Style," *PMLA* 83 (1968): 1386–99; M. A. K. Halliday, "Linguistic Function and Literary Style: An Inquiry into the Language of William Golding's *The Inheritors,*" in *Literary Style: A Symposium,* ed. Seymour Chatman (New York, 1971), pp. 330–6.

General surveys of the problem of defining style in relation to language may be found in Seymour Chatman, "The Semantics of Style," *Social Science Information* 6 (1967): 77–99, and Graham Hough, *Style and Stylistics* (London, 1969). Hough's book includes brief critical discussions of the work of a number of recent theorists and practitioners of stylistic criticism; there is an annotated bibliography. See also Richard W. Bailey, "Statistics and Style: A Historical Survey," and the appended Bibliography, in *Statistics and Style,* ed. Lubomír Dolezel and R. W. Bailey (New York, 1969), pp. 232–36, and *Literary Style,* ed. Chatman, passim.

5. See Sir Alan Gardiner, *The Theory of Speech and Language* (Oxford, 1951), chap. 1; Roger Brown, *Words and Things* (Glencoe, Ill., 1958), "Introduction," pp. 7–16, and chap. 3, "Reference and Meaning," pp. 82–109; Mortimer Adler, *The Difference of Man and the Difference It Makes* (New York, 1967), chaps. 8–11.

6. On spotted creatures in Moore, see chap. 6, p.111. I discuss "Virginia Britannia" on pp. 127–31.

7. See chap. 2, p. 40.

8. According to Robert Penn Warren, "the poem is about the kind of heaven the poet wants, the kind of dream—after labor—he wants and expects" ("The Themes of Robert Frost," in *The Writer and His Craft* [Ann Arbor, 1954], p. 129). John Lynen says that "After Apple-Picking" and other poems show "that [in back-country New England] the life of the imagination can be made to coincide with the humble business of living" (*The Pastoral Art of Robert Frost* [New Haven, 1960], p. 178). For Reuben Brower, "the poem is absorbed with 'states-between,' not only of winter sleep, but of all similar areas where real and unreal appear and disappear" (*The Poetry of Robert Frost: Constellations of Intention* [New York, 1963], p. 26). Richard Poirier describes "After Apple-Picking" as "a dream vision" which "proposes that only labor can penetrate to the essential facts of natural life" (*Robert Frost: The Work of Knowing* [New York, 1977], p. 293). I discuss the poem in "Robert Frost: To Earthward" (*Frost: Centennial Essays II,* ed. Jac Tharpe [Jackson, Miss., 1976], pp. 21–39); "If he were there to be asked, the woodchuck would have to say that the night's sleep to which the speaker looks forward is not at all like hibernation . . . What vitiates it is an anxiety bound up with the responsibilities to which only human beings are subject, the ideals of behavior making them at once less fortunate than animals and—I think Frost would agree—more interesting and important" (p. 28).

9. My interpretation of the poem is much the same as Robert Pack's. "The theme of 'Metaphors of a Magnifico' can be most accurately expressed as a question: how does the mind act when it is trying to concentrate on an abstract idea? The idea in this poem is the relationship of the one to the many . . . . The point of the poem is that the mind must always turn to perception for the foundation of its thought, and Stevens' success is that he dramatizes this truth, reveals the workings of the mind, without having to generalize about it" (*Wallace Stevens: An Approach to His Poetry and Thought* [New Brunswick, 1958], pp. 170, 172–73). Ronald Sukenick speaks of "that reality of 'Metaphors of a Magnifico' which keeps resisting abstract thought and finally resolves itself in its particular details" (*Wallace Stevens: Musing the Obscure* [New York, 1967], p. 51). Bruce King, in "Wallace Stevens' 'Metaphors of a Magnifico,' " explicates the poem in detail, but with a negative emphasis I consider unjustified. The "awareness of vivid, intense, unintellectualized experience" attained at the end of the poem "fades before the mind can assimilate it within the intelligence. Thus the poem ends on a note of defeat as the images fade into the tell-tale dots of uncompleted intellectual process" (*English Studies* 49 [1968]: 450–52).

10. For sound-symbolic words in Stevens, see pp. 68–71; for the grammatical sense of "dynamic," see pp. 96–97.

11. R. A. Sayce, in "The Definition of the Term Style" (*Proceedings of the Third Congress of the International Comparative Literature Association* [The Hague, 1962], pp. 156–66), notes that "a reader of Tolstoy, . . . who knows no Russian, clearly grasps much in the way of plot, character, description and so on, and equally clearly loses something . . . . As long as some sort of equivalent can be achieved in different languages, the absolute identity of form

and content can hardly be maintained" (p. 161). In my terms, this reader enters the Tolstoy novel at the level of formulation; the significant relations between this and other more general or abstractive levels of the form of the original are thus accessible to him.

12. I speak of "levels," rather than of "phases" or "stages" such as might imply a succession in time. My account of form does not in any way purport to describe the mental activity of the composing poet, whether conscious or unconscious. In the actual process of composition, as everybody knows, the idea of the passage may precede the idea of the poem; the choice of a rhyme-sound may suggest a descriptive detail. Yet in all purposeful activity, there is a sense in which a generalized impulse to act precedes and governs the manner of the action. One is inevitably reminded of the account of language given by transformational grammar, with its generalized "deep structures" and its particular "constructions" at the verbal surface. Whether the levels posited there or here represent an actual sequence of events within the brain will probably never be known.

Shortly after writing the above, I came upon these remarks by T. S. Eliot in a letter to Lytton Strachey dated June 1, 1919: "Whether one writes a piece of work well or not seems to me a process of crystallisation—the good sentence, the good word, is only the final stage in the process. One can groan enough over the choice of a word, but there is something much more important to groan over first" (quoted in *Lytton Strachey, A Critical Biography,* II: *The Years of Achievement,* by Michael Holroyd [New York, Holt, Rinehart and Winston, 1968], p. 364).

13. Roland Barthes, in "Style and Its Image" (*Literary Style,* ed. Chatman, pp. 3–10), suggests that discourse is "a construction of layers" like an onion rather than "a species of fruit with a kernel," as the old form-content analysis had it; these "layers (or levels, or systems)" are related finally only to each other (p. 10). I agree that all levels of form in a poem are interrelated, but would argue that the dramatic form in which their interrelationships are manifest is grounded in cultural tradition (including language) and experience.

CHAPTER TWO

1. See, e.g., John Lynen, *The Pastoral Art of Robert Frost* (New Haven, Conn., 1960), p. 2: "On the surface, [Frost's] work has a disarming simplicity which sets it apart.... No obscurity here, ... no esoteric learning or thickets of private symbolism.... The illusion of simplicity is so strong that it is hard to place Frost in the present century." Lawrance Thompson in *Fire and Ice* (New York, 1961) describes the early shift in Frost's style from poetic diction to simplicity and directness of language (pp. 93–99). Philip L. Gerber's handbook, *Robert Frost* (New York, 1966), speaks of "Robert Frost's reputation as a poet of 'simplicity'" (p. 88). Although this and other qualities of Frost's verbal style have often been noted, little has been done by way of describing his language in detailed factual terms. The most sustained discussion is Lynen's (chap. 3, "The Yankee Manner: Style as Symbol"), which contains many pertinent observations and is valuable especially for its definitive statement on the almost total lack of specifically regional language in Frost's poetry (pp. 86–87). Lynen rejects the "mechanical" investigation of language in favor of an analysis of the dramatized persona from whom, as he rightly maintains, stems the felt life of Frost's words. But certain aspects of diction susceptible of "mechanical" investigation are directly relevant to this very persona, as this study, I hope, will demonstrate. Reginald L. Cook's *The Dimensions of Robert Frost* (New York, 1968) and Reuben A. Brower's *The Poetry of Robert Frost: Constellations of Intention* (New York, 1963), both valuable for the student of Frost, are concerned with language per se only peripherally; Brower, in passing, characterizes Frost as "a poet of distinct and clear statement" (p. 3). A certain amount of confusion has resulted from a widespread tacit identification of *simple* language with *colloquial* language in Frost, as in Babette Deutsch's statement that "his diction is simple and colloquial" (*Poetry*

in Our Time [New York, 1956], p. 61). Cf. Lynen, p. 2: "Frost's sentences are always clear, . . . his language close to everyday speech." The distinction is in fact important; simple language may not be colloquial (Tennyson's "Morte Arthure"), and colloquial language may not be simple (Kenneth Koch's "Fresh Air").

2. My primary authority for etymologies and definitions is *The Shorter Oxford English Dictionary*, 3d ed. (1973) (*SOED*), which I have used in conjunction with *The Oxford Dictionary of English Etymology* (1966) (*ODEE*). Supplementary information, especially on early recorded use and historical developments in meaning, has been taken from the unabridged *Oxford English Dictionary* (*OED*). Volumes 1 (1972) and 2 (1976) of *A Supplement to the Oxford English Dictionary* treat words beginning with A–G and H–N, respectively; updated information on words beginning with the letters O–Z is available in the Addenda to *SOED*. For words and meanings in American English, I have also consulted *A Dictionary of American English* (*DAE*), ed. Sir William A. Craigie and James R. Hulbert (Chicago, 1938–44); *A Dictionary of Americanisms on Historical Principles,* ed. Mitford M. Mathews (1951) (*DA*); *Webster's New International Dictionary,* 2d ed. (1934) (*Webster's 2d*); *Webster's Third New International Dictionary* (1961) (*Webster's 3d*); and *Webster's New Collegiate Dictionary,* 8th ed. (1973) (*WCD8*).

The distinction between "Latinate" and "of Latin derivation" is essential for an understanding of the relation between etymology and stylistic value in English. It depends on the fact that French words are "derived from" Latin originals in two quite different ways: by transmission in the spoken language (chiefly from that branch of vulgar or popular Latin spoken in Gaul in early times) and by literary borrowing. English borrowings from French include words of both these types. Thus, the near-synonyms *faith* and *fidelity* correspond to two Old French words both of which ultimately "derive from" Latin *fides.* The Old French prototype of *fidelity* was a literary borrowing from Latin *fidelitas;* hence, *fidelity* in my terms is Latinate, whether or not its immediate source in English is French; *faith,* also "derived from" Latin, is Romance. The Latinate element in English includes Latinate French as well as direct Latin borrowings. American dictionaries do not distinguish between Latinate and Romance derivation in Old French words, the one exception known to me being *The American College Dictionary* (New York, 1955) (see, in their introductory materials, the statement on "Descent vs. Adoption" in "Treatment of Etymologies" by Kemp Malone, p. xxvi). However, this information is generally accessible in *SOED* and *ODEE.* In both, Romance transmission from Latin is indicated by the colon-dash (:–), Latinate transmission by the dash only. In earlier editions of *SOED,* Latinate French words are described as "adoptions of" (*a.*) or "adaptations of" (*ad.*) their Latin originals. In addition to words of Latin derivation, the "Romance" component of French includes words of Germanic and Celtic origin, and a few words whose origins are obscure.

In the passage quoted from "The Lesson for Today," *limit, extension,* and *fate* are direct Latin borrowings in English; *nation* and *total* are Latinate French. *Careers, race,* and *liable* are Romance. In the passage from "The Strong Are Saying Nothing," *farm* (twice), *carries,* and *cry* are Romance. The remaining words in the two passages are "native," a category in which all Germanic sources are counted together with Old English (*they* in "The Strong Are Saying Nothing" is from Old Norse). Since the correlation between word origins and stylistic values with which I am concerned here has its basis in the English language as it reemerged into high social and cultural status after the Conquest, Latin loan words in Old English such as *creed* and *cup* must be classed as "native" rather than "Latinate." See the "Note on Method" preceding Appendix A.

3. I exclude from consideration in this study Frost's dramatic monologues and "eclogues," where the Romance-Latinate level is, if anything, even lower. It was these poems that Frost was referring to when he said he had "dropped to an everyday level of diction

that even Wordsworth kept above" (*Selected Letters of Robert Frost,* ed. Lawrance Thompson [New York, 1964], pp. 83–84). But the remark is of obvious interest for the style of Frost's lyrics in the "simple" mode, as is the comment that immediately follows: "You are not going to make the mistake . . . of assuming that my simplicity is that of the untutored child. I am not undesigning" (ibid.). The longest sequence of native words I have found in Frost occurs in "The Pauper Witch of Grafton": there are eighty-seven native words between *rocks* and *courage* in the last eleven lines of the poem. At the "low" extreme of diction, one has to reckon with the fact that many Romance words in particular, and some Latinate words, have been so thoroughly assimilated into the language that they are indistinguishable from the most common and everyday words of native origin (e.g., in the sequence *bed* [OE], *chair* [R], *table* [L]). But enough words of Romance origin are associated with the more refined and aristocratic realms of experience so that this generally recognized correlation exists; it is true of any correlation that it may fail to predict a particular case.

4. The critic's "preliminary grasp of the whole" is itself dependent on an understanding of the parts and, notably, on the intuitive recognition of "saliency" or key significance in details which, statistically viewed, are so many "features." A definitive account of the complementary relationship between the grasp of form and the perception of detail is given by Leo Spitzer in the title essay of *Linguistics and Literary History* (New York, 1962), pp. 1–39. This essay, although its examples are drawn chiefly from the Romance languages, is indispensable for the critic concerned with the relationship between language and style in English or, indeed, any literature. (One need not, as Spitzer does, locate the formal principle sought in "the soul of the artist" [p. 19]; a sufficient goal for stylistic criticism is an account of the authorial "second self"—the fictional character discoverable in the language of the work. For an illuminating discussion of this distinction, see Wayne C. Booth, *The Rhetoric of Fiction* [Chicago, 1961], pp. 70–77.) At its best, the process of criticism may involve modification, even correction, of the overriding sense of the whole by a respectful attention to the parts. To quote again from Wallace Stevens, "Alpha continues to begin. Omega is refreshed at every end."

5. This may safely be called the majority view (see, e.g., Elizabeth Drew, *Poetry: A Modern Guide to Its Understanding and Enjoyment* [New York, 1959], p. 63; and Lawrance Thompson in *Seven Modern American Poets: An Introduction,* ed. Leonard Unger [Minneapolis, 1959], p. 15). Radcliffe Squires, in *The Major Themes of Robert Frost* (Ann Arbor, Mich., 1963), finds the theme of "breaking down traditional barriers" unsuccessfully presented in the poem and states, further, that such a thematic interpretation "takes us to a position which nothing else in Frost's poetry supports" (p. 76). This latter opinion is, I believe, radically erroneous. S. L. Dragland, in the *Explicator,* vol. 25, no. 39 (1967), argues that the wall stands for a civilizing "progress" necessary for "individuation"; the speaker, as a man of the modern era, finds it "no longer a simple matter either to condemn or to endorse barriers." John Lynen (pp. 28–29) paraphrases the question raised by the poem as follows: "Should man tear down the barriers which isolate individuals from one another, or should he recognize that distinctions and limits are necessary to human life?" For Lynen, "Frost does not really provide an answer," though "the poem presents the speaker's attitude more sympathetically than the neighbor's" (p. 29). Carson Gibbs, in the *Explicator,* vol. 20, no. 48 (1962), makes what I consider an important distinction between what the speaker says about the wall and the fact that he wishes to keep it repaired (see my discussion of this point, p. 26). But Gibbs's conclusion that "the speaker prefers walls and their preservers to their destroyers, natural or human," is unjustified on the symbolic level. All these critics twist the meaning of the poem to some extent by stating its theme in epistemological rather than ethical terms. The value of "distinctions and limits" or "individuation" may be ambiguous, but human impulses of reconciliation and sympathy are clear moral goods.

6. In the words of Richard Poirier, "Just as early spring 'sends' or 'spills' what is firmly placed, so the 'notions' of the speaker are meant to displace the settled ideas in his presumably block-headed friend" (*Robert Frost: The Work of Knowing* [New York, 1977]. p. 105).

7. The "father's saying" is not to my knowledge recorded as a bona fide proverb, although it resembles one in verbal form and in the prudential character of its message. The idea itself is expressed in traditional proverbs. "A hedge between keeps friendship green" and "Love your neighbor, yet pull not down your hedge," the latter from George Herbert's *Jacula Prudentum,* are cited in *The Home Book of Proverbs, Maxims and Familiar Phrases,* ed. Burton Stevenson (New York, 1948), pp. 1674–75, s.v. "Neighbor," 13, together with a German analogue somewhat closer to Frost's in wording, "Zwischen Nachbars Gärten ist ein Zaun gut"; the line from "Mending Wall" is also cited (cf. *The Oxford Dictionary of English Proverbs,* 1948 ed., pp. 289, 392, s.vv. "Hedge," "Love"). The word *fence* in the formulation used by Frost is of interest here because of its etymology: as an aphetic form of *defense,* it implies the threat of violence signified also by the hunters and the "weapon"-bearing neighbor. The New Testament associations of the word *neighbor,* which are especially conspicuous in Herbert's formulation, are ironic (see p. 31).

8. Complete etymological breakdowns of the poems discussed will be found in Appendix A. The reader wishing to check my statistics is asked to read the Note on Method which precedes the figures presented there. Other poets besides Frost, of course, have used language whose Romance-Latinate content represents the "low" extreme for English text; in fact, such language is easier to find in poetry than in prose, even the prose of everyday conversation. Some modern examples are Housman's *A Shropshire Lad* and Dylan Thomas's "A Winter's Tale" and "Fern Hill." In Housman's "Loveliest of Trees," the only non-native word is *cherry* (2x), and the first five stanzas of "Farewell to Barn and Stack and Tree" contain only the Latinate proper names *Terence* and *Maurice* (see also the poets exemplifying the "tradition of simple elevation" in English, p. 32 above). Like any other striking aspect of language in a characteristic and effective style, "simplicity" in Housman and Thomas will presumably be functional dramatically as it is in Frost, but its functions will not necessarily be the same; they can be understood only from a full study of the poetry of each. At the other end of the scale, Romance-Latinate percentiles regularly correlate with an impression of literary, specifically of "learned," diction. An example is W. H. Auden's "In Memory of W. B. Yeats," where the first 500 words (out of 526) yield percentiles of 18, 24, 14, 22, and 27, despite the repeated playing off of elevated language against simple ("The day of his death was a dark cold day"). The "high" extreme for English text generally is, as one would expect, found in the scientific and technical prose of learned journals and books, where successive Romance-Latinate percentiles may run as high as the mid-40s.

9. I know that such hypothetical "alternatives" disregard metrical form as an overriding condition of the poet's choice of words and that an effective relationship between metrical form and the sounds of words, on the one hand, and dramatic expressiveness, on the other, is a *sine qua non* in poetry worthy of the name. But to object that Frost "could not have used" *barriers* instead of *wall,* and *antipathy* instead of "does not love," because the result would not have been metrical is to overlook the fact that Frost, like any master of the poet's craft, was able in general to say what he wished to say in the sort of language he wished to use, without loss of metrical effectiveness.

10. My account is oversimplified, chiefly in the tacit identification of "formal" with "written" words. Literature, and with it distinctively formal language, came into existence long before writing, and even today such language may be learned orally, as when children memorize and recite the Pledge of Allegiance (*allegiance, republic, nation, indivisible*) or

the Lord's Prayer (*hallowed, trespasses*). Yet it remains true that formal language is more often seen than heard.

The range envisaged here between distinctively colloquial and distinctively formal extremes will be recognized as based on a scheme of what have sometimes been called "functional varieties" in language. The confusion of functional classifications with normative judgments, less widespread now than formerly, was effectively criticized by John S. Kenyon in "Cultural Levels and Functional Varieties of English," *College English* 10 (1948): 31–36. Further discussion of the relationship between stylistic and cultural levels can be found in Martin Joos, *The Five Clocks* (New York, 1961; New York, 1967); "Usage and Variety in English," in W. Nelson Francis, *The English Language: An Introduction* (New York, 1963), pp. 218–63; "What Is Standard English?" in Randolph Quirk, *The Use of English* (London, 1968), pp. 79–96; and "Registers, Repertories, Roles, and Reputations" in Dwight Bolinger, *Aspects of Language,* 2d ed. (New York, 1975), pp. 358–69.

"High formal" language is distinguished from "formal" language generally at a later stage of this study. For references, see the Index.

11. The classic discussion of word origins as related to cultural history and stylistic values in English is Otto Jespersen's *Growth and Structure of the English Language,* 9th ed. (New York, 1938). J. A. Sheard's *The Words of English* (New York, 1966; originally published by Oxford University Press, 1954, as *The Words We Use*) contains informative discussions of the main groups of loan words which have come into the language from Old English times on. Still useful, though dated in its normative view of the colloquial (functional) level of language, is James Bradstreet Greenough and George Lyman Kittredge's *Words and Their Ways in English Speech* (New York, 1901). None of these writers distinguishes systematically between Romance and Latinate French borrowings, though all remark on the presence in Old French of colloquial and learned doublets deriving from a single Latin original and the concomitant possibility that both members of such pairs may appear as loan words in English (see Jespersen, pp. 119–22, Sheard, pp. 245–46, and Greenough and Kittredge, pp. 94–97). Stephen Ullmann, in *Semantics: An Introduction to the Science of Meaning* (New York, 1962), pp. 145–48, describes the "double" and "triple scales" according to which synonyms in English are grouped in stylistically differing pairs like *answer* (OE) / *reply* (French) and *bodily* (OE) / *corporeal* (Latin) and, less frequently, in triplets like *food* (OE) / *nourishment* (French) / *nutrition* (Latin); many other examples are given (*nourishment,* like *nutrition,* is derived ultimately from Latin *nutrire* and is Romance; *nutrition* is a direct Latin borrowing in English, but *nutritive* is Latinate French).

12. By sentence sounds (a compound he sometimes hyphenated and sometimes did not) Frost meant the combination of such features of language as intonation, tone of voice (including irony), stresses, and pauses, especially those "rhetorical" stresses and pauses above and beyond the phonemic grades of stress and juncture, as these give dramatic expressiveness to language. When a poet is skilled at creating sentence sounds, we instinctively impose such patterns on his lines in reading them aloud or to ourselves. The sounds themselves need not be formally complete sentences; witness Frost's example "You, you—!" in *Selected Letters,* p. 140, and his use of it in the poem "Beyond Words." To the extent that these patterns are heard primarily or exclusively in speech, they are distinctively colloquial; what Frost does is to superimpose them on common diction and syntax. His style is thus both like and unlike that of Browning, in which recognizable sentence sounds and colloquial syntactic features are combined with a learned and eccentric vocabulary. For Frost's account of what he means by sentence sounds, see, e.g., *Selected Letters,* pp. 107–8 and 110–14. The value he attached to this aspect of poetic composition is shown in his assertion that "a man is all a writer if *all* his words are strung on definite recognizable

sentence sounds" (ibid., p. 111) and by his claim that one of his least successful poems is "almost saved by a striking sentence-sound" (ibid., p. 112). To balance an element of exaggeration in this view, we may cite Edward Thomas, one of Frost's most perceptive and appreciative early critics, who in a review of *North of Boston* in 1914, while praising Frost's poems for their beauty, even grandeur, observed that "many, if not most, of the separate lines and sentences are plain and, in themselves, nothing" (quoted by W. W. Robson in "The Achievement of Robert Frost," *Southern Review*, n.s. 2 [1966]: 737).

13. The most relevant discussion, though primarily concerned not with English style but with Latin, is in Erich Auerbach's immensely illuminating essay "Sermo Humilis," in *Literary Language and Its Public in Late Latin Antiquity and in the Middle Ages* (New York, 1965), pp. 25–66. Auerbach discusses the impact of the Christian message on the earlier concept of a threefold classification of levels of style based on subject matter (see esp. p. 38). This concept, according to Auerbach, was modified by Saint Augustine, who shifted the emphasis from subject matter to the author's purpose, holding that "a Christian orator recognizes no absolute levels of subject matter . . . . [His] subject is always Christian revelation, and this can never be base or in-between" (p. 35). The point "is of fundamental importance: in the Christian context humble everyday things . . . lose their baseness and become compatible with the lofty style; and conversely, as is made clear in Augustine's subsequent remarks, the highest mysteries of the faith may be set forth in the simple words of the lowly style which everyone can understand" (p. 37). The paradox of elevated humility is inherent in Christianity itself; its stylistic concomitant, a solemn simplicity pregnant with biblical allusion, can be found in English literature from its beginnings. As early as the end of the fourteenth century, following the incorporation into the language of a sizable Romance-Latinate vocabulary and the assimilation by English poets of Continental literary influences, one can observe the playing off of simple language against erudite language in works written in the high style; witness the conclusion of the following passage from *The Clerk's Tale:*

> Noght fer fro thilke paleys honurable,
> Wher as this markys shoop his mariage,
> There stood a throop, of site delitable,
> In which that povre folk of that village
> Hadden her beestes and hir herbergage.
>
> . . . .
>
> Amonges thise povre folk ther dwelte a man
> Which that was holden povrest of hem alle;
> But hye God somtyme senden kan
> His grace into a litel oxes stalle.
>
> (Lines 197–201, 204–7)

14. For *swale hay* and *swale grass*, see the attributive uses of *swale* cited in *DAE; swale hay* is cited from a Massachusetts source, *swale grass* from Vermont. The relevant definition of *swale* in *DAE* is "a marshy or moist depression in a level or rolling area." *OED* (s.v. "swale" sb.³) confuses the issue somewhat by an emphasis on "prairies" in the primary definition, but there is a helpful citation under attributive uses: "Their crop is swale hay; in other words swamp grass."

15. See Elizabeth Shepley Sergeant, *Robert Frost: The Trial by Existence* (New York, 1960), p. 82.

16. For fuller discussion of the economic and imaginative dimensions in Frost, see Marie Borroff, "Robert Frost: To Earthward," in *Frost: Centennial Essays II,* pp. 21–39.

17. In "The Tuft of Flowers" we should note the presence of a few "poetic" words of Romance or Latinate origin—*scene, isle, tremulous*—such as Frost avoids in all but his

earliest poems. The Romance words *reply* and *aid* in the same poem seem merely elevated synonyms of native *answer* and *help* "used for the sake of the rhyme," again an effect unusual in the later Frost.

18. An account similar in many respects to this, arrived at from the direction of thematic analysis rather than language, is given in Cook, chap. 3 ("The Organic"), pp. 69–93. Cook makes the point that, "although [Frost's] poetry inheres in empirical experience, its substance is certainly not simply direct observation. It is some truth hardily won out of personal experience" (pp. 74–75). I should wish to insist more than Cook does on what is dramatically portrayed in the poem itself, as against the process of composition which is an aspect of the poet's life. A man may win truth out of personal experience, and yet write about it in poems whose structure does not embody this process.

19. To the bibliography given by George Knox in his article on the poem, "A Backward Motion toward the Source" (*Personalist* 47 [1966]: 365–81), p. 381n., should be added Brower's discussion, pp. 226–42 (n. 1 above), and James P. Dougherty's "Robert Frost's 'Directive' to the Wilderness," *American Quarterly* 18 (1966): 208–19.

20. For the American use of the word *panther* to designate the animal also called *catamount* or "cat of the mountain," see "panther," sense 2, in *OED* (cf. "catamount," sense 2); "panther," sense 1a. (cf. "catamount," sense b) in *DAE*. Citations in the latter indicate that the American panther survived in New England well into the nineteenth century. Some would say well into the twentieth; a claim that he sighted a mountain lion in Maine in the 1940s or 1950s, while in the company of the photographer Kosti Ruohomaa, is made by Lew Dietz in *Down East: The Magazine of Maine* 16 (October 1969): 60, 65. I have found the place name "Catamount Mountain" (also called "Catamount Hills") in nineteenth-century New Hampshire gazetteers; Frost refers to a "Catamount" (Hill) in "Paul's Wife."

21. Elizabeth Shepley Sergeant quotes Frost as saying to his Amherst students, "What is education? What is poetry? Why is it written? Which of you know when I'm fooling and when I'm serious? Better find out." She adds, "He would put on a Yankee drawl to say it" (p. 201).

22. This point is made by Dougherty, pp. 208–9.

23. See n. 14 on p. 487 of S. P. C. Duvall's valuable article "Robert Frost's 'Directive' Out of *Walden*," *American Literature* 31 (1960): 482–88.

24. Margaret M. Blum, in "Robert Frost's 'Directive': A Theological Reading," *Modern Language Notes* 76 (1961): 524–25, sees the "two lost cultures" of the poem "as two religions, one possibly Judaism, the other certainly Christianity" (p. 524). For her, "the ruined playhouse of the children . . . is the Christian mythus. The main house that 'was no playhouse but a house in earnest' is the earlier religion" (pp. 524–25). This interpretation, though too rigidly exclusive, identifies an important aspect not only of "Directive" but the thematic working of Frost's poems generally.

25. See Cook, chap. 4 ("The Parablist"), pp. 95–115. Cook distinguishes between parable and allegory as follows: "The parable embodies its interpretation in the narrative; the allegory emphasizes ideas as abstractions. Frost's poetic parables more nearly resemble the symbolic than the linguistic metaphor" (p. 101).

26. See Duvall, p. 487. He quotes Frost as saying, in connection with the passage from Saint Mark, "It seems that people weren't meant to be saved if they didn't understand figures of speech." In his discussion of the ending of "Directive," Brower observes that "the speaker and reader arrive at salvation not through embracing a doctrine or through argument . . . but through poetry" (p. 240).

CHAPTER THREE

1. The peculiarities of Stevens's diction have been duly noted, and attacked or defended on various grounds, in the published criticism both early and late, *Harmonium* being of course the prime offender from the point of view of the attackers. Of *Harmonium*, Paul Rosenfeld wrote, "So novel and fantastic is the tintinnabulation of unusual words, and words unusually rhymed and arranged, that you nearly overlook the significations, and hear outlandish sharp and melting musics . . . . His music is a music signaled as vain, an exaltation, not as much 'without sound' as without . . . signification" (*Men Seen: Twenty-four Modern Authors* [New York, 1925], pp. 151, 159). Daniel Fuchs opens his profoundly respectful study of Stevens's poetry by acknowledging that "reading Stevens poses an immediate problem. The reader is dazzled by a display of verbal pyrotechnics, a shower of exotic colors, wondrous sound-effects, inkhorn words, hoo-hoos and rum-tum-tums . . . " (*The Comic Spirit of Wallace Stevens* [Durham, N.C., 1963], p. 3). Among more recent critics, Edward Kessler feels it necessary to say that Stevens's "preoccupation with curious and curious-sounding words is not evidence of obscurantism, but of the poet's desire to help the reader find pleasure in 'things unintelligible, yet understood' " (*Images of Wallace Stevens* [New Brunswick, N.J., 1972], p. 227). But there has been little systematic discussion of Stevens's diction, or indeed of any other aspect of his language, as such. A useful analysis of certain key aspects of syntax and sentence structure and their significance is presented in chap. 1, "The Pensive Man: The Pensive Style," of Helen H. Vendler's *On Extended Wings* (Cambridge, Mass., 1969), pp. 13–37 (see also Adalaide K. Morris, *Wallace Stevens: Imagination and Faith* [Princeton, 1974]).

The negative view has been presented most recently by Hugh Kenner, who discusses Stevens in conjunction with William Carlos Williams, to the disadvantage of the former, in chap. 3, "Something to Say," of *A Homemade World* (New York, 1975), pp. 50–90. "If any poems have been simply confected from words," Kenner says, "words shaggy, smooth, humdrum, exotic, words stroked and smoothed and jostled, words set grimacing, they would seem to be Stevens' poems" (p. 56). But words in Stevens have broken loose from reality in sinister fashion; his language reflects "an autonomous verse-tradition" of elevated rhetoric in which "learning to write . . . no longer teaches you to see, because its way of seeing . . . is no longer believed in" (p. 70). The Victorian poet Edward Lear, realizing this, concluded that poetry had better "shut itself up completely in its own cocoon of suggestion." Stevens, like Lear, is a nonsense poet for whom the sounds of words determine what is said; his Canon Aspirin and Professor Eucalyptus are comparable to Lear's Dong with the luminous nose and the Jumblies who went to sea in a sieve (ibid.). One may find Kenner's critique witty and provocative, yet perverse; what he seems to miss is the *experiential* reality of Stevens's poetry, its affecting portrayal of important states of human consciousness. As a means to this end, Stevens's odd language is not merely eccentric—or, if it is, it reveals the eccentric to be the base of design.

2. Unless otherwise specified, page references are to *The Collected Poems*. For Stevens's other works, I shall use the following short titles: *N.A., The Necessary Angel* (1951); *O.P., Opus Posthumous* (1957); *Letters, Letters of Wallace Stevens,* ed. Holly Stevens (1966); and *Palm, The Palm at the End of the Mind: Selected Poems and a Play,* ed. Holly Stevens (1971).

3. The term *collocation* has been used by the British linguist J. R. Firth and others to refer to the lexical aspects of word combinations and the conventions governing these (see, e.g., Angus McIntosh, "Patterns and Ranges," in *Patterns of Language,* ed. McIntosh and M. A. K. Halliday [Bloomington, Ind., 1966], pp. 183–99). Any innovative metaphor, such as Stevens's "corridors of clouds" (p. 134) or "the corals of the dogwood" (p. 400), will involve a strange but intelligible collocation. But there are limits to the "tolerance of compatibility" or

"potential of collocability" among words, as McIntosh's invention, "The molten postage feather scored a weather" well demonstrates (pp. 186–87). This sentence is grammatically unambiguous but resists resolution on any level of meaning. Yet the words of which it is composed are compatible or "collocable" stylistically—all of them could easily belong to a single context. If it were altered to read "The deliquescent postage feather clobbered a weather," it would exhibit incompatibilities of diction as well as of meaning, and it would resemble the sort of word combination I am talking about in Stevens. The point is that words have two different though interrelated kinds of expressive value: they are signifiers of meanings in relation to "subjects of reference" (more broadly, subject matter) whose identity is known or inferred, and they are aspects of conventional modes of verbal behavior. I call them *terms* in the first of these capacities, and *tags* in the second. See chap. 1, above, pp. 11–13.

4. The designation "Latinate" as used throughout this study applies to a number of words whose immediate source in English is French. The distinction between "Romance" and "Latinate" is explained in n.2 to chap. 2.

Many Latin words were themselves borrowed from Greek. An example among the Latinate words listed above is *syllable*, which goes back through Anglo-French *sillabe*, and Latin *syllaba*, to Greek συλλαβή. The source of a word in Latin, however, is not relevant to its Latinate status in English, nor is there a special correlation between etymology and stylistic status in English for Latinate words whose source was Greek. English words borrowed directly from Greek are so rare that little would be gained by adding Greek to Romance and Latinate as a third category in carrying out etymological breakdowns.

5. I have borrowed this useful distinction from Stephen Ullmann, who develops it in *The Principles of Semantics*, 2d ed. (New York, 1957) and elsewhere. According to Ullmann, a word is "motivated" when it is "self-explanatory" in the sense that there seems to be an "intrinsic and synchronously perceptible reason for [its] having this particular form" (*Principles*, pp. 86–87). To speak of the connection between sense and shape as "synchronously perceptible" is to exclude "diachronic" considerations of historical development or derivation, the relationship of a present-day word or form to an earlier source. "Phonetic motivation," as one would expect, consists in a relationship of correspondence felt to exist between "the sounds [of words], their acoustic or articulatory features," and the meanings they express; "it is essentially intuitive and incomplete" (p.87).

The correspondence between sound and meaning takes many different forms, and I have used the term "sound symbolism" to refer to all of them. It includes not merely simple onomatopoeia, in which the sound of a word is felt to resemble a sound denoted by the word, but correspondences between the sounds of words and nonacoustic perceptions of size, texture, motion, etc., and correspondences between the physical actions involved in articulating a word and some action denoted by the word or associated with its meaning. *Flick* and *gulp,* cited above from Stevens, belong to the second and third of these types, respectively (see also chap. 4, "Transparent and Opaque Words," in Ullmann, *Semantics: An Introduction to the Science of Meaning* [Oxford, 1962; reprint ed., 1970], pp. 80–115, and chap. 3, "Semantics and Etymology," in Ullmann, *Language and Style* [Oxford, 1964], pp. 40 ff.). Ullmann distinguishes "primary onomatopoeia" ("simple onomatopoeia" as described above) from "secondary onomatopoeia," in which "a movement . . . or some physical or moral quality, usually unfavorable," is evoked by the sounds of a word, citing *dither, wriggle, grumpy,* and *mawkish,* among others, as examples of the latter (*Semantics,* p. 84). Cf. *Language and Style,* pp. 69–70.

A reader's or listener's sense of the intrinsic correspondences between phonetic shape and meaning would seem to be in large part intralingual and culturally conditioned, with some subjective variation of response in marginal cases. For valuable general discussions, see the chapter of "Sound Symbolism" in Otto Jespersen, *Language* (New York, 1964), pp. 396–411; J. R. Firth, "Modes of Meaning," in *Essays and Studies . . . Collected for the English Association*, ed. Geoffrey Tillotson (London, 1951), pp. 118–49, esp. 121–23; and the chapter on "Phonetic Symbolism and Metaphor" in Roger Brown, *Words and Things* (Glencoe, Ill., 1958), pp. 110–39. Some excellent remarks on the subject may be found in Dwight Bolinger, *Aspects of Language* (New York, 1975), pp. 22–25; Bolinger discusses "phonesthemes," or sound-symbolic combinations of phonemes shared by groups of words, on pp. 218–20. For a detailed account of the sound-symbolic vocabulary of English, see chap. 7, "Phonetic Symbolism," in Hans Marchand, *The Categories and Types of Present-Day English Word-Formation: A Synchronic-Diachronic Approach*, 2d ed. (Munich, 1969), pp. 397–428.

Sound-symbolic "motivation," as I have said, is synchronic rather than diachronic. But the impulse to coin words of phonetically expressive character, for all that it subverts the essentially conventional character of the perceived shapes of words (Saussure's "l'arbitraire du signe"), is a force of considerable importance in the history of at least the English language. The felt expressiveness of the sounds of a word may enhance its life or influence the evolution of its meaning; see the discussions of *bosh, patter, husky* "hoarse" and other examples in Jespersen, pp. 401–2, 406–7. The relevance of sound-symbolic considerations to philological inquiry is demonstrated by G. V. Smithers's article, "Some English Ideophones" (*Archivum Linguisticum* 6 [1954]: 73–111), which is largely, though not exclusively, concerned with early Middle English words.

6. *Honky-tonk* is defined in *DA* as "a cheap burlesque show, a place of low amusement. Also attrib." The last citation given is, "Across the narrow street a honkatonk orchestra blared from the open door of a saloon." The relevant definition appears in the addenda to *SOED:* "Ragtime music as played in honky-tonks . . . also *attrib.* or quasi-*adj.*, as in *honky-tonk* piano, an out-of-tune or tinny sounding piano." The word is similarly defined in *WCD8*. Its sound-symbolic character is indicated by its form: it is an iterative of the rhyming type (see n.19 below and p. 51).

7. Stevens's language may thus be described as "foregrounded" in the sense in which that term has been made well known by literary theorists of the Prague school. By foregrounding (*aktualisace*) is meant "the use of the devices of the language in such a way that this use itself attracts attention and is perceived as uncommon" (Bohuslav Havránek, "The Functional Differentiation of the Standard Language," in *A Prague School Reader on Esthetics, Literary Structure, and Style*, ed. and trans. Paul Garvin [Washington, D.C., 1964], p. 10). Foregrounding is the opposite of automatization, "such a use that the expression itself does not attract any attention" (p. 9); it is characteristic of the language of poetry as opposed to that of science (p. 12). In the words of Jan Mukařovský, "the function of poetic language consists in the maximum of foregrounding of the utterance" ("Standard Language and Poetic Language," ibid., p. 19).

Some difficulties arise when we attempt to apply this concept to both the self-signalizing, gaudy language of Stevens and the lucid, natural language of the early Frost. Significantly, Mukařovský responds to the hypothetical objection that in some poetry the subject matter rather than the language seems to be foregrounded by maintaining that "there is no fixed border, nor, in a certain sense, any essential difference between the language and subject matter" of poetry (p. 22); language is thus reductively identified with form at all levels.

8. This combination is singled out by Kenner (p. 51) as illustrating Stevens's penchant for creating "nonsense verse" by putting "queer words" together.

Combinations of outrageously disparate elements of diction have been used systematically for comic effect since the sixteenth century, as witness the following from Nashe's "The Prayse of the Red Herring" (1599): "Now king Dionisius being a good wise-fellow . . . no sooner entered their temple, & saw [the enshrined herring] sit vnder her Canopie so budgely, ... but to him he stept, and pluckt him from his state with a wennion ["vengeance"], then drawing out his knife most iracundiously, at one whiske lopt off his head" (*The Works of Thomas Nashe,* ed. from Original Texts by Ronald B. McKerrow [London, 1910], 3:194). The technique is used in the present day, for various purposes and with various effects, by S. J. Perelman, Tom Wolfe, and Donald Barthelme, among others.

9. "Like the comic style of Laforgue and the early Eliot, Stevens's comic style is full of travesty and self-irony, full of integrations of the frivolous and serious . . . . There is a constant tension in his poetry between the promulgation of a new seriousness and the deflation of a grandeur which he can see only as ridiculous" (Daniel Fuchs, *The Comic Spirit of Wallace Stevens,* pp. 24–25).

10. See chap. 1, where it is argued that the relationship between form and content in language is a variable one, such that the two can be distinguished at levels closer to, or more distant from, the verbal surface of a text, according to the perceptions and interests of the critic. The terms *verbalization, formulation, development,* and *conception* are suggested there as designations for form at arbitrarily chosen points on what is in fact a continuum.

11. *On Extended Wings,* pp. 243–44.

12. For definitions of "Romance" and "Latinate," see n.2 of chap. 2.

13. The passages quoted at the beginning of this chapter as illustrating Stevens's use of different kinds of words have the following Romance-Latinate counts: (1) "The major abstraction is the idea of man": one Romance word, ten Latinate, for a total of eleven words out of twenty-eight, or between 39 and 40 percent. (2) "He was more than an external majesty": two Latinate words, for a total of two out of forty-four, or between 4 and 5 percent. (3) "It is the visible rock, the audible": eight Romance words, five Latinate, for a total of thirteen words out of twenty-seven, or between 48 and 49 percent. (4) "For myself, I live by leaves": two Romance words, for a total of two out of twenty-four, or between 8 and 9 percent. (I have thought it best not to attempt to etymologize the ithy oonts and longhaired plomets.) The average for all these figures is about 25 percent, a figure that corresponds neither to the high percentiles in the passages nor to the low ones. The thirty 100-word passages for which detailed statistics are given in Appendix A have Romance-Latinate percentiles of between 6 and 34, and average out to almost 20 percent. Given the wide range of the figures, the average tells us little about the language of any particular poem among those sampled; nor does it have predictive value. It does, however, contrast significantly with the average of 9 percent for all the Frost passages tabulated. That it should amount to almost 20 percent, despite the presence of a number of very low percentiles pulling it down, is evidence for the prevailing tendency toward elaborate formality in Stevens's language.

14. The traditional account of levels of language in terms of a range between formal and colloquial, with a corresponding three-part division of words and other features into formal, colloquial, and common (presented for example in the introduction to *SOED*), has seemed sufficient for the purposes of this part of my study. In recent theorizing about language varieties, the concept of "register" has been especially prominent. A detailed exposition and history, with reference to Firth (whose concepts of "context of situation" and "restricted languages" were seminal), McIntosh and Halliday, and others, may be found in J. Ellis and N. Ure, "Language Varieties: Register," in *Encyclopaedia of Linguistics, Information and Control,* ed. A. R. Meetham (Oxford, 1969), pp. 251–59. Register is described by Ellis and Ure as depending, not on social class or locality, but on "the use we are putting language to and other circumstances of the 'immediate situation of utterance'" (p. 251). They identify four "dimensions" in distinguishing among registers (pp. 253–54): field, correlating with "variations in the type of subject-matter, where the difference is not merely a direct reflection of the particular reference"; mode, "correlating with the medium of utterance and

the general communicative relation between the participants"; role, "correlating with the social or other function of the utterance or text"; and formality, "correlating with the personal relation between the participants."

Such an apparatus seems in general less suitable for literary than for scientifically or sociologically oriented investigations of language, though the data yielded by investigations based on it might well be useful to the literary critic. One would like to see a detailed analysis of registers in "The Waste Land," or Berryman's *Dream Songs*. For an account of the kinds of linguistic features identifiable as aspects of register, with detailed analyses of specimen passages, see David Crystal and Derek Davy, *Investigating English Style* (London, 1969).

See also the summary chapter, "Varieties of English," in *A Concise Grammar of Contemporary English* by Randolph Quirk and Sidney Greenbaum (New York, 1973), pp. 1–9, where formality is discussed under the heading "Varieties according to attitude." The "essential aspect" of such variety is said to be "the gradient between stiff, formal, cold, impersonal on the one hand and relaxed, informal, warm, friendly on the other" (p. 7). Between these extremes, there is a "common core"; the resultant classification is diagrammed as follows: "(rigid~) FORMAL~(neutral)~INFORMAL (~familiar)" (ibid.).

In studying the styles of Frost, Stevens, and Moore, I have found it important to distinguish "high" or ceremonial formality from formality in the broad sense. High formal language is solemn in tone; it works by conferring the dignity its idiom has inherited from the past on the voice of authority in the present. Some poets use high formal language consistently, as Wallace Stevens does; some use it sporadically, as Robert Frost and Marianne Moore do.

15. The first English grammar to make systematic use of "test frames" was Charles Carpenter Fries's *The Structure of English* (New York, 1952). The frames were defined by Fries as "minimum free [i.e., grammatically independent] utterances" containing "significant positions" into which a number of words could be fitted "without a change of the structural meaning" (p. 74). The first such utterance devised by Fries was "The concert was good" ("Frame A"); words that could be substituted, as specified above, for *concert* were called "Class 1" words (pp. 75–79). These, of course, correspond in general to "nouns" in traditional grammatical terminology, or, in more recent position-based terminology, to "nominals." A brief and clear account of the parts of speech in English, distinguishing inflection-based from position-based methods of definition, may be found in James Sledd, *A Short Introduction to English Grammar* (Chicago, 1959), chap. 2.

16. It is perhaps worth remarking that the fact that *laughter* happens to rhyme with *after* has led to some memorable (as well as many nonmemorable) instances of its use in poetry; one thinks, among others, of

> What is love? 'Tis not hereafter;
> Present mirth hath present laughter;

and

> April, April,
> Laugh thy girlish laughter;
> Then, the moment after,
> Weep thy girlish tears.

17. See *SOED*, s.v. -*er*[5], *suffix*, and -*le*, *suffix*, 3. Frequentative verbs in -*er* and -*le* are discussed in Otto Jespersen et al., *A Modern English Grammar on Historical Principles*, Part VI, *Morphology* (London, 1946), secs. 15.3₁ ₂ and 22.5₄, respectively, and in Marchand (n.5 above), secs. 4.29 and 4.59.1–6, respectively (cf. Smithers, n.5 above, p. 84).

18. Frequentatives in -*er* are called by Jespersen "Echo-Verbs." Concerning frequentatives in -*le*, Jespersen states that "new formations of a more or less echoic character are frequent

in all periods [after Old English]," that many such verbs may be "arbitrary echoic formations" rather than derivatives formed by adding suffixes to stems, and that "the echoic character of the suffix is seen *i.a.* in its occurrence in reduplicative forms such as . . . *tittle-tattle.*" According to Marchand, the frequentative suffix *-er* "is suggestive of reiteration, continuation, or the like . . . [Frequentatives] in *-er* are compounds of several symbolic elements one of which is final *-er*"; verbs in *-le,* like those in *-er,* "should more correctly be called compounds of several symbolic elements" than derivatives of existing stems.

19. Iteratives are discussed and classified by Jespersen in chap. 10 of *A Modern English Grammar,* Part VI, under the general heading "Reduplicative Compounds" (see also Marchand, sec. 2.16, "Reduplicative Compounds," and chap. 8, "Ablaut and Rime Combinations").

20. All these iteratives may be found in *SOED,* with the exception of *he-he (hee-hee),* which seems to be an Americanism (see *Webster's 2d* and *Webster's 3d*). More recent than *yuk-yuk* in American English is the extended iterative *har-de-har-har,* used colloquially as a sarcastic imitation of a hearty laugh, with exaggerated, drawling emphasis. This formation is not recorded in any dictionaries I have seen.

21. Jespersen introduces his discussion of iteratives by noting that "repetition of the same syllable . . . comes natural to all human beings and is found very often in all languages as a means of strengthening an utterance." Concerning the shift from short *i* to short *a* or short *o* in iteratives exhibiting vowel gradation, he says, "You begin with what is light and indicates littleness and nearness and end with the opposite . . . . The alternation often serves to express the sound produced by a movement to and fro . . . hence vacillation, indecision, etc., and contemptible things in general." For a fuller exposition of Jespersen's views, see his *Language,* pp. 402 ff. According to Marchand, iteratives of the reduplicative subtype in English are almost all "expressive sound words"; he describes rhyming iteratives as "essentially non-serious" in character; those having vowel gradation have an underlying "symbolism . . . of polarity which may assume various semantic aspects." Smithers, on pp. 82–84, discusses iteratives having "apophony" (i.e., vowel gradation) and rhyme as sound-symbolically motivated, and distinguishes "gradation" in this sense from the ancient gradation-patterns having grammatical significance which are represented in English, e.g., in forms of strong verbs like *drink, drank, drunk.* Ullmann discusses iterative formations as an aspect of sound symbolism (*Semantics,* pp. 84–85; cf. the iteratives cited from non–Indo-European languages by Smithers, pp. 83–84, and Morris Swadesh, *The Origin and Diversification of Language* [Chicago, 1971], pp. 144–45).

22. See *OED,* s.v. *guffaw* sb. and v.; evidence for a connection between *guffaw* and a group of sound-symbolic words including *gab* (in the archaic sense "to speak mockingly"), *gaff* "nonsense," and *guff* "empty talk" is presented in Smithers, pp. 104, 111.

23. There is also a considerable body of "scenic" frequentatives, mainly visual and auditory (*sparkle, glimmer, twitter, babble*), to which these tonal restrictions obviously do not apply and which have had wide currency in the traditional language of poetic description. Cf. from Wordsworth's "The Green Linnet,"

> Amid yon tuft of hazel trees,
> That *twinkle* to the gusty breeze,
> Behold him perched in ecstasies,
>   Yet seeming still to *hover;*
> There! where the *flutter* of his wings
> Upon his back and body flings
> Shadows and sunny *glimmerings*
>   That cover him all over.

24. As a counterinstance to the principle involved here, one may think of the reiterated "burr, burr, burr" (for which see *SOED,* s.v. *burr* sb.⁶) of Wordsworth's Idiot Boy. But this poem, though no doubt serious in import, is scarcely solemn in tone.

25. I am indebted for information on this point to Professor Robert K. Adair. The sentence in *Finnegans Wake* from which the word was taken is "Three quarks for Muster Mark"; it presumably suggested itself to Gell-Mann partly because the particle as originally conceived had three varieties. There is further evidence of the trend toward simplicity in the terminology of atomic physics in the recent classification of quarks as having or lacking "charm," "color," and "strangeness."

26. Honeycomb in biblical imagery stands not only for sweetness and pleasure, but, by virtue of its association with the return of the resurrected Christ to the disciples, for the confirmation of faith (Luke 24:42–43: "And they gave him a piece of a broiled fish, and of an honeycomb. And he took it, and did eat before them").

27. Cf. Charles C. Butterworth, *The Literary Lineage of the King James Bible, 1340–1611* (Philadelphia, 1941), esp. chap. 12. Butterworth states that "between 1500 and 1540 the normal manner of speech and writing was more like the English of the Bible than at any other time" (p. 12). In assessing the contributions to the Authorized or King James Version of the previous translations, he concludes that "the chief place of honor is undoubtedly Tyndale's [d. 1536]. It was he who gave to our biblical speech its organic features, shaping it out of the language of his time" (p. 233). The translators of the King James Bible were explicitly instructed to use the wording of the Bishops' Bible (1568) "as little altered as the Truth of the original will permit"; certain earlier versions, including those of Tyndale (1525–34) and Coverdale (1535), were to be followed "when they agree[d] better with the text" (Butterworth, pp. 227–28). The use of simple rather than learned and ornate language in rendering the Bible into English from Old English times on accords with the aim of educating the common man, whether through reading aloud or making a printed text available. Cf. the well-known story told of Tyndale in John Foxe's Book of Martyrs: "Master Tyndall happened to be in the company of a learned man and ... disputing with him ... said: 'If God spare my life, ere many years I will cause a boy that driveth the plough shall know more of the Scripture than thou dost'" (quoted in F. F. Bruce, *The English Bible: A History of Translations from the Earliest English Versions to the New English Bible,* rev. ed. [New York, 1970], p. 29).

28. Another group of archaisms of native origin in English is specifically poetic: *e'er* and *ne'er, o'er, e'en, 'gainst, 'mid,* and the like. These were originally reduced forms belonging to the spoken language, directly comparable with *p'raps* for *perhaps, can't* for *cannot, 'pears* for *appears,* and the like, in current use. They became obsolete in speech but were retained in poetry as metrical variants, and as a result migrated eventually from the distinctively colloquial to the distinctively formal end of the spectrum of diction.

29. For the sake of clarity, I have confined my examples to words of native (Germanic) origin. The vocabulary of biblical and poetic archaisms in modern English does in fact include a number of Romance words (e.g., *cry* "call out," *pass* in *come to pass* "happen," *perish* "die," *render* "give," *suffer* "allow," and *travail* "suffering") and some Latinate words as well (e.g., *exceeding* "very," *multitude* "crowd," and *contemn* "despise").

30. New dictionaries regularly include new sound-symbolic words that have become established at the colloquial level. The following are in *Webster's 3d* but not in *Webster's 2d: beep* "sound from a horn," *blah* "dull and unattractive," *blip* "a short crisp sound," *boo-boo* "a foolish ... error," *clobber* "to pound mercilessly," *conk* "to break down," *dribs and drabs* "miserably small ... amounts," *goop* "sticky substance," *guck* "something unpleasant ... oozy sloppy dirt," *gunk* "greasy matter," *hassle* "heated argument," *icky* "sticky," *plonk* "a socially awkward ... person," *tizzy* "excited ... state of mind,"

yak "voluble talk," *yak* "laugh," *yuk,* interjection used reduplicatively to express amusement or derision. In *WCD8* we find the following, which are not in *Webster's 3d: barf* "vomit," *chugalug* "to drink a whole container without pause," *glitch* "malfunction, . . . a minor technical problem," *glop* "messy mass," *zap,* interjection used to indicate a sudden . . . occurrence, *zap* "overwhelm," *zilch* "zero." *The Barnhart Dictionary of New English since 1963,* ed. Clarence L. Barnhart et al. (New York, 1973) and *6000 Words: A Supplement to Webster's Third New International Dictionary* (Springfield, Mass., 1976) list *klutz* "a clumsy, awkward person," which is in none of the above; *6000 Words* also lists the derivative *klutzy.* Other sound-symbolic words which I have heard in talk or seen in print but which, so far as I am aware, have not yet attained the status of dictionary entry, are *boing* "resonant vibration," *boing-boing,* reduplicative use of the above, *dork* "stupid or comatose person," *gop* "gooey mess," *goppy/gopsy* "gooey, messy," *gork,* same as *dork,* above, *nerd* "stupid person," *snarf* "gobble up," and *swack,* in phrase *swacked out* "knocked out, overcome with amazement." By the time this is published, there will be others.

CHAPTER FOUR

1. The relation of Stevens's language and thought to traditional Christianity is fully discussed in Adalaide K. Morris, *Wallace Stevens: Imagination and Faith* (see esp. chap. 1, "Lineage and Language," pp. 9–44). In Morris's words, "The imagination's explication of reality [in Stevens] . . . often assumes shapes traditionally given to the expression of religious piety . . . . The major biblical forms that Stevens uses in his poetry are the parable, the proverb, the prayer, the hymn, and the psalm" (pp. 17–18); "Stevens' poetry, like his prose, consciously incorporates biblical wording and echo" (p. 41).

2. Of the eleven 100-word sequences contained in "Credences of Summer," nine have percentiles of 20 or over, the highest being 34 percent. The average for the eleven sequences is about 23.5 percent. For complete statistics and lists of Romance and Latinate words, see Appendix A.

3. This is not to say that words belonging to the common level of diction are lacking in Stevens's language; on the contrary, they predominate numerically over their more elevated brethren. The point is that the latter are present in sufficient numbers, along with the stylistically neutral common words, to be sensed as markers of a pervasive formality of style. The comparative statistics yielded by spot checks of Stevens and Robert Frost are revealing. For example, Stevens uses *desire* (n. and v.) 84 times and *want* (n. and v.) 47; there are 6 occurrences of *desire* in Frost vs. 145 of *want.* Stevens uses *distances(s)/distant/distantly* a total of 50 times and *far* 30; there are 11 occurrences of *distance/distant* in Frost (none of *distances/distantly*) and 105 of *far.* And Stevens uses *edifice* 5 times and *buildings(s)* 12, while Frost uses *building* once and *edifice* not at all. (These data are taken from Thomas F. Walsh, *Concordance to the Poetry of Wallace Stevens* [University Park, Pa., 1963], and Edward C. Lathem, *A Concordance to the Poetry of Robert Frost* [New York, 1971].)

4. The word *canto* also suggests *The Divine Comedy* and thus indirectly reinforces the Christian allusiveness of the opening line. But the wording of that line, "In the first canto of the final canticle," has additional implications. The word *canto* ("song") resembles the word *canton* ("division") (to which, however, it is not related, having descended from a different Latin source), and successive cantos are successive "divisions" of a narrative poem. That Stevens was conscious of an affinity of sound and meaning between the two is shown by the opening line, "I sang a canto in a canton," of "Country Words." This poem dramatizes a dissatisfied and "rebellious" state of mind in which the speaker desires a unifying revelation. In "The Hand as a Being," Stevens reverses the relationship between *canto* and *canticle,* using the latter word, which is actually the diminutive of the former, to signify the larger whole.

5. The variegated and innovative character of Stevens's vocabulary can be shown in capsule form by a comparison of Stevens's words for laughing and crying with Frost's. Going from the formal to the colloquial end of the spectrum, we find that Stevens has *cachinnation, hilarious* (in its literary sense), *ridicule, laugh, laughing, laughter, funny, guffaw, chuckle,* and *titter; lament, lamentable, lamenting, weep, weeping, tears, cry, crying, sob,* and *blubber.* Frost has *merry* (only in the phrase "merry Christmas"), *mirth, laugh, laughter, laughing, laughingly, laughter,* and *funny; lament, weep, weeping, tears, teardrops, cry,* and *crying.* In addition, Stevens adapts the French word *ricanerie* "mocking laugh" as *ricanery* (p. 253), uses the French *pleure* ("weeps," p. 186), and makes an iterative *chu-chot-chu* out of the French *chuchoter* ("whisper"), itself a sound-symbolic word, to signify the rasping noise made by the breath in sobbing (p. 253).

6. As is to be expected, sound-symbolic words of a purely colloquial sort are absent from Stevens's vocabulary, though his altered forms are occasionally reminiscent of more ordinary ones. Thus he uses *belch* (p. 29) but not *burp, blob* (p. 197) but not *gob, dizzle-dazzle* (p. 530) but not *razzle-dazzle, fitful-fangled* (p. 455) and *fire-fangled* (*O.P.,* p. 118) but not *newfangled, slop* (p. 209) but not *slurp, whimper* (p. 477) but not *sniffle.* And Bonnie and Josie, dancing around a stump in Oklahoma in "Life Is Motion," shout "Ohoyaho, / Ohoo," not "Yippee-i-ay." In this last example, we should note the phonetic similarities between outcry and place name as symptomatic, in a poem by Stevens, of a vital union between spirit and world. But the anticolloquial strangeness of the interjection is important in itself; it makes more striking and removes from the realm of mundane circumstance an action which is not to be conceived of in realistic terms.

7. Harold Bloom says of Stevens that he "is uniquely the twentieth century poet of that solitary and inward glory we can none of us share with others. . . . He celebrates an apprehension that has no social aspect whatsoever and that indeed appears resistant to any psychological reductions we might apply" ("Wallace Stevens: The Poems of Our Climate," *Prose* 8 [1974]: 12–13).

8. In an illuminating article on "Wallace Stevens' Later Poetry" (*ELH* 25 [1958]: 137–54), Frank Doggett speaks of "assertions of resemblance which appear to be statements of equalization. . . . series of modifications which seem to be reconsiderations . . . . In apposition the poet seems to deliberate about his original concept. He appears to reconsider it by seeking an equivalent in another and another version, continuously altered yet presented as though it were the same" (pp. 145–46). The last remark in particular expresses an insight of basic importance for Stevens's poetry as a whole.

9. To these as to other aspects of the longer poems, Helen H. Vendler's *On Extended Wings* will be found an indispensable guide, though hers is a more somber figuration of Stevens than that presented here.

10. To see Stevens's poetry as essentially a record of affirmation and sustained power is to take issue with what Harold Bloom has called "all merely canonical misreading that continues to give us Stevens as an ironist, as a wry celebrant of a diminished version of Romantic or Transcendental selfhood." For Bloom, "Stevens is the authentic twentieth-century poet of the Sublime . . . . Perhaps no other modern poet was as unlikely to revindicate the Sublime as Stevens was, and yet the actual burden of his major poetry is the movement both towards a possible wisdom and towards a possible ecstasy, between which Stevens refuses to choose, though Yeats had insisted that an individual could hope to move only towards one or the other" ("Wallace Stevens: The Transcendental Strain" in *Poetry and Repression* [New Haven, 1976], p. 282).

CHAPTER FIVE

1. See the reproduction on p. 94. I have cheated somewhat in deleting the opening

"Why," an idiom never used in Moore's poems, and part of the first paragraph, including some trite phraseology ("dainty striped wimple, bright silk kerchief") and patently fake enthusiasm ("There's another, ... And another! This must be weeks from England. But no ... ").

2. That Moore's poetic language resembles prose is a commonplace of the published criticism, and was recognized from the first. An adverse review of Moore's first collection, *Poems* (London: Egoist Press, 1921) accused her of writing "as a matter of fact, a clumsy prose.... She seems, indeed, entirely ignorant of the first poetic truth—that form and expression must harmonize and help each other" (*Times Literary Supplement,* 21 July 1921, p. 471). T. S. Eliot, an important early admirer, wrote in his Introduction to *Selected Poems* (New York, 1935), "She seems to have saturated her mind in the perfections of prose, in its precision rather than its purple" (see *Marianne Moore: A Collection of Critical Essays,* ed. Charles Tomlinson [Englewood Cliffs, N.J., 1969], p. 62). Most of Moore's later critics have found occasion to make the same point. Jean Garrigue says of Moore's "voice" that, "bringing a new diction to another kind of 'subject matter,' it employed the cadences of prose in a rhythm based on speech" (*Marianne Moore* [Minneapolis, 1965], p. 8). George Nitchie cites "To Military Progress" and "New York" as examples of traditional metrical form and free verse, respectively, but adds that "more frequent and more characteristic are those [poems] written in the peculiar prosody of "Bird-Witted" and "The Monkeys," with stanzas based on syllable count and inconspicuous rhyme working against a cadence that is essentially that of elegant and precise prose" (*Marianne Moore: An Introduction to the Poetry* [New York, 1969], p. 29). And Donald Hall, who finds in Moore's poems "the flavor of prose brought to spare perfection," quotes the opening of "Critics and Connoisseurs" and remarks "These lines might be found in an essay" (*Marianne Moore: The Cage and the Animal* [New York, 1970], p. 38).

3. In preparing this and certain other sections of my study of Moore's language, I have benefited greatly from Geoffrey N. Leech's comprehensive *English in Advertising* (London, 1966), to be referred to hereafter as "Leech."

4. "When the word 'advertising' is mentioned, most of us automatically think of what might be more accurately called 'commercial consumer advertising': advertising directed towards a mass audience with the aim of promoting sales of a commercial product or service.... Advertising differs from other types of loaded language (such as political journalism and religious oratory) in having a very precise material goal. Changing the mental disposition of the audience is only important in so far as it leads to the desired kind of behaviour—buying a particular kind of product" (Leech, pp. 25–26).

5. I suggest a pictorial analogue with the descriptive style of certain passages in Moore where the language is especially reminiscent of advertising on p. 112. For a brilliant and detailed "explication" of pictorial and verbal elements in an advertisement for Sunkist orange juice, see Leo Spitzer, "American Advertising Explained as Popular Art," in *Essays on English and American Literature,* ed. Anna Granville Hatcher (Princeton, 1962), pp. 248–77.

6. I take the term "disjunctive" from Leech, who describes the disjunctive mode as having "an important bearing on advertising language" (p. 90). As compared with "discursive grammar," "disjunctive grammar" is formally incomplete; "a sentence need not contain a finite predicator, and this in turn means that a single nominal group or a single adverbial group may be grammatically independent. Either of these groups may in turn consist of a single word" (p. 93).

7. Under the heading "Role Borrowing," Leech speaks of various "disguises" assumed by the advertisement, quoting a passage which "has all the appearance of a popular documentary" (p. 100); he goes on to say that "disguise in copywriting reaches its extreme

in the 'chameleon technique' whereby an advertisement is made to resemble, both in language and lay-out, a feature or article of the publication in which it appears" (p. 101).

8. These data are taken from *A Concordance to the Poems of Marianne Moore,* ed. Gary Lane (New York, 1972) and *Concordance to the Poetry of Wallace Stevens,* ed. Thomas F. Walsh (Cambridge, Mass., 1969).

9. Three that come to mind are "What Are Years?" and the less powerfully imagined "In Distrust of Merits" and " 'Keeping Their World Large'." All make use *passim,* of simple diction and biblical allusion, as in the following passage, in which only two words out of twenty-three, *crown* and *halo,* are of other than native origin:

> There is hate's crown beneath which all is
> death; there's love's without which none
> is king; the blessed deeds bless
> the halo.

> (p. 136)

But these poems do not approach the statistically low extreme for Romance-Latinate diction in English represented by the pastoral lyrics of Robert Frost. See the tabulations in Appendix A.

10. *Punctualize* is not in *Webster's 2nd, Webster's 3rd, WCD7, WCD8,* or *SOED. Officialize* is in *Webster's 2nd* and *3rd, OED,* and *SOED,* but is not in *WCD7* or *8,* nor is it in *The American Heritage Dictionary of the English Language* (1969).

11. My grammatical terminology is taken for the most part from *A Grammar of Contemporary English,* by Randolph Quirk, Sidney Greenbaum, Geoffrey Leech, and Jan Svartvik (New York, 1972), to be referred to as "Quirk et al." For the definition of "open class" and the distinction between "closed-system items" and "open-class items," see secs. 2.14–15. Sets of closed-system items "cannot normally be extended by the creation of additional members," whereas the open classes are "indefinitely extendable. New items are constantly being created and no one could make an inventory of all the nouns in English (for example) and be confident that it was complete." For the sake of clarity, I have identified the four open classes as "the nouns, the verbs, the adjectives, and the adverbs," but this is in fact too simple a description. Quirk et al. point out that "although they have deceptively specific labels, the parts of speech tend in fact to be rather heterogeneous. The adverb and the verb are perhaps especially mixed classes, each having small and fairly well-defined groups of closed-system items alongside the indefinitely large open-class items. So far as the verb is concerned, the closed-system subgroup is known by the well-established term 'auxiliary.' . . . With the adverb, one may draw the distinction broadly between those in *-ly* that correspond to adjectives . . . and those that do not" (sec. 2.15). Quirk et al. use the designation "lexical verbs" as an alternative to "open-class verbs"; see secs. 3.7, 3.41. Cf. the discussion of "Word Classes" in Dwight Bolinger, *Aspects of Language,* 2d ed. (New York, 1975), pp. 142–56 and table 6-2.

I differ from Quirk et al. in restricting the term "clause" to structures containing finite verbs. In their terminology, three types of "clauses" are identified: finite, non-finite (containing infinitives or participles), and verbless. See secs. 11.4–5, 11.7.

12. In his innovative and important study, *The Structure of English* (New York, 1952), Charles Carpenter Fries used "test frames" to identify four "functioning units" or parts of speech which he called Class 1, Class 2, Class 3, and Class 4 words, corresponding roughly but by no means precisely with the "nouns," "verbs," "adjectives," and "adverbs" of traditional grammar. The words that did not belong to these classes he called "function words" (see pp. 65–86). Later grammarians kept the designation "function word" and used "lexical word" or "content word" for the four major parts of speech. See the definition of "Function Word" in the Glossary appended to *The Structure of American English* by W. Nelson Francis (New York, 1958), p. 592; for the distinction between function words and

lexical words, see p. 231. See also James Sledd, *A Short Introduction to English Grammar* (Chicago, 1959), p. 213, and the Summary of definitional criteria on pp. 110–11. For "content words," see Bolinger, *Aspects of Language,* p. 121. Charles Hockett, in *A Course in Modern Linguistics* (New York, 1958), distinguishes between "functors" (which include not only "function words" but inflectional endings) and "contentives." The latter, as he puts it, "*do* purport to deal with the world around us" (pp. 263–65).

13. Bolinger, discussing "the general question of the interdependence of thought and language," pays tribute to the writings of the American linguist Benjamin Lee Whorf, who turned his attention to "the framework of whole languages. He was not the first to take this step—Fritz Mauthner in 1902 declared that 'if Aristotle had spoken Chinese or Dakota, his logic and his categories would have been different.' Others, including Wilhelm von Humboldt and Whorf's own teacher, Edward Sapir, held similar opinions. But Whorf was the most successful in dramatizing it . . . . Instead of a perfectly flexible rubber mask that shapes itself to reality, each language is somewhat like a Greek mask, with its own built-in scowl or grin" (*Aspects of Language,* pp. 240–41; see the eighth chapter, "Mind in the Grip of Language," for further historical and theoretical discussion). Whorf's best-known essay is probably "The Relation of Habitual Thought and Behavior to Language" (*Language, Thought, and Reality; Selected Writings of Benjamin Lee Whorf,* ed. John B. Carroll [Cambridge, Mass., 1956], pp. 134–59).

14. As Bolinger puts it, "Nouns are thing-like, verbs are event-like, adjectives are quality-like . . . . Our earliest experiences are grouped around actions and things, and the corresponding classes of verbs and nouns are found in all the languages of the world. We get a sense of detachable qualities as soon as we can see differences playing on samenesses—at least as early as our games of marking and coloring. This is a physiological peg for adjectives" (*Aspects of Language,* p. 149).

15. Cf. the "three ranks" identified in the grammatical interrelationships of words by Otto Jespersen. In *A Modern English Grammar,* vol. 2 (Heidelberg, 1914), sec. 1.21, he used the terms "principal," "adjunct," and "subjunct," shifting to the alternative designations "primary," "secondary," and "tertiary" in *Essentials of English Grammar* (New York, 1933), sec. 8.1$_1$. "If we compare the two expressions *this furiously barking dog* and *this dog barks furiously,* it is easy to see that while *dog* is primary, *this* secondary, and *furiously* tertiary in both, the verb *bark* is found in two different forms, *barking* and *barks;* but in both forms it must be said to be subordinated to *dog* and superior in rank to *furiously;* thus both *barking* and *barks* are here secondaries" (*Essentials,* 8.1$_3$). In other words, the adverb *furiously* presupposes either the finite verb *barks* or the verbal adjective *barking,* while either *barks* or *barking* presupposes the noun *dog.* Jespersen distinguishes between "ranks" and "classes" (parts of speech), but observes that nouns are habitually primary, adjectives secondary, and adverbs tertiary (8.1$_2$).

16. Fries undertook in *The Structure of English* to "examine anew the functioning units" of the sentence (p. 66). "Unfortunately we cannot use as the starting point of our examination the traditional definitions of the parts of speech. What is a 'noun,' for example? The usual definition is that 'a noun is the name of a person, place, or thing.' But *blue* is the 'name' of a color, as is *yellow* or *red,* and yet, in the expressions *a blue tie, a yellow rose, a red dress* we do not call *blue* and *yellow* and *red* 'nouns.' . . . *Run* is the 'name' of an action, as is *jump* or *arrive. Up* is the 'name' of a direction, as is *down* or *across.* [Yet these words] . . . are not called nouns in such expressions as 'We *ran* home,' 'They were looking *up* into the sky,' 'The acid made the fiber *red*'" (p. 67). Cf. Sledd, *A Short Introduction to English Grammar:* "The traditional definitions plainly do not enable us to classify our words as belonging to one part of speech rather than another. For one thing, definitions like that of the noun are in terms of meaning, while others, like that of the pronoun, are in terms of function or use.

Nouns and verbs are defined by what they mean, but the other parts of speech ... are defined by what they do'' (p. 61). Cf. also the section of "Word Classes" in Bolinger, *Aspects of Language,* pp. 142–56.

For Fries's use of "test frames" to determine word classes, see chap. 3, n.15.

17. In *Eras and Modes in English Poetry* (Berkeley, 1957), Josephine Miles analyzed samples of the works of a series of English poets from Langland to Auden in terms of distinctions among types of sentence structure. "The first or phrasal type employs an abundance of adjectives and nouns, in heavy modifications and compounding of subjects, in a variety of phrasal constructions, including verbs turned to participles . . . . The second or clausal type emphasizes compound or serial predicates, subordinate verbs in relative and adverbial clauses, action, and rational subordination . . . . Theoretically, there might be a third type between these two: not merely a scale of degrees between extremes, but a mode of statement characterized by a balance between clausal and phrasal elements. And actually, . . . we find a kind of poetry in which sentence structure is balanced between the two" (pp. 2–3). Miles's interests are in large part diachronic; within each century, from 1500 to 1900, she finds shifts in the predominant sentence type, beginning with one of the two extreme types and ending with the balanced type (p. 3). The poetry of Swinburne, Bridges, Thompson, Phillips, and Hopkins, which exemplifies the balanced mode, is followed in the twentieth century by "the clausal revival of the Donne tradition, in Housman, Hardy, Cummings, Frost, Auden" (p. 4).

Tables at the end of Miles's book (pp. 218–30) give the numbers of adjectives, nouns, and verbs found in an average ten lines in the works of each poet. "A proportion of one adjective and one verb per line indicates a balanced structure; more adjectives than verbs per line indicate a dominantly phrasal structure; more verbs than adjectives, a dominantly clausal structure" (p. 215). The proportions for Frost, Stevens, and Moore are 8-15-11 (clausal), 9-18-9 (balanced), and 9-17-6 (phrasal), respectively. These findings correspond to mine in that the proportion of verbs in Moore is the lowest of the three. I have not counted adjectives or nouns, but I have noted that Stevens's style is heavily qualitative and Moore's heavily informative, while Frost's is neither. It is thus not surprising that both Stevens and Moore use more adjectives than Frost. It might be said that in Stevens the heavy use of qualitative terms is "balanced" by the strongly dynamic tendency of his syntax; the former characteristic makes for high proportions of adjectives, the latter for high proportions of verbs.

18. Roger Brown, *A First Language: The Early Stages* (Cambridge, Mass., 1973), p. 75. Brown describes the aim of the book, which is the first of two projected volumes, as follows: "I want to attempt . . . a kind of overview, or general plan, of the design of English with respect to sentence construction and the meanings carried by constructions. This overview is in five parts ordered in what I believe to be the order of development in children of the knowledge in question and corresponding to Stages I through V" ("An Unbuttoned Introduction," p. 3). In the section entitled "Stage I. Semantic Roles and Grammatical Relations" (pp. 63–245), Brown analyzes the sentences spoken by children at "Stage I . . . when multi-word utterances begin" (p. 58). The explicit and implicit constituents of the actual sentences recorded as data for the study are described in Table 28 (p. 205) in relation to a five-part paradigm "agent-action-dative-object-locative." "Mommy fix," for example, is analyzed as a three-part sentence in which "agent" and "action" are expressed, but "object" is omitted. It seems significant that "action" (expressed by a finite verb element) is omitted in only two of the twelve recorded combinations (pp. 204–5).

As Brown points out, the earliest speech of the child is not only "simple," it is "telegraphic." Children "generally do not use prepositions, conjunctions, articles, or auxiliary verbs," words Brown, following Hockett, distinguishes as "functors" (roughly equivalent to closed-system items) from the "contentives" (open-class items) (pp. 74–75). My examples of "simple sentences," in that they include closed-system items, are thus childlike in structure only; they are not realistic imitations of the child's earliest speech.

19. These generalizations are supported by the findings of A. Busemann, though Busemann's syntactic investigations were not limited to the finite verb element, nor did they bear on the proportion of any one of the grammatical open classes to the total number of words in a passage. As described by Friederike Antosch, the method developed by Busemann was designed to determine "the exact relation of the 'active' and 'qualitative' aspects of a literary text. Busemann established a formula

$$\frac{\text{Active Statements}}{\text{Qualitative Statements}}$$

and called it the *Aktionsquotient*. Active statements are statements on activities and are expressed in words that 'imply action'; qualitative statements are statements expressing properties . . . . V. Neubauer and A. Schlismann . . . considerably simplified the method by restricting 'active statements' to verbs and 'qualitative statements' to adjectives and adjective-modifiers. Thus the formula for the ratio was altered to a simplified form:

$$\text{Verb-Adjective Ratio (VAR)} = \frac{\text{Number of Verbs}}{\text{Number of Adjectives}} .$$

All verbal forms (with the exception of the auxiliary verbs *haben, sein,* and *werden*) are counted as verbs" ("The Diagnosis of Literary Style with the Verb-Adjective Ratio," *Statistics and Style,* ed. Lubomír Dolezel and Richard W. Bailey [New York, 1969], p. 57). According to Antosch, "Busemann found the VAR is higher in the spoken language. He attributes this result to the slower speed of writing as compared to the speed of speech" (ibid.).

David P. Boder, using Busemann's work as a starting point, examined a number of different kinds of texts in English to determine what he called the "Avq." or "Adjective-Verb Quotient" in each ("The Adjective-Verb Quotient: A Contribution to the Psychology of Language," *Psychological Record* 3 [1940]: 310–43). "The Avq. . . . designates the number of attributive adjectives *per hundred verbs* in a given text, e.g., an Avq. of 15 means that the number of adjectives in the text amounts to 15% *of the number of verbs*" (p. 317). Of the thirteen kinds of text examined by Boder, advertisements had the second highest Avq. (the highest of all was found in Ph.D. theses). "Private letters" by "inexperienced writers" ranked eleventh; those by "experienced writers" ranked seventh (see his table I, p. 318). Boder did not tabulate samples of taped conversation. The lowest Avqs. he found (not included in table I) occurred in scenes from plays; their distribution indicated that such quotients were "not the property of separate roles but of the dialogue as a whole" (pp. 318–20).

Joseph A. DeVito carried out comparative analyses of the proportions of the four major parts of speech in written and spoken language dealing with the same subject matter, using as his materials articles by ten professors of speech and interviews with them discussing these same articles, for a total of 5,000 written and 5,000 spoken words ("A Linguistic Analysis of Spoken and Written Language," *Central States Speech Journal* 18 no. 2 [1967]: 81–85). Translated into percentiles, his table I (p. 83) indicates that the spoken passages contained an average of 13.7 percent finite verb elements, whereas the average for the written passages was 11.2 percent. These figures should be compared with those I cite on p. 95; see also n.25 below.

Rudolf Flesch has worked with the proportions of the parts of speech as one measure of "readability" or "level of abstraction" ("Measuring the Level of Abstraction," *Journal of Applied Psychology* 34 [1950]: 384–90). He mentions Boder's article, among others, as bearing out the generally accepted notion that "an abstract style contains relatively more descriptive adjectives, indefinite pronouns, and subordinating conjunctions, while a concrete style contains relatively more proper nouns, limiting adjectives, finite verbs, personal pronouns, and coordinating conjunctions" (p. 384).

Rulon Wells, in "Nominal and Verbal Style" (*Style in Language*, ed. Thomas A. Sebeok [Cambridge, 1960], pp. 213–20), remarks on "the ... fact that nominality is contrary to conversational style" (p. 218).

20. See n.34, below.

21. In particular, we should note the anti-colloquial effect of such rhetorical repetition of finite verbs as occurs in Stevens's "Martial Cadenza":

<blockquote>
Only this evening I saw it again,
At the beginning of winter, and I walked and talked
Again, and lived and was again, and breathed again
And moved again and flashed again, time flashed again.
</blockquote>

More in keeping with the spoken idiom are the opening lines of Frost's "Out, Out—":

<blockquote>
The buzz saw snarled and rattled in the yard
And made dust and dropped stove-length sticks of wood,
</blockquote>

and the echo later in the poem:

<blockquote>
And the saw snarled and rattled, snarled and rattled,
As it ran light, or had to bear a load.
</blockquote>

22. The passages of taped conversation were taken from Edward C. Carterette and Margaret Hubbard Jones, *Informal Speech* (Berkeley, 1974). Carterette and Jones were interested chiefly in the phonology of speech; their method was to bring five participants together and instruct them to make conversation as if they had met at a party. Fifty 100-word passages were tabulated, some taken from long single speeches, some from rapid conversational interchange. (I omitted *uh* and *um*, as being noises rather than words, though I counted bona fide interjections such as *oh*. I also omitted a number of inadvertent reiterations or dittologies, as extraneous to grammatical structure.)

The first 1,000 words of five feature articles were tabulated; I give full titles, short titles, and the location of the relevant reference in Moore:

Frank Davis, "A Page for Collectors: The Chinese Dragon," *Illustrated London News* 177 (1930): 346 (Davis). Cited by Moore in Notes to "The Plumet Basilisk," p. 264.

Robert T. Hatt, "Pangolins," *Natural History* 34 (1934): 725–32 (Hatt). Cited by Moore, with erroneous date 1935, in Notes to "The Pangolin," p. 281.

Berthold Laufer, "Ostrich Egg-Shell Cups from Mesopotamia: The Ostrich in Ancient Times," *Open Court* 40 (1926): 257–68 (Laufer). Cited by Moore in Notes to "He 'Digesteth Harde Yron,'" p. 277.

W. P. Pycraft, "The World of Science: The Frilled Lizard," *Illustrated London News* 180 (1932): 210 (Pycraft). Cited by Moore (as "The Malay Dragon and the 'Basilisks'") in Notes to "The Plumet Basilisk," p. 265.

John J. Teal, Jr., "Golden Fleece of the Arctic," *Atlantic Monthly* 201 (March 1958): 76–81 (Teal). Cited by Moore in the headnote to "The Arctic Ox (or Goat)," p. 193.

The first 1,000 words of five scientific articles were tabulated:

Gwendolyn T. Brock, "The Morphology of the Ostrich Condocranium," *Proceedings of the Zoological Society of London* 107B (1937): 225–43.

E. Horne Craigie, "The Cerebral Cortex of the Ostrich (Struthio)," *Journal of Comparative Neurology* 64 (1936): 389–411.

G. C. Robson, "Notes on the Cephalopoda," *Annals and Magazine of Natural History*, ser. X, 6 (1930): 544–47.

Harold L. Weatherford, "Some Observations on the Tusks of an Indian Elephant—The Innervation of the Pulp," *Anatomical Record* 76 (1940): 81–93.

George B. Wislocki, "Note on the Hypophysis of an Adult Indian Elephant," *Anatomical Record* 74 (1939): 321–28.

23. In selecting the poems by Moore to be analyzed for Romance-Latinate percentiles and f.v.e. counts, I did not look for passages containing a minimum number of verbs. Had I done so, I might have chosen "Those Various Scalpels," the first 200 words of which contain a total of two f.v.e.'s, one in each 100. But Moore chose to write the poem in the form of a catalog. This fact in itself largely rules out the use of finite verbs, so that the f.v.e. counts do not tell us anything about Moore's language in passages of conventional description.

24. The fact that Frost's f.v.e. counts are considerably lower than those found in samples of tape-recorded conversation, differing from Stevens's scarcely at all (Frost's average is in fact the lower of the two, though not by much), ought not to pass without remark. Clearly, the relationship between f.v.e. counts and Romance-Latinate percentiles in the two poets contradicts the negative correlation described earlier; that is, the correlation is exemplified in Stevens, but not in Frost. The reason, which I can do no more than touch on here, is that despite the fact that Frost was obsessed by change and wrote about real events in a down-to-earth manner, his syntax is heavily stative. For him the assertion of human values in labor was an attempt to create a temporary stasis in a world of process and decay. Poetry, as "a momentary stay against confusion," is part of this effort, and grammatical stativeness works in Frost to imply an unchanging validity in description or aphorism. In Stevens, change itself is the greatest value. His syntax is more dynamic than we expect elaborate syntax to be (note the f.v.e. counts in "The Idea of Order at Key West," tabulated in Appendix A), just as Frost's is more stative than its simplicity would seem to permit.

25. The scope of my statistical tabulations is too small to enable me to claim anything more than tentative results. However, I believe that the average of about 9 percent f.v.e.'s I have found in feature article prose would not be greatly modified if a much larger amount of similar material were analyzed. Nor do I believe that the high average of 16.4 percent I found in taped conversations will be exceeded in other genres, at least other nonliterary genres. I should be interested to know if the average f.v.e. count in the language of another poet or poets proved to be lower than the 8.1 percent I have found in Moore.

Large-scale and complete investigations of the proportions of all the parts of speech, minor as well as major, have now been made feasible by computer programs in which the stored words of a text are labeled according to various systems of grammatical classification. No computer can analyze the grammar of a passage fully without human assistance, but the EYEBALL system designed by Professor Donald Ross, Jr., has advanced further toward that goal than the layman might think possible. See Donald Ross, Jr., and Robert H. Rasche, "EYEBALL: A Computer Program for Description of Style," *Computers and the Humanities* 6 (1972): 213–21; Donald Ross, "Beyond the Concordance: Algorithms for the Description of English Clauses and Phrases," in *The Computer and Literary Studies* (Edinburgh, 1973), pp. 85–99; and "Description of EYEBALL" (rev. ed., 1976), available from Professor Ross, Department of English, University of Minnesota at Minneapolis.

Two investigations by Ross of the language of literary texts using the EYEBALL program are "An EYEBALL View of Blake's *Songs of Innocence and of Experience*," *Computers in the Humanities*, ed. J. Lawrence Mitchell (Edinburgh, 1974), pp. 94–108, and "Dialogue and Narration in Joyce's *Ulysses*," coauthored with Mary Beth Pringle, presented at the Third International Conference on Computers and the Humanities, Windsor, Ontario, August 1977. I am indebted to Professor Ross, in a personal communication, for giving me a more detailed breakdown of his statistics on Blake's songs: the average percent of finite verbs per poem in Blake's *Songs of Innocence* is 15; the average for the *Songs of Experience* is 13.5 These findings are in accord with my theory that simple, biblically allusive language is syntactically simple, hence "high" in f.v.e. counts, as well.

26. See Quirk et al., sec. 2.6, where the distinction is introduced with reference to verbs, and sec. 2.16, where it is applied to all four of the open classes. See also the fuller discussion of stative and dynamic verbs in secs. 3.40–41, and the discussion of stative and dynamic adjectives in sec. 5.38. Bolinger, pp. 277–78, uses the terms " 'state' verbs" and " 'process' verbs" with the same meaning. Cf. Brown, *A First Language,* pp. 327–28.

27. For the use of the simple present tense in "timeless statements," see Quirk et al., sec. 3.25.

28. Quirk et al. point out that "although it is convenient to speak of 'dynamic' and 'stative' verbs, it . . . would be more accurate to speak of 'dynamic' and 'stative' uses of verbs" (sec. 3.41).

I am disregarding the use of the simple present with dynamic significance in colloquial and literary narrative, called the "instantaneous simple present" by Quirk et al., sec. 3.25 (2). Cf. the concluding section of Wallace Stevens's "The Bouquet," beginning

> A car drives up. A soldier, an officer,
> Steps out. He rings and knocks. The door is not locked.
> He enters the room and calls.

All the verbs in these lines, except *is,* are dynamic. The section as a whole contains 15 finite verbs in a total of 62 words, or about 25 percent.

29. See the diagram in Quirk et al., sec. 2.16, with regard to which it is said that "nouns can be characterized naturally as 'stative' in that they refer to entities that are regarded as stable, whether these are concrete (physical) . . . or abstract (of the mind). . . . At the opposite pole, verbs can be equally naturally characterized as 'dynamic': they are fitted (by their capacity to show tense and aspect, for example) to indicate action, activity and temporary or changing conditions." The diagram would seem to indicate that adjectives and adverbs are comparable to nouns and verbs, respectively, on the stative-dynamic scale. My own view is that adjectives and verbs are intrinsically more dynamic than nouns, and that adverbs are intrinsically more dynamic than verbs and adjectives, because adjectives and verbs are "secondary" and adverbs "tertiary" in the ontological hierarchy implied by the English parts-of-speech system (see pp. 90–91, and note 17 above).

Since the stative/dynamic distinction applies to lexical verbs only, the modal auxiliaries belong, strictly speaking, in neither category. However, in that they do not designate actions directly but qualify them in terms of necessity, possibility, obligation, and so on, the modals are clearly akin in significance to the stative verbs proper. The subjunctive mood, too, in that it presents action at one remove from actuality, is more "stative" than the indicative mood.

30. Leech notes that "the future auxiliary *will* . . . is one exception to the general infrequency of auxiliary verbs in advertising language. The other exception is the modal auxiliary *can.* The relevance of these items to advertising can be summed up in the words 'promise' and 'opportunity'" (p. 125).

31. Quirk et al. discuss "existential" sentences with *have* in sec. 14.31.

32. Discussing Moore's "The Fish," Kenner remarks that "the English sentence . . . has two uses for nouns, as doer and as thing done to, . . . and can cope with the odd noun used otherwise ('The dog *treed* the cat'), but loses mobility beneath such a rain of nouns as this poem pours through it" (Hugh Kenner, "Disliking It," *A Homemade World: The American Modernist Writers* [New York, 1975], p. 101). The reference to "losing mobility" is of interest with relation to the stative character of Moore's grammar.

33. " 'Like a Wave at the Curl' " is the title of a poem by Moore which appeared in *The New Yorker,* 29 Nov. 1969, after the publication of *The Complete Poems.*

34. As the concept of the grammatically "stative" and its dramatic implications seems made for Marianne Moore's poetry, the concept of the grammatically "dynamic" seems made for the poetry of Wallace Stevens. It is a fundamental tenet in Stevens that truth can never be fixed but must be sensed as perpetually in process: "A mountainous music always seemed / To be falling and to be passing away" (p. 179). If Moore converts action into pictures, Stevens converts pictures into action, as in "Study of Two Pears": "The yellow glistens. / It glistens with various yellows." Limitations of space forbid me to do more than touch on this topic, but one example of the significance of dynamic syntax in Stevens is the opening of "On the Road Home." Here, rejection of "the" truth (i.e., any definitive truth) is immediately followed by a new beginning, the emergence of "a" truth belonging to a certain time and place. This temporary truth takes the form of two events signified by two clauses, the second containing a dynamic verb:

> It was when I said,
> "There is no such thing as the truth,"
> That the grapes seemed fatter.
> The fox ran out of his hole.

Cf. my discussion of "Metaphors of a Magnifico" in chap. 1.

35. Leech remarks that "nominal groups, at least in pre-modification, are often complex" in advertising language, "but verbal groups are mostly of maximum simplicity" (p. 120). In *Investigating English Style* (London, 1969), David Crystal and Derek Davy devote an entire chapter to "The Language of Newspaper Reporting," a genre stylistically similar in many respects to the feature article. They point out the presence in news articles of "much more complex pre- and post-modification than we normally hear or write" (p. 186).

36. See Quirk et al., chaps. 4, "Nouns, Pronouns, and the Basic Noun Phrase," and 13, "The Complex Noun Phrase." The basic noun phrase is described as "consisting of pronouns and numerals . . . and of nouns with articles or other closed-system items that can occur before the noun head . . ." (sec. 4.1).

37. For bibliographical information on the five feature articles used as source materials here, see n.22, above. Advertisements are cited by title of periodical, month, day, and year, and page number. The short titles *Geog., ILN, Sun,* and *Times* in citations of advertisements refer to the *National Geographic,* the *Illustrated London News,* the *New York Sun,* and the *New York Times,* respectively.

38. Sledd, in *A Short Introduction to English Grammar,* cites several sentences from the *Reader's Digest,* including the following, as examples of overexpanded nominal constructions: "Outside the hotel squatted the usual little group of swarthy, turbaned men surrounded by disturbing bags, ready with their bulb-shaped oboe-toned pipes to charm their swaying cobras, or eager to put on a battle between a snake and one of the red-eyed, badger-gray mongooses which clung about them like cats." Sledd comments: "Again, a bulb-shaped, disturbing bag of a simple sentence is devoted almost wholly to the gaudy expansion of a single nominal" (p. 301).

39. Randolph Quirk, in *The Use of English* (London, 1968), cites as a peculiarity of journalistic writing "a piling up of adjectives and relative clauses, even though the information so conveyed is frequently not properly relevant to the rest of the sentence" (pp. 173–74). As an illustration, he quotes a paragraph of newspaper prose in which the following sentence occurs: " . . . the modest, 17-year-old Craig—who celebrated his recent double century against the South Africans by week-ending at his local Youth Club camp—is considered a certainty for the England tour" (ibid., p. 174).

40. Leech describes the "designative, or categorising function" of premodifiers on p. 128. Quoting the phrase "Natural Teak and Antique Soft-glow Formica decorative laminate," he remarks that "in this group (itself an outstanding instance of piled up pre-modification),

decorative does not have the usual sense 'pleasing to look at': instead, it helps to specify more exactly the kind of material referred to as 'laminate' " (ibid.).

41. For "gradability" and "non-gradability" in adjectives, and for "non-gradable" as a subclass of "stative," see Quirk et al., secs. 5.39, 5.70; cf. "intensifiable" and "unintensifiable" in Bolinger, *Aspects of Language,* pp. 147–48. Leech says that "the class of designative adjectives is probably identical with that of 'non-gradable' adjectives" (p. 128).

42. Leech discusses "attributive" (i.e., qualitative) adjectives in the premodifying sequence. One kind of "cluster" in which such adjectives appear "consists of an approbatory adjective followed by one of more concrete meaning: 'this wonderful new toothbrush' "; in another, exemplified by "Rugged Western style Jeans," "the first adjective is chiefly evaluative in import . . . whereas the second element (compound or adjective) specifies the class of garment more exactly" (pp. 129–30).

43. A reverse combination in advertising language, in which a qualitative noun is preceded by an objective noun as premodifier, was described by Anna Granville Hatcher; two of these are included in the title of her article "Twilight Splendor, Shoe Colors, Bolero Brilliance" (*Modern Language Notes* 61 [1946]: 442–47). "Twilight splendor" is from Tennyson's poetry; Hatcher believes that this sort of combination is "an artistic device," first used in poetic language to "suggest the crystallisation of an ideal quality." Combinations like "shoe colors" are of a different order, reflecting "simply . . . an increasing desire to classify, to label . . . the various aspects . . . of modern civilization." Combinations in advertising like "bolero brilliance" (Hatcher also cites "ice-cream perfection" and "leg loveliness") illustrate "the deliberate imitation of the poetic type" (pp. 444–45). I have noted no such combinations in Moore.

44. For the adjectival noun as premodifier in the language of advertising, see Leech, pp. 133–34; for the adjectival compound, pp. 135–40; for the inflected genitive, p. 133. Leech remarks that "in advertising English, lexical restraints on compound formation are less stringent than elsewhere"; this explains "the profusion of *ad hoc* compounds" in the genre (pp. 136–37). Crystal and Davy cite phrases that "function almost as compound nouns," including "forecast chart" and "pressure distribution," in the language of newspaper reporting (p. 186), and remark on "the coining of new and sometimes outlandish adjectival formations," including "weather-conscious," "seven-to-ten-hour," "faster-arriving," and "computer-made" (ibid.). They find "only a hint," in the samples used as data for the chapter, "of the premodifying genitive where it would not normally go—as in *The University of London's James Smith said* . . . —a feature which is common in the American press" (p. 187).

45. These, if nothing else, may count as evidence against Spitzer's statement that " 'the poetry of advertising' can never be vanguard poetry: in the period of a Frost it can never be 'Frostian,' but only Emersonian, Tennysonian, Swinburnian, Elizabethan; it must have a familiar ring, must reproduce the stock poetic devices which the average reader of advertising has been taught to accept as poetic—the folklore of poetry, as it were" ("American Advertising Explained as Popular Art," p. 260, n.15).

CHAPTER SIX

1. In saying this, I mean to deny neither the intrinsic interest of Moore's use of source materials nor the value of source studies in shedding light on her methods of composition and on the meaning of obscure poems and passages. Such studies were greatly facilitated by the establishment in 1969 of the Marianne Moore Collection at the Rosenbach Foundation in Philadelphia; the Collection, available to scholars, includes notebooks, early drafts of poems, diaries, correspondence, and other papers. The *Marianne Moore Newsletter (MMN),* edited by Patricia C. Willis, began publication under the auspices of the Foundation

in the spring of 1977. Clive E. Driver, Moore's literary executor, is now writing a full-length biography.

For a full description of the collection and its setting, see "The Marianne Moore Collection at the Rosenbach Foundation" (*MMN* 1 [1977]: 3–5). The second issue of *MMN* contains, inter alia, a letter from Moore to Barbara Kurz revealing that she had in mind Brooklyn (where a steeplejack named C. J. Poole had attempted to repair the steeple of the Lafayette Avenue Presbyterian Church), "various New England seacoast towns," and "perhaps" Sheepshead Bay in writing "The Steeple-Jack." In the same issue, Professor Laurence Stapleton identifies the source of the quoted phrase "neatness of finish" in "An Octopus" as William Carlos Williams's *Kora in Hell,* where, however, it appears as "neatness *and* finish." It seems safe to predict that the more fully its operations are chronicled, the more the plastic stress of Moore's creative intelligence will be revealed.

2. The statement about Xenophon as it appears in Laufer's "Ostrich Egg-Shell Cups from Mesopotamia" is "Xenophon, when he accompanied the army of Cyrus through the desert along the Euphrates, in northern Arabia, noticed numerous wild asses and many ostriches which he calls 'large sparrows' as well as bustards and antelopes" (p. 266).

3. See "The Ford Correspondence," *A Marianne Moore Reader* (New York, 1961), pp. 215–24.

4. Not surprisingly, Moore had a gift for sketching. Drawings of a kiwi and egg, and of a katydid, appear on the title pages of the first and second issues of *MMN* (1977), respectively. Interesting evidence for the analogy between Moore's "eye-catching" descriptive techniques and conventional techniques of visual representation is provided by a set of rules, with accompanying drawings, by Arthur L. Guptill (reprinted in *Rendering in Pencil,* ed. Susan E. Meyer [New York: Watson-Guptill; London: Pitman, 1977], fig. 50). Headed "Means of Gaining Attention," they are: "1. Living subjects, especially when in motion, catch the eye far more quickly than inanimate subjects. 2. Unfamiliar subjects demand far more attention than familiar things. 3. Subjects of striking or restless shape draw the eye. 4. People (or objects) seen in unusual positions or circumstances exert a strong attractive force. 5. (A) Vigorous technique gains attention. (B) Extreme means of portraying textures are very conspicuous. 6. Detailed treatments have a power to attract." Rule 2 is accompanied by a drawing of a lemur!

5. R. P. Blackmur describes Moore as "an expert in the visual field at compelling the incongruous association to deliver, almost startlingly to ejaculate, the congruous, completing image"; he quotes from "The Monkey Puzzle," among other phrases, "this porcupine-quilled, complicated starkness" ("The Method of Marianne Moore," *Marianne Moore,* ed. Tomlinson, p. 79).

6. Moore's comment, "painted as a Turk, it seems," is evidently based on a misunderstanding of Smith's coat of arms, on which three Turks' heads are represented. Smith was assigned this emblem in recognition of his services against the Turks in several successful military engagements. See Edward Arber, ed., *Travels and Works of Captain John Smith* (Edinburgh, 1910), 2:840–41, 842–45. I owe this explanation to Professor Anne Parten.

7. "Lines such as 'this little hedge- / sparrow that wakes up seven minutes sooner than the lark,' simply distract. A little gratuitous information makes one chuckle, but it doesn't do anything for the poem" (Donald Hall, *Marianne Moore: The Cage and the Animal* [New York, 1970], p. 104). Hall goes on to say, however, that "the poem has beauties that may make up for all confusion" (ibid.).

8. Hugh Kenner, "Disliking It," *A Homemade World,* p. 98.

9. By William Maccall. See *The Home Book of Quotations,* ed. Burton Stevenson, 10th ed. (New York, 1967), p. 507, no. 4.

10. It is interesting that Moore was impressed by a letter from the Federal Reserve Board of

New York describing certain minute differences between genuine and counterfeit notes, to the point of quoting it at length ("Humility, Concentration, and Gusto," *A Marianne Moore Reader,* p. 126).

11. Kenneth Burke finely says of Moore's themes that the relation among them, as among the themes of all genuine poetry, "is *substantial*—which is to say that all the branches spread from a single trunk . . . because of this substantiality, the surfaces [of her poems] are derived from depth. . . . And the objects treated have the property not simply of things, but of volitions. They derive their poignancy as motifs from their relation to the sources of motive" ("Motives and Motifs in the Poetry of Marianne Moore," *Marianne Moore,* ed. Tomlinson, p. 96).

12. I am grateful to Clive E. Driver for informing me that Moore "visited Virginia several times during the period when her brother was stationed at Norfolk," and that "one of her notebooks records visiting the places mentioned in the poem 'Virginia Britannia'" (personal letter, 20 June 1977).

13. Cf. the eloquent tribute of George Nitchie: "The poem closes in a superbly controlled formality . . . . Miss Moore's most Wordsworthian line [i.e., 'are to the child an intimation of what glory is'] brings the poem back, with grace and firmness, from the contemplation of vastness to the human world of 'What Are Years?' If the latter poem is her 'Character of the Happy Warrior,' this perhaps is her 'Lycidas.' It is surely one of our great poems" (*Marianne Moore: An Introduction to the Poetry* [New York, 1969], p. 126).

14. Randall Jarrell notes that "a good deal of her poetry is specifically (and changingly) about armour, weapons, protection, places to hide; and she is not only conscious that this is so, but after a while writes poems about the fact that it is so. As she says, 'armour seems extra,' but it isn't; and when she writes about 'another armoured animal,' about another 'thing made graceful by adversities, conversities,' she does so with the sigh of someone who has come home" ("Her Shield," *Marianne Moore,* ed. Tomlinson, p. 119).

15. A. Kingsley Weatherhead remarks on "the kind of obliquity [in Moore] in which the statement being made by the poem is offered as the speech or thought of a person or an animal or as what the animal reveals by its acts, as if not the poet herself but someone or something else were 'the central intelligence'" (*The Edge of the Image: Marianne Moore, William Carlos Williams, and Some Other Poets* [Seattle, 1967], p. 84). Hugh Kenner makes much the same observation: "Her cats, pangolins, jerboas, elephants are not beings she half-perceives and half-creates. Their accomplishments are wholly their own" ("Disliking It," *A Homemade World,* p. 116). Kenneth Burke's word for the tendency is *objectivism:* "In objectivism, though an object may be chosen for treatment because of its symbolic or subjective reference, once it has been chosen it is to be studied in its own right" ("Motives and Motifs," p. 88). But Burke adds that "We can call Miss Moore 'objectivist' . . . only by taking away the epithet in part. For though many details in her work seem to get there purely out of her attempt to report and judge of a thing's intrinsic qualities, . . . the fact remains that, after you have read several of her poems, you begin to discern a strict principle of selection motivating her appraisals" (p. 89).

16. "Idiosyncrasy and Technique," *A Marianne Moore Reader,* p. 171.

17. "Interview with Donald Hall," *A Marianne Moore Reader,* p. 258.

18. Quoted by Donald Hall, *Marianne Moore,* p. 34.

19. In *Tell Me, Tell Me: Granite, Steel, and Other Topics* (New York, 1966), p. 46.

20. "We perceive the occasion and seize the nearest peg to hang the form on, which happened to be the very slight peg of inverted commas" (R. P. Blackmur, "The Method of Marianne Moore," p. 68).

21. "A Note on the Notes," *Complete Poems,* p. 262.

SELECTED
BIBLIOGRAPHY

Adler, Mortimer. *The Difference of Man and the Difference It Makes.* New York: Holt, Rinehart and Winston, 1967.

Antosch, Friederike. "The Diagnosis of Literary Style with the Verb-Adjective Ratio." In *Statistics and Style,* pp. 57–65. Ed. Lubomír Doležel and Richard W. Bailey. New York: American Elsevier Publishing Co., 1969.

Arber, Edward, ed. *Travels and Works of Captain John Smith.* Edinburgh: J. Grant, 1910.

Auerbach, Erich. *Literary Language and Its Public in Late Latin Antiquity and in the Middle Ages.* Trans. Ralph Manheim. New York: Pantheon Books, 1965.

Bailey, Richard W. "Statistics and Style: A Historical Survey." In *Statistics and Style,* pp. 200–36. Ed. Lubomír Doležel and Richard W. Bailey. New York: American Elsevier Publishing Co., 1969.

Bloom, Harold. *Poetry and Repression: Revisionism from Blake to Stevens.* New Haven: Yale University Press, 1976.

———. "Wallace Stevens: The Poems of Our Climate." *Prose* 8 (1974): 5–24.

Blum, Margaret M. "Robert Frost's 'Directive': A Theological Reading." *Modern Language Notes* 76 (1961): 524–25.

Boder, David P. "The Adjective-Verb Quotient: A Contribution to the Psychology of Language." *Psychological Record* 3 (1940): 310–43.

Bolinger, Dwight. *Aspects of Language.* 2d. ed. New York: Harcourt, Brace and World, 1975.

Booth, Wayne C. *The Rhetoric of Fiction.* Chicago: University of Chicago Press, 1961.

Borroff, Marie. "Robert Frost: To Earthward." In *Frost: Centennial Essays II,* pp. 21–39. Ed. Jac Tharpe. Jackson: University Press of Mississippi, 1976.

Brower, Reuben A. *The Poetry of Robert Frost: Constellations of Intention.* New York: Oxford University Press, 1963.

Brown, Roger. *A First Language: The Early Stages.* Cambridge: Harvard University Press, 1973.

———. *Words and Things.* Glencoe: Free Press, 1958.

Bruce, F. F. *The English Bible: A History of Translations from the Earliest English Versions to the New English Bible.* New York: Oxford University Press, 1970.

Butterworth, Charles C. *The Literary Lineage of the King James Bible, 1340–1611.* Philadelphia: University of Pennsylvania Press, 1941.

Carterette, Edward C., and Margaret Hubbard Jones. *Informal Speech: Alphabetic and Phonemic Texts with Statistical Analyses and Tables.* Berkeley: University of California Press, 1974.

Chatman, Seymour, ed. *Literary Style: A Symposium.* New York: Oxford University Press, 1971.

———. "Milton's Participial Style." *PMLA* 83 (1968): 1386–99.

———. "The Semantics of Style." *Social Science Information* 6 (1967): 77–99.

Cook, Reginald L. *The Dimensions of Robert Frost.* New York: Rinehart, 1959.

Crystal, David, and Derek Davy. *Investigating English Style.* London: Longmans, 1969.

Deutsch, Babette. *Poetry in Our Time.* New York: Columbia University Press, 1956.

DeVito, Joseph A. "A Linguistic Analysis of Spoken and Written Language." *Central States Speech Journal* 18 (1967): 81–85.

Doggett, Frank. "Wallace Stevens' Later Poetry." *ELH* 25 (1958): 135–54.

Doughery, James P. "Robert Frost's 'Directive' to the Wilderness." *American Quarterly* 18 (1966): 208–19.

Dragland, S. L. "Frost's 'Mending Wall.'" *Explicator* 25 (1967), no. 39.

Drew, Elizabeth. *Poetry: A Modern Guide to Its Understanding and Enjoyment.* New York: W. W. Norton, 1959.

Duvall, S. P. C. "Robert Frost's 'Directive' Out of *Walden*." *American Literature* 31 (1960): 482–88.

Ellis, J., and N. Ure. "Language Varieties: Register." In *Encyclopaedia of Linguistics, Information, and Control.* Ed. A. R. Meetham. Oxford and New York: Pergamon Press, 1969.

Firth, J. R. "Modes of Meaning." In *Essays and Studies . . . Collected for the English Association,* pp. 118–59. Ed. Geoffrey Tillotson. London: J. Murray, 1951.

Flesch, Rudolf. "Measuring the Level of Abstraction." *Journal of Applied Psychology* 34 (1950): 384–90.

Francis, W. Nelson. *The English Language. An Introduction: Background for Writing.* New York: W. W. Norton, 1965.

———. *The Structure of American English.* New York: Ronald Press, 1958.

Fries, Charles Carpenter. *The Structure of English: An Introduction to the Construction of English Sentences.* New York: Harcourt, Brace, 1952.

Frost, Robert. *The Poetry of Robert Frost.* Ed. Edward Connery Lathem. New York: Holt, Rinehart and Winston, 1969.

———. *Selected Letters of Robert Frost.* Ed. Lawrance Thompson. New York: Holt, Rinehart and Winston, 1964.

Fuchs, Daniel. *The Comic Spirit of Wallace Stevens.* Durham: Duke University Press, 1963.

Gardiner, Sir Alan. *The Theory of Speech and Language.* Oxford: Clarendon Press, 1951.

Garrigue, Jean. *Marianne Moore.* Minneapolis: University of Minnesota Press, 1965.

Gerber, Philip L. *Robert Frost.* New York: Twayne Publishers, 1967.

Gibb, Carson. "Frost's 'Mending Wall.'" *Explicator* 20 (1962), no. 48.

Greenfield, Stanley. "Grammar and Meaning in Poetry." *PMLA* 82 (1968): 377–87.

Greenough, James Bradstreet, and George Lyman Kittredge. *Words and Their Ways in English Speech.* New York: Macmillan, 1901.

Hall, Donald. *Marianne Moore: The Cage and the Animal.* New York: Pegasus, 1970.

Halliday, M. A. K. "Linguistic Function and Literary Style: An Inquiry into the Language of William Golding's *The Inheritors.*" In *Literary Style: A Symposium,* pp. 330–36. Ed. Seymour Chatman. New York: Oxford University Press, 1971.

Hatcher, Anna Granville. "Twilight Splendor, Shoe Colors, Bolero Brilliance." *Modern Language Notes* 61 (1946): 442–47.

Havránek, Bohuslav. "The Functional Differentiation of the Standard Language." In *A Prague School Reader on Esthetics, Literary Structure and Style.* Ed. and trans. Paul Garvin. Washington: Georgetown University Press, 1964.

Hockett, Charles. *A Course in Modern Linguistics.* New York: Macmillan, 1958.

Hough, Graham. *Style and Stylistics.* London: Routledge, 1969.

Jespersen, Otto. *Essentials of English Grammar.* New York: Henry Holt, 1933.

———. *Growth and Structure of the English Language.* 9th ed. Garden City, N.Y.: Doubleday Anchor Books, n.d.

———. *Language: Its Nature, Development and Origin.* New York: W. W. Norton, Language Library, 1964.

———, et al. *A Modern English Grammar on Historical Principles.* 7 vols. 1909–49.

Selected Bibliography

Joos, Martin. *The Five Clocks*. New York: Harcourt, Brace, Harbinger Books, 1967.

Kenner, Hugh. *A Homemade World: The American Modernist Writers*. New York: Alfred A. Knopf, 1975.

Kenyon, John S. "Cultural Levels and Functional Varieties of English." *College English* 10 (1948): 31–36.

Kessler, Edward, *Images of Wallace Stevens*. New Brunswick: Rutgers University Press, 1972.

King, Bruce. "Wallace Stevens' 'Metaphors of a Magnifico.'" *English Studies* 49 (1968): 450–52.

Knox, George. "A Backward Motion toward the Source." *Personalist* 47 (1966): 365–81.

Lane, Gary, ed. *A Concordance to the Poems of Marianne Moore*. New York: Haskell House, 1972.

Lathem, Edward Connery, ed. *A Concordance to the Poetry of Robert Frost*. New York: Holt Information Systems, 1971.

Leech, Geoffrey N. *English in Advertising: A Linguistic Study of Advertising in Great Britain*. London: Longmans, 1966.

Lynen, John F. *The Pastoral Art of Robert Frost*. New Haven: Yale University Press, 1960.

McIntosh, Angus. "Patterns and Ranges." In Angus McIntosh and M. A. K. Halliday, *Patterns of Language: Papers in General, Descriptive and Applied Linguistics*. London: Longmans, 1966.

Marchand, Hans. *The Categories and Types of Present-Day English Word-Formation: A Synchronic-Diachronic Approach*. 2d ed. Munich: Oscar Beck, 1969.

"The Marianne Moore Collection at the Rosenbach Foundation." *Marianne Moore Newsletter* 1 (1977): 3–5.

Miles, Josephine. *Eras and Modes in English Poetry*. Berkeley: University of California Press, 1957.

Moore, Marianne. *The Complete Poems*. New York: Macmillan/Viking, 1967.

———. *A Marianne Moore Reader*. New York: Viking Press, 1961.

———. *Tell Me, Tell Me: Granite, Steel, and Other Topics*. New York: Viking Press, 1966.

Morris, Adalaide Kirby. *Wallace Stevens: Imagination and Faith*. Princeton: Princeton University Press, 1974.

Mukařovský, Jan. "Standard Language and Poetic Language." In *A Prague School Reader on Esthetics, Literary Structure and Style*. Ed. and trans. Paul Garvin. Washington: Georgetown University Press, 1964.

Nitchie, George. *Marianne Moore: An Introduction to the Poetry*. New York: Columbia University Press, 1969.

The Oxford Dictionary of English Proverbs. Comp. William George Smith. Oxford: Clarendon Press, 1970.

Pack, Robert. *Wallace Stevens: An Approach to His Poetry and Thought*. New Brunswick: Rutgers University Press, 1958.

Poems, by Marianne Moore, rev. of *Times Literary Supplement*, 21 July 1921, p. 471.

Poirier, Richard. *Robert Frost: The Work of Knowing*. New York: Oxford University Press, 1977.

Quirk, Randolph. *The Use of English*. London: Longmans, 1968.

———, and Sidney Greenbaum. *A Concise Grammar of Contemporary English*. New York: Harcourt Brace Jovanovich, 1973.

———, Sidney Greenbaum, Geoffrey Leech, Jan Svartvik. *A Grammar of Contemporary English*. New York: Harcourt, Brace, Jovanovich; Seminar Press, 1972.

Robson, W. W. "The Achievement of Robert Frost." *Southern Review*, n.s. 2 (1966): 735–61.

Rosenfeld, Paul. *Men Seen: Twenty-four Modern Authors.* New York: L. MacVeagh, Dial Press, 1925.

Ross, Donald. "Beyond the Concordance: Algorithms for the Description of English Clauses and Phrases." In *The Computer and Literary Studies,* pp. 85–99. Edinburgh: University of Edinburgh Press, 1973.

———, and Robert H. Rasche. *Description of EYEBALL.* Rev. ed. Minneapolis: Department of English, University of Minnesota, 1976.

———. "EYEBALL: A Computer Program for Description of Style." *Computers and the Humanities* 6 (1972): 213–21.

———. "An EYEBALL View of Blake's Songs of Innocence and of Experience." In *Computers in the Humanities,* pp. 94–108. Ed. J. Lawrence Mitchell. Edinburgh: University of Edinburgh Press, 1974.

Sayce, R. A. "The Definition of the Term Style." *Proceedings of the Third Congress of the International Comparative Literature Association,* pp. 156–66. The Hague, 1962.

Sergeant, Elizabeth Shepley. *Robert Frost: The Trial by Existence.* New York: Holt, Rinehart and Winston, 1960.

Sheard, J. A. *The Words of English.* New York: W. W. Norton, Language Library, 1966.

Sinfield, Alan. *The Language of Tennyson's "In Memoriam."* Oxford: Blackwell, 1971.

Sledd, James. *A Short Introduction to English Grammar.* Chicago: Scott, Foresman, 1959.

Smithers, G. V. "Some English Ideophones." *Archivum Linguisticum* 6 (1954): 73–111.

Spitzer, Leo. "American Advertising Explained as Popular Art." *Essays on English and American Literature.* Ed. Anna Granville Hatcher. Princeton: Princeton University Press, 1962, pp. 248–77.

———. *Linguistics and Literary History: Essays in Stylistics.* Princeton: Princeton University Press, 1948.

Squires, Radcliffe. *The Major Themes of Robert Frost.* Ann Arbor: University of Michigan Press, 1963.

Stevens, Wallace. *The Collected Poems of Wallace Stevens.* New York: Alfred A. Knopf, 1954.

———. *Letters of Wallace Stevens.* Ed. Holly Stevens. New York: Alfred A. Knopf, 1966.

———. *The Necessary Angel: Essays on Reality and the Imagination.* New York: Alfred A. Knopf, 1951.

———. *Opus Posthumous.* Ed. Samuel French Morse. New York: Alfred A. Knopf, 1957.

———. *The Palm at the End of the Mind: Selected Poems and a Play.* Ed. Holly Stevens. New York: Alfred A. Knopf, 1971.

Sukenick, Ronald. *Wallace Stevens: Musing the Obscure.* New York: New York University Press, 1967.

Swadesh, Morris. *The Origin and Diversification of Language.* Ed. Joel Sherzer. Chicago: Aldine, Atherton, 1971.

Thompson, Lawrance R. *Fire and Ice: The Art and Thought of Robert Frost.* New York: Henry Holt, 1942.

———. "Robert Frost." *Seven Modern American Poets: An Introduction.* Ed. Leonard Unger. Minneapolis: University of Minnesota Press, 1959, pp. 9–44.

Tomlinson, Charles, ed. *Marianne Moore: A Collection of Critical Essays.* Englewood Cliffs, N.J.: Prentice-Hall, 1969.

Turner, G. W. *Stylistics.* Harmondsworth, Middlesex, England: Penguin Books, 1973.

Ullmann, Stephen. *Language and Style: Collected Papers.* Oxford: Blackwell, 1964.

———. *The Principles of Semantics.* Glasgow: Jackson, 1951.

———. *Semantics: An Introduction to the Science of Meaning.* New York: Barnes and Noble, 1962.

Unger, Leonard, ed. *Seven Modern American Poets: An Introduction.* Minneapolis: University of Minnesota Press, 1967.

Vendler, Helen Hennessy. *On Extended Wings: Wallace Stevens' Longer Poems.* Cambridge: Harvard University Press, 1969.

Walsh, Thomas F., ed. *Concordance to the Poetry of Wallace Stevens.* University Park: Pennsylvania State University Press, 1963.

Warren, Robert Penn. "The Themes of Robert Frost." In *The Writer and His Craft.* Ed. Robert Morss Lovett. Ann Arbor: University of Michigan Press, 1954.

Weatherhead, A. Kingsley. *The Edge of the Image: Marianne Moore, William Carlos Williams, and Some Other Poets.* Seattle: University of Washington Press, 1967.

Wells, Rulon S. "Nominal and Verbal Style." In *Style in Language,* pp. 213–20. Ed. Thomas A. Sebeok. Cambridge: Massachusetts Institute of Technology Press, 1960.

Whorf, Benjamin Lee. "The Relation of Habitual Thought and Behavior to Language." In *Language, Thought and Reality: Selected Writings of Benjamin Lee Whorf,* pp. 134–59. Ed. John B. Carroll. Cambridge: Massachusetts Institute of Technology Press, 1956.

Wimsatt, W. K., Jr. *The Prose Style of Samuel Johnson.* New Haven: Yale University Press, 1941; paperback, 1963.

INDEX
OF POEMS

This list does not include poems mentioned as exemplifying features of style. See the features listed for each poet in the "Index of Topics and Proper Names."

Index of Poems

INDEX
OF TOPICS AND PROPER NAMES